ZIONISM, ISRAEL & THE ARABS

Hal Draper

ISBN 0-916695-09-03

Second Printing

Center for Socialist History
PO Box 626 Alameda CA, 94501
Tel: (510) 601-6460
www.socialisthistory.org
mlipow@pacbell.net

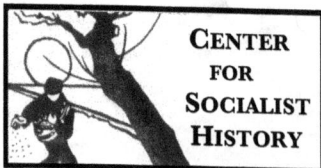

CENTER
FOR
SOCIALIST
HISTORY

CONTENTS

Preface

A personal word may help to explain some minor aspects of this collection. It does not offer a systematic analysis of Zionism and Israel, with a complete overview, but rather only studies in certain sides of the subject. There is a reason for this.

My intensive concern with the question of Zionism began only when the issue was thrust on me—as on the socialist movement, and on the rest of the world—by the outbreak of war in the Middle East over the 1948 partition of Palestine and the establishment of the state of Israel. Zionism had never been of special interest to me: my own secular-minded Jewish family was as uninfluenced by Zionist ideas as by religious beliefs; and I had never even personally run into anti-Semitism, at least not knowingly. In general, my parents, immigrants from East Europe, reflected a milieu which has now vanished almost completely—the world of the socialistic-minded needle-trades workers of New York, like most of the other militants of the Shirt Workers Union and its successor Amalgamated Clothing Workers. They viewed Jewishness as purely a cultural artifact; they looked to build their Zion here; they looked with something like contempt on the idea of running away from the class struggle here to dream of a nationalistic utopia far away.

During the 1930s, at any rate about 1932 to 1937, I had often worked closely in the activities of the socialist student movement with young socialist Zionists (belonging, I think, to Hashomer Hatzair); but I do not recollect ever getting into an argument, or discussion, with them about Zionism. As a Marxist I held a dim view of Zionism, as negative then as it is now. I was not particularly well prepared to grapple with the problem in 1948.

The 1948 partition was generally approved by socialists as a practical-political necessity; and of course everyone was under the impress of the Holocaust horror. Still, the outbreak of war raised a new problem of policy, as war always does. As far as I recall, there was no sentiment in the Independent Socialist League—the third camp socialist organization of which I was a member— opposed to supporting Israel's defensive stance. It was a question of the context in which the war was seen: critical or uncritical of the Israelis' policies vis-à-vis the Arabs? (Remember that the American public knew little about these policies, and we knew little more.)

It turned out, or we found out, that we had a wing of the League that was—well, not exactly pro-Zionist, but soft-on-Zionism; for example, inclined to gloss over and apologize for whatever the new "Jewish state" wanted to do, with a minimum of criticism. The spokesman of this tendency in our ranks was one Al Findley, whose political approach tended to waver from soft-on-Zionism to harder-on-Zionism, depending on the level of nationalistic hysteria in the Jewish community, to which he was very sensitive.

This spectrum (soft-on to harder-on) had a stronger influence on the organization as a whole—it turned out—than I had known. To anticipate events a little: this was shown at the ISL convention of 1949. There were two resolutions on Israel and the Jewish question presented there, even though in previous years there had been no objection to a straight anti-Zionist line. One resolution was mine; it is available now because it was adopted later (in 1951) and published in the New International. A counter-resolution was submitted by Findley, to express a viewpoint which teetered on the brink of endorsing an essentially Zionist view of Israel with fuzzier words. Neither resolution gained a majority at the 1949 gathering; but the Findley thesis garnered more votes than mine. And influential leaders, who had not previously been known as sympathetic to Zionism, now abstained from the vote: in particular, Max Shachtman and N. Gould. Obviously our group was temporarily reeling under the wave of Jewish-nationalist sentiment unleashed by the establishment of Israel. I say temporarily, for at the next convention in 1951 I reintroduced the same resolution word-for-word, and this time got a unanimous vote in favor (including even Findley—temporarily).

This 1949 episode was the last time the group as such staggered on the question, though on later occasions—as when England, France and Israel ganged up to attack Suez—our small soft-on-Zionism wing went through its heart-burnings.

But let us return to early 1948; the delicate state of affairs in the ranks was still unknown to me. I had just returned to New York from a five-year sojourn in the Los Angeles area, had just taken on editorship of the New International—the monthly journal of the organization—and become a member of the ISL's resident political committee. In this situation, the very first heavy political issue I faced was the one on the Palestine partition and the new war.

It turned out (to skip many details) that in the political committee it devolved on me to work out the appropriate policy on the Middle East war. And I did work this policy out. It was embodied in two pieces: first, an unsigned editorial in our weekly paper Labor Action (May 24 and 31) headed "War of Independence or Expansion?" Then a signed article in the New International (July) on "How to Defend Israel."

This policy statement is included in the following pages. Why reprint it here? In the first place, I still think it is a key analysis in thinking out the

Middle East puzzle. In the second place, I am very proud of it for a special reason. Many years later, during the 1960s, a revolutionary socialist group called Matzpen arose in Israel out of native Israelis—principledly anti-Zionist, third-camp in politics, home-grown (before it was torn apart by burrowing sects, Maoist and Trotskyist). And a Matzpen representative in this country made my day when he read those old pieces about 1948 and expressed his astonishment that the ISL back in 1948 had worked out exactly the same analysis of the "war of independence" that Matzpen itself had worked out a couple of decades later...

This policy statement on the war was fundamentally a warning. It explained in advance why socialists could not continue to support the national-chauvinistic policies of Israel vis-à-vis the Arab world. In editing Labor Action from 1949 on, my relative ignorance about the politics and history of Zionism was a handicap, however—though I had begun to read about the subject. Two aids came to the rescue in part.

Firstly: Labor Action had contact inside Israel with (non-Stalinist) critics of Zionism, and we printed their reports whenever we could get them. One was J. Artusky of the old "Polish" Jewish Bund, who was a leader of a Bund group in Israel; and another was M. Stein, who was then especially involved in combating the regime's official policy of suppressing Yiddish as a language. (For a whole period, Israel was the only country in the world that forbade the publication of a newspaper in Yiddish.)

Secondly: I made the acquaintance, right in New York, of a great-hearted man—William Zukerman, the editor and publisher of the Jewish Newsletter. Here was a totally honest, as well as knowledgeable, voice on all aspects of the "Jewish question,"at home as well as in the Middle East. In the course of the 1950s, Labor Action was going to reprint many news items and commentaries from the columns of Zukerman's modest paper. Besides, I came to know Zukerman well as a friend and mentor (though he must have been twenty years older), and thus I gained in the understanding of the background that had produced Zukerman; the background which, as it happened, was the same as or allied to the secular-humanist outlook of the now-vanished Jewish world that had also been that of my shirtworker-parents. Except that Zukerman represented the intellectuals' side of that society, while the shirtworkers and ILGWU operatives represented the labor movement's end.

The least I can say about Zukerman's Jewish Newsletter (and the allied materials it led me to) is that it kept me straightened out on the problems of the Middle East and their relations to the Jewish people. It had weaknesses, to be sure; for one thing, Zukerman was a mild social-democrat in general politics, though I never noted any antirevolutionary knee-jerk in his reactions. In any case, the Jewish Newsletter was a basic recourse for me, during all the years from April 1949 (when I became editor of the weekly Labor Action) until the middle of 1957, when the political collapse of the ISL sent me back to the West Coast.

In the middle 1950s (it must have been about 1955) I was thrown still deeper into the complex of problems clustering around Israel. This resulted directly from an article I refused to print in Labor Action. I had seen references to the discriminations and harassments against Israeli Arabs by the "Jewish state," but it was impossible to find any information on this subject in the American press; presumably such offenses against its Arab population did not exist in Israel.

One day I received an article from one of my contributors in Israel, in Hebrew, on precisely the subject in question: the treatment of the Israeli Arabs in Israel. (I omit the writer's name for reasons to be seen in a moment.) The article was translated into English in record time; I read it eagerly; and then stared at it in puzzlement. The situation it described sounded authentic; but as for its detailed facts—there was something "off" about most of them. The translator and I started checking individual facts—and most of them checked out a little askew, some a lot askew. Other facts, unchecked, sounded exaggerated, even if essentially true. I got the impression of a research job that was careless, unbuttoned, eminently refutable in detail if not in essence. An article like this could discredit us, and make a return to the subject very difficult.

Yet there was very important material floating in that stew; could something be salvaged? This was how I got acquainted with the magnificent Zionist Library in New York City, which not only carried Zionist and Jewish-related periodicals from all over the world but also compiled a Zionist Periodical Index. At first I thought my lack of Hebrew might be an insuperable obstacle, but the Periodical Index pointed to numerous translations (into English, French, etc.) of important articles originally published in Hebrew, like certain essays in the Israeli Haaretz. I worked away in this wonderful library, part-time of course, for somewhere near two months; and by that time I was sure of what I had. The result was the production of two long studies published in The New International, "Israel's Arab Minority: The Beginning of a Tragedy," and with the same main title, "The Great Land Robbery." For that matter, I had copious notes for follow-up articles, which I never got around to producing.

There was one other outstanding contribution to my education. I discovered that a doctoral dissertation had been published on my subject,

"Israel and the Arab Refugees," by Don Peretz (Columbia, 1954), available in two mimeographed volumes. It was a magnificent job of research, and at that time the sole honest-scholarly inquiry into the question. Peretz was a disciple of Judah L. Magnes, founder of the Ichud. (His work was later published, in revised form, as a book.) I got personally acquainted with Peretz, who helped whenever called on for information.

o   o   o

At the present moment in 1990, thirty-forty years after some of these studies were originally published, the most unexpected fact is the following: most of the material thus published has not yet been superseded. This is shocking, and betokens the extent to which the facts about Israel have been long suppressed.

Take the subject of the plight of the Israeli Arabs: because so much archival documentary material has been so recently opened to examination, there are now three books (three outstanding books) that marshal a good deal of the true picture of what happened in 1947/48–1949. These three books were published only in 1986/87—so late!

But astonishingly, even these three books do not duplicate the material which I dredged out of the Zionist Library in 1955. For what these new books have to offer is material which was secret in that year, hidden in secret archives and confidential collections, and only now made public. What is contained in my two studies on "Israel's Arab Minority" is, on the contrary, material that was quite public in 1955, open to the general public—already published for anyone to find who wanted to look. What I find still difficult to understand is why nobody wanted to look.

The three aforementioned books, which today are indispensable for the history of the truth, have been little reviewed, suppressed in a small way. But their contents will percolate through the public. They are:

Segev, Tom. 1949. The first Israelis. Arlen Neal Weinstein, English language editor. New York: Free Press; London: Collier Macmillan, 1986. [Original published in Hebrew.]

Flapan, Simha. The birth of Israel. Myths and realities. New York: Pantheon Books, 1987.

Morris, Benny. The birth of the Palestinian refugee problem, 1947–1949. (Cambridge Middle East Library) Cambridge University Press, 1987.

To this, add the above-mentioned pioneer:

Peretz, Don. Israel and the Palestine Arabs. Washington, D.C.: Middle East Institute, 1958.

And the following book is unique as a Marxist work on the broad subject which is at the same time skillfully-scholarly done:

Weinstock, Nathan. Zionism: false messiah. Trans. & ed. by Alan Adler. London: Ink Links, 1979. [This is the English version only of Part I of the French original, below]

Weinstock, Nathan. Le sionisme contre Israël. Paris: François Maspero, 1969. [Part II remains untranslated: Les Israéliens à la recherche d'un avenir (1948–1968)]

If you read the three books first mentioned, by Segev, Flapan and Morris, you will realize two things about the historical picture offered by the contents of this book: (1) virtually every aspect covered, in every article, is fully confirmed by the new revelations, except (2) for one qualification, namely, the truth was stated mildly and moderately back then, as compared with the greater harshness of the reality. What I mean is this sort of thing: where I intimated that official statements should be taken with a pinch of salt, the fact is I should have said roundly that we were dealing with a Big Lie. I tended to accept the view held by Peretz, for example, that the official Israeli policy of expulsion and exclusion of Israeli Arabs developed only gradually at first, and did not harden into a conscious and systematic state policy until (say) 1949. There is still some truth to this, but documents that were once secret now reveal that more Zionist leaders than we thought (especially Ben-Gurion) understood from the very beginning the direction that events would have to take, and why the Zionists wanted them that way.

o   o   o

Politically there is one all-important difference in the situation—a difference between the period when these essays were written as compared with the present day. My debate with Clovis Maksoud immediately suggests this difference, for at issue was the preoccupation of Arab socialist elements with the "militant" line of crushing Israel out of existence, rather than changing its policies. We Independent Socialists refrained from giving political support to any of the Palestinian political groups, precisely because their official policies were formulated in terms of "destroying" Israel. (Thus, Zionist apologists denounced us as "pro-Arab" while some Arab socialists like Maksoud denounced us as pro-Zionist: but this pattern was inevitable and did not bother us.) Politically we stated our support in terms of a series of demands by the Palestinians, as was done in articles included here (see especially "To Break the Vicious Spiral").

On this question too, we won in the end—"won" so to speak, for the pressure leading to the change was not our doing but a triumph of the young people who carried on the great intifada waged in the occupied territories. We can say now, and with great satisfaction, that the general line being followed by the PLO leadership under Arafat and by the Palestinian movement of rebellion is essentially the line that we advocated among both Jewish-Zionist and Arab-nationalist socialists. This is simply a matter of "pointing with pride,"you understand, since there is no claim about influencing events; but the pride involved bears on the general nature of our Independent Socialist and "third camp" politics as a guide to an era.

I make only this claim: that there is no political tendency other than that of Independent Socialism that can reprint its main political documents thirty-forty years later with such total confirmation of its political programmatic ideas and analyses. These ideas are still the best guide to politics.

January 1990, H.D.

Chapter 1
WAR OF INDEPENDENCE OR EXPANSION?

The UN, set up with fanfare to bring peace to the world, is again showing that it cannot prevent or halt war even by fifth-rate powers, such as the states of the Middle East—let alone war by the major warmakers who control its deliberations.

Compelled by the falling apart of the British Empire to recognize the independence of Palestine on paper, the UN drew a braided line through that tortured country of mingled nationality, erecting a state-boundary wall between already suspicious and jealous peoples. The Jews were assured of a state of their own—a state completely outfitted with salients, corridors, enclaves and angles sticking into the sides of the surrounding Arab world, with military lines athwart each other and commercial routes interpenetrating. The Jews cheered.

Then Washington ran out on its own partition plan, and the Arab leaders in turn were encouraged to proceed with their plans to enforce a Pan-Arab Palestine by force of arms in the interests of reactionary Arab landlordism. When this had already gone virtually to the point of invasion, the White House flipflopped, backtracked and reversed gear again in a precipitous recognition of the new Jewish state of Israel, again encouraging the Jews.

If meanwhile the British line was more consistent, it was more consistently directed toward fomenting the Pan-Arab reaction against the partition.

As long as the two peoples can thus be "sicced" against each other, the shadow of imperialist domination does not leave the scene. This is the end of UN policy.

If there is to be peace at the eastern end of the Mediterranean, and if the Jews and Arabs are to live in fraternal unity, no one can look toward the United Nations or to American and British imperialism to bring this about. If there is to be peace, it has to be made by the peoples.

The partition of Palestine into two non-viable states was not calculated to achieve any real solution of the Palestine question, and cannot. Before partition, the road to a basic solution lay only in the joint struggle by the socialist workers of the Jewish community together with the oppressed Arab peasantry to throw off the yoke of their common oppressor—British imperialism, based on the two ruling classes, Arab landlords and Zionist capitalists; and such Arab-Jewish cooperation from below could have forged a united Palestine in the fire of anti-imperialist struggle.

Now that partition is virtually an accomplished fact, this basic road only takes a different form.

There is a war on—not yet full-scale war as this is written, but not far from it. The socialist working class of the Jewish territory has chosen to follow its Zionist leadership in achieving a separate state. As Marxist socialists—that is, as the only consistent democrats—we believe in and accept the democratic right of all peoples (including the Palestinian Jews) to self-determination, to work out their own destiny as they see fit. We said this even while advising against the exercise of this right to the point of separation.

The politics from which the Pan-Arab war and threats of invasion flow is perfectly clear—the aim of depriving the Jews precisely of this right to self-determination. There is therefore not the slightest iota of common ground between the Arab landlords' opposition to partition and our own. While we are more firmly than ever of the opinion that the Jews' choice of separatism was a mistake and a setback for the only long-range solution, we believe that the imposition of "unity" upon Palestine by Abdullah, the Mufti or the Arab League would be a reactionary solution even more disastrous in its consequences and a violation of the democratic rights of peoples.

To recognize the right of the Jews to self-determination, if it is not merely to be a pious obeisance to a formula, requires socialists also to recognize the right of the Jews to defend their choice of separate national existence against any and all reactionary attempts to deprive them of that right, whether by Arab feudal lords or UN imperialism. That is why we demanded recognition of Israel by the government, and why our British comrades particularly must demand similar action by the Labor government—as the concretization of the demand that the imperialists keep out. That is why we demand the lifting of the imperialist embargo on arms to the new Jewish state.

But the defense of Israel's right of self-determination against a reactionary war of invasion is only one side of the picture. Surely even the Zionist leaders do not believe that the "Palestine question" will be over if only Abdullah stops short of Israel's borders! On the contrary, it only enters a new stage. On the one hand, the Jews face the possibility of permanent guerilla warfare, unending "border incidents," and, above all, such permanent national hostility with the Arab world as would make national existence a nightmare for the Jewish splinter state. On the other hand, the unreproved demands by the Irgun and Stern gang for the conquest of all of Palestine raises the same question of future relations. For the socialist working class of Palestine that question is posed in terms of the present struggle as follows:

2

Are the Jews—socialist workers in their majority—to wage a war of nationalist expansionism, or a revolutionary war for the reunification of Palestine from below against both the Jewish and Arab ruling classes?

Today their struggle is a war of defense in the immediate circumstances. But tomorrow their struggle will inescapably be transformed into one or the other!

Before this question can be answered, the first illusion that needs destroying is the illusion that the splinter state of Israel can "go it alone." To be sure, given Haganah military victories, Israel can succeed in maintaining its formal independence. But world imperialism—British, American and Russian—will remain on the scene with their fingers in the pie as long as the Balkanization of the Middle East continues.

The present situation in Palestine, the fruit of partition and the end product of Zionist policy in the country, can only continue to inflame nationalist hostility on both sides.

Even if the Arab legions' invasion is beaten back, the new state of Israel exists in an impossible economic and political situation. Its leaders will be forced to seek to fortify the stability of the new state in face of an encirclement of hatred—and they will look for aid and comfort only toward the imperialists. Such will be the inevitable drift for these "practical" politicians whose conception of statesmanship will consist of attempts to maneuver with the imperialist interests which hold Palestine in a net. And the price of such statesmanship can only be their willingness to act as an imperialist outpost in the Middle East for one or the other of the contending forces, hoping for protection and support in exchange.

Behind all this is the sorry fact that Israel cannot exist as a splinter state quivering in the flesh of the Arab Middle East without constant war-skirmishing or imperialist entanglements or both. This is guaranteed both for economic and political reasons.

This is why the only road that can save the Jews from subservience to imperialism or destruction by the Arabs is a course directed toward the reunification of Palestine on a basis which will permit the two peoples to live together in fraternal harmony. Such an outcome is simply impossible on the basis of the present policy of the Israeli leadership. And it is equally impossible as long as the Arab masses are under the unchallenged domination of their semi-feudal dynasties, landlords, effendis and militarists.

The reunification of Palestine and of the two peoples in it can take place only through a struggle from below. The conditions for such a struggle are present as they were before partition—the class struggle within Jewish society, and the grinding exploitation of the Arab peasants by their lords and masters.

We believe that the main (not exclusive, but the main) responsibility for taking the initiative in this direction lies with the Jewish workers—precisely because, as the Zionist leaders boast on any occasion, it is the Jews who are the more advanced socially and culturally, because it is they who claim to be socialists, etc.

While opposing any attempt by the Arab landlord regimes to overthrow the Jewish state and impose their own reactionary sway on the whole land, it is the duty of real socialists in Israel to fight for a policy, a program and a government of the working people which can bring about such reunification instead of deepening the nationalist gulf.

The key to such a program is in the first place the policy of the people of Israel toward the Arabs now within their own borders. Israel must demonstrate that they are fighting not against the Arab people but against the Arab dynasts and landlords who are also the oppressors of the Arab people themselves. It must demonstrate that it seeks the alliance of the Arab masses against their own exploiters—an alliance of classes.

It can demonstrate this only by sharply reversing the whole Zionist policy toward the Arab people—accepting them as equals and collaborating in the building up, not of a Jewish state, but of a binational state. We use the term "binational" (which has been used with various senses) to designate merely the aim of a state which is the home of two peoples and comports itself a such, the forms to be worked out in common agreement.

Complete equal rights to the Arabs within the state of Israel; equality, not Jim Crow, in the Jewish-controlled trade unions; the abandonment of the economic nationalism which has reigned in the Jewish community hitherto; the constitutional and de facto guarantee of the Arabs' fully recognized status as a national people—here are the elementary beginnings of such a program in Israel which can demonstrate in action the basis for a reunited Palestine.

Only such a government in Israel could seek to stir up the Arab masses of the invading nations against their own oppressors, raising in the first place its sympathy with the demand for land to the Arab fellaheen and the other social interests of the submerged mass of the Arab semi-feudal world.

Such a state, which appears in the Middle East not as the representative of Jewish nationalist chauvinism but of the social aspirations of all the people, Jewish and Arab, could fight for a reunified Palestine—and live.

Such is the program for a revolutionary war against the Arab feudal lords, not a war of nationalist expansion against the Arab people. Such a

4

program cannot be expected from the present rightist government of Israel, dominated by the Jewish capitalist class and tail-ended by the bourgeois labor leaders of the Histadrut, which in the longer run can only stumble from disaster to stalemate to subservience under outside imperialism.

Such a program demands the fight for a workers' government in Israel as the vanguard of the future United Socialist States of the Middle East.

Without such a program all the heroic sacrifices of the Jewish people and all the military victories of the Haganah will not be able to make of Palestine anything but a death trap of the peoples and a happy hunting ground of revived imperialist influence.

Labor Action, May 24 & 31, 1948

Chapter II
HOW TO DEFEND ISRAEL

An uneasy four-week truce has just been signed by both sides in Palestine. It may mean the end of formal, declared hostilities; it may mean only a lull. If the title of this article were to be read as promising military advice, its relevance would therefore be in doubt.

But we shall concern ourselves exclusively with politics, not with military strategy; and whether the present truce is indefinitely continued or not, a state of war and imminence of war will continue to exist in Palestine. Abdullah, after agreeing to the truce, declares loudly that no permanent settlement is possible while the Jewish state exists; he may only be bargaining for a diminution of Israel's borders and a restriction of its sovereignty, especially with regard to immigration, but over this there will be a struggle also. The consideration of a political program for the defense of the Israelis' right to self-determination is equally important for either war or peace.

*

A new state has been set up. A people have declared that they want to live under their own government and determine their own national destiny. They have taken a blankcheck made out to the Right of Self-Determination and have signed their name to it: Israel. And they have sought to cash it in.

They have done this in the teeth of the opposition— direct, concealed or weaselly— of the imperialist capitals. And invading their defenses and threatening their independence came the reactionary onslaught of some of the most backward and reactionary kingships and dynasties of the world, the semi-feudal oppressors of the Arab people.

This reactionary invasion was launched with but one end in view—precisely to deprive the Israeli people of their right to self-determination.

Now the decision to set up a new national state in the world of today is no light matter. It may be a wise decision or a mistaken one, quite regardless of the fact that one has the right to make the decision. We have explained why, in our opinion, the decision was a mistaken one. This we did both before and after partition; and insofar as the question has significance now, after the accomplished fact, we consider that the course of events since partition has been proving that that opinion was correct.

We advocated a different course, a socialist plan to achieve a viable life for the peoples of Palestine, Jewish and Arab, and one which could not but meet with the opposition of the rulers of both peoples, the Zionist capitalists and the Arab effendis. We advocated that the workers, landworkers and peasants of both communities, joining their strength from below in common struggle, launch a united struggle for independence their then common master, British imperialism; and that they fight for the creation of a free, democratic Palestine based on universal suffrage and a fully democratic constituent assembly.

The national antagonisms between Jew and Arab do not exist only at the tops—today more than ever is this true, unfortunately!—but they stem, not from the interests of the exploited, but from the interests of the top rulers. In such a joint struggle for national liberation, the already strong tendencies toward Arab-Jewish cooperation from below could flower, the fellaheen could be torn away from their ties with the Arab landlords and money masters, the Jewish workers could be pried loose from the chauvinistic aims of the Zionist leadership, and a united democratic Palestine achieved in which both peoples could live with full national rights assured. This in brief.

The Zionist leadership (at first) and the Arab cabal also opposed partition, because they too had an alternative. Their alternative was the complete conquest of Palestine and the subordination of the other people, by force of arms if necessary. This was their reactionary, chauvinistic alternative to partition—one that was at the opposite pole from ours. If the Zionists accepted the partition—including elements like the Hashomer Hatzair which had to make a flipflop to do so—it was because the main Jewish leaders looked upon it as a necessary installment toward this end.

There was no such reason for our disagreement with partition to come to an end with the UN decision. As compared with the program we advocated, partition represented a setback on the road to the unity of the Jewish workers and Arab peasants. The creation of the Jewish state has indeed set up a state wall between them and has inflamed national feelings—or rather, has given the most reactionary elements in both camps the best opportunity to inflame them.

This is why we rejected partition as a solution for the Palestine problem. Nor has it solved the problem. It has only posed new conditions under which that solution must be sought.

That is why socialist thinking on this subject must start by understanding the distinction between (a) the Jews' right to self-determination, and (b) the correctness or advisability of exercising this right to the point of separation under given conditions. We need only refer to the fact that, before and after the Russian Revolution, the Bolsheviks' program called for defense of Finland's right to self-determination: before the revolution, Marxists in Finland advocated separation; after the revolution, the Communists in

Finland advocated unity with Russia; but both before and after, there was no question in their minds but that the Finns had the right to separate if they so willed. Never under Lenin did the Soviets attempt to deprive them of that right by force of arms.

But in the present case we do not even have the complication of a workers' state being involved. Far from it! The attack upon the Jews' right to self-determination comes from a deeply reactionary social class—the Arab lords—whose reactionary aims in this case are not alleviated by the fact that they themselves suffer from the exploitation of British imperialism (at the same time that they cling to that imperialism in order to defend their privileges against their own people).

In this conflict, as socialists—that is, as the only thoroughgoing and consistent democrats, we not only support the Palestine Jews' right to self-determination but draw the necessary conclusions from that position; for full recognition of the Jewish state by our own government; for lifting the embargo on arms to Israel; for defense of the Jewish state against the Arab invasion in the present circumstances.

But for us this is not the end of the question but only the beginning:

*

Defense of Israel, then. But, against whom must the Jews defend themselves?

The Arab Legion, of course. But since even the Zionist leaders know that, we make bold to point out that there is a second enemy.

In the eyes of partisans of freedom, what is going on in Palestine is a death struggle between a people fighting for their rights and a reactionary invader. But this struggle is taking place on a stage where the preliminaries of the Third World War are being acted out. Bending over the scene are the giants of world imperialism—the Big Three—themselves locked in battle (without guns) for the really big stakes of power.

And if we look at the same scene through their imperialist eyes, we see in Palestine: two dogs snapping and tearing at each other for a miserable bone. They sic on now one, now the other; bet on the outcome; nudge their favorites—and wait only for one thing: to be the one to carry off the stakes. Through their eyes there is no aura of democratic or national rights (and certainly not of humanitarianism) over the scene, any more than in a cockfight.

And ill will it be for Israel if, by dint of blood and sacrifice and heroic toil, they beat back the Arab invader only to fall over on the other side into the net of imperialism!

Now we Marxists are notoriously cynical about the motives and designs of all the capitalist and imperialist governments. But the role that Britain, specifically Laborite Britain, has been playing makes cynicism pale. The Labor party, which up to its assumption of power was denouncing the British government for its "betrayal" of the Jews of Palestine, has taken over the filthy, oil-reeking job of propping up the Abdullahs and Arab landlord-princes of the Middle East against the Jewish state.

Why? Because Ernie Bevin is a scoundrel? Far from it. It is because the "socialist" Laborites, after one day in office, discovered that "justice to the Jews" conflicted with their higher loyalty—loyalty to the interests of British imperialism, of which they are the current caretakers.

We cynical Marxists have been a bit less shocked than the Zionist leaders. We never looked to British imperialism to give justice to the Middle East, as they did. We never promised to be good British cat's-paws if only they granted a Jewish homeland, as did the Zionist leaders for decades, crawling on their bellies before Whitehall. We were never taken in by the fish story about the British Labor Party building a socialist England. "Perfidious Albion" is perfidious only to those who have been taken in by it: by its own lights, which have nothing to do with any ideals of freedom or justice, its leaders (Conservative or Laborite) have been consistently loyal and faithful servitors of the real rulers of England, the London City.

We knew that the coming of Bevin meant only a different signature under British imperialism, and said so in advance. Now a lot of other people have found it out too. How much more must the rank-and-file Zionists find out, how many more disappointments with "friends of the Jewish people" must they go through before they too understand and say:

No interference from the imperialists in Palestine, singly or collectively in the UN!

We can expect nothing from these Greeks bearing gifts—not even from the "fair" proposal of an embargo on both sides. This basis for the present truce, presented by the British, was rightly denounced by the Israeli leaders when first proposed. How equitable it is to embargo both sides with even-handed impartiality!—after the Arabs had stockpiled British arms and equipment with feverish haste for months, while the Israelis were still scurrying around for rifles and mortars. How equitable it is to forbid the importation of men for both sides!—in a situation where men for Israel must come through the British blockade, while men for the Arab Legion

10

need only cross over the land routes from the neighboring states. One might as well propose another perfectly impartial agreement, evenly applied to both sides—a proposal, for example, that both sides immediately stop worshipping Allah ...

We say to the imperialists: Lift the embargo! Get out of the lives of the Middle East peoples! Keep hands off! The Jewish and Arab peoples' road to fraternity may be a hard one, but you will intervene only to put both in your pocket!

And that must go for all of them. The British-proposed truce basis, so roundly denounced by the Jews before accepting it, came after long consultations with Lewis Douglas, U.S. ambassador to Britain, and was accepted (not too demonstratively) by the U.S. Truman, unlike Bevin, recognized the new state—bringing fulsome tributes from Zionist wheelhorses like Abba Hillel Silver—but what stopped him from immediately lifting the embargo on arms for the defense of this state whose existence he "recognized"?

"Perfidious Albion,"indeed! The British policy at least had been consistent with itself. Perfidious Washington has meanwhile been trying to carry water on both shoulders.

How many illusions can a Zionist retain? We are thinking of the fairly large number of Jewish socialists who consider themselves even "left-wing" Zionists. Can one give up illusions about "Socialist" Britain and retain the idea that Wall Street's government has any other intention except that of meddling in the situation in order to snare Palestine in its own net?

Or that Russia, which puts Zionists in slave camps, and whose satellites have not refrained from running guns to the Arab legions, has any other interest except to put Palestine under its own heel?

The truth is that all of the imperialist Big Three are playing for the Palestine stakes. Britain is betting on the Arabs. Russia, it would seem at the moment, is mainly wooing the Jews, at least in the diplomatic channels. The United States relies on a force without nationality, neither Arab nor Jewish nor even American—the force of gold. And it expects that whoever wins is going to be gathered into its golden fold and anointed with oil.

To all those disillusioned Zionists who are now par-boiling over the perfidy of "Socialist" Britain: not a particle more trust in Wall Street! We want no Greeks bearing gifts from Washington either.

For Israel to become the cat's-paw, the outpost, for any of the Big Three means its doom for any really independent existence. It will then be assigned to play the role in the Middle East that Czechoslovakia played in Eastern Europe between the First and Second World Wars. And if the

Middle East is allowed to remain the playground of imperialism up to the Third World War, then it may well be, as was written, that Armageddon will be in Palestine.

If not to the big powers, where then shall Israel turn for succor? Shall it rely only on its own arms? Can it rely only on the miliary forces of the Haganah, while the Arabs are supported by their secondhand ally, Britain? Is its own military defense enough?

Far be it from us to pooh-pooh the fact that wars are won with guns and cannon and aircraft and the independence of states defended by armed force. Wars are won with guns and cannon—but not all wars are won only with guns and cannon.

There was a war (in 1919 and the following years) waged by a people seeking to defend their independence, and it was fought with muskets against machine guns and swords against tanks and, almost, popguns against airplanes. That was the war fought by revolutionary Russia against the Allied intervention after the First World War—and they won. Because they had another weapon, and they used it.

There was another war (in 1936-38) fought, to be sure, with guns and cannon but against superior force. That was the war of the Spanish loyalist government against Franco. That war was lost. They too had another weapon, and did not use it.

The Spanish government relied only on bullets and bravery. Powerful weapons! But at hand was a greater one—the possibility of exploding an arsenal of weapons behind Franco's own lines. The loyalist government, restrained by the combine of bourgeois politicians and Stalin's counter-revolutionaries, refused to give its freedom to Morocco—and the Moors remained with Franco to the end. They refused to tell the peasants to take the land—and behind Franco's lines the peasants remained mainly quiet and passive. Because, much as they hated Franco, they were given no cause for great joy in a loyalist victory.

Facing the enemy on fourteen fronts and almost without an army, the Russian Revolution turned back the combined assault of the military powers of the world—because they demonstrated in action to the people and to the soldiers of both sides that their victory had a social meaning.

I mention this to show that there is something else to be relied on besides guns and cannon and instead of a sellout for imperialist aid. What is that weapon in Palestine?

The road to a lasting victory in Palestine is for the Israelis to wage the war as a war against the Arab landlords and dynasts and not as a war against the Arab people. And this not in tender expressions of sympathy and tolerance but in demonstrated deeds.

The present situation in Palestine—the fruit of partition and the end product of Zionist policy toward the Arabs—can only continue to inflame national hostility and chauvinism on both sides. On the one hand, there is the disgraceful portent of the Deir Yassin massacre of Arab women and children by the Irgun, unpunished by the official Israeli leadership and therefore, in the eyes of the Arabs, endorsed. On the other hand, there is the godsent opportunity for the effendis to inflame the antagonism of the mass of Arab peasantry toward the Jews as such.

Under these conditions, with all its economic life intertwined with its Arab neighbors', with its supply lines and commercial routes interpenetrating, with its national life economically dependent and helpless—what can be the future of a splinter country separated from the world on all sides and surrounded by a wall of hatred?

Only a chronic nightmare existence, a new horror of the twentieth century, a state-wide ghetto, a death trap for the Jews!

This is the direction in which the present rightist-bourgeois government of Israel is heading. And along these lines, its only avenue of escape—no, not escape, but its only possibility of even alleviating that nightmare is complete capitulation to one of the predatory imperialisms; to become its outpost in the Middle East, the harlot Jerusalem.

This is not a chimera conjured up. This is a reality of Israel's adventure into statehood. From these vicious alternatives of destruction, imperialist overlordship or permanent nightmare in a Balkanized Middle East, the Israeli people can escape only by relying on the only other force that they can seek to lean on: the mass of Arab workers and peasants who are exploited and oppressed by the very same rulers who invade Palestine.

The key is right at hand. It is the 30-40 per cent of Israel which is now Arab. Israel's future will be determined in the first place by how it acts toward them. It is not enough to "leave them be." The Israelis must demonstrate that they seek the alliance of the Arab masses, that they are carrying on a social war—not Jew against Arab, but a war of classes.

It must seek to integrate the Arabs into the country on a completely equal basis with the Jews:

(1) An end to the Jim-Crow trade unions by which those Arab workers who are organized are kept in "parallel" unions.

(2) Stamp out the policy of kibbush avoda—the ousting of Arab labor—in every sphere.

13

(3) Stamp out the policy of boycotting Arab goods.

(4) An end to every other form of economic nationalism.

(5) Organize the state as the home of both peoples with equal national status: in schools, in the government, in the use and teaching of both languages, in every aspect of national life.

(6) State aid to the Arab peasants, as to the Jewish colonists.

(7) Distribution to the Arab peasants of all lands vacated by Arab landlords and under Israeli control.

(8) The formation of a bi-national army and police.

This outcome can be made possible by the successful prosecution of the other steps.

Such a program, we are perfectly aware, means a complete overturn of the policy of the Jewish leaders. But only such a program, of which the above points represent not the whole but a beginning and a token, can transform the war of defense into a social war, a war with the dynamic power to tear apart the national unity behind the Arab rulers' legions. Only such a program can prepare for the reunification of the splintered land into a community where Jew and Arab can live in fraternity.

Such a reunited state cannot come about while the Arab effendi, landlord and militarist remains in control of his Arab vassal. It cannot come about while Zionist nationalism rules Israel. It can come about only if the working masses of both people unite, from below, and tear themselves away from their own ruling classes. The working-class movement among the Jews is powerful; the majority of its calls itself socialist, many even left-wing socialists. Here is the only consistent socialist program for a reunited Palestine.

This is the program for transforming the war into a revolutionary war against the Arab feudal masters—and striking down the perpetrators of Deir Yassin massacres who call for Jewish expansionism against the Arab people. It has to be fought for against the present leaders of Israel, dominated by the Jewish capitalist class and trailed by the bourgeois labor leaders of the Histadrut.

New International, July, 1948

Chapter III
ISRAEL'S ARAB MINORITY;
THE BEGINNING OF A TRAGEDY

Tell it not in Gath, publish it not in the streets of Askelon; lest the daughters of the Philistines rejoice, lest the daughters of the uncircumcised triumph.   2 Samuel 1:20

All well-wishers of Israel, including the official Zionists themselves, are accustomed to the platitude that its peace and security depend upon normal relations with the Arab world which surrounds it. Instead there has been increasing hostility, in a vicious circle of reciprocal hatred, which threatens to embroil the region, perhaps the world, in war. It is to be feared that the outcome of the Zionist "fulfillment," so far from being the solution to the Jewish problem that was heralded by Zionism, may mean a new act in the tragedy of the Jewish people.

To break out of the vicious circle requires an attempt to win the support and friendship of the Arab masses away from and against the Arab rulers, from below, toward the goal of a binational state. For Israel this program begins at home: Israel will never be at peace with the surrounding Arab world, even if it makes a deal with the Colonel Nassers, as long as it is at war with its own Arab minority. This is the place to start.

The very existence of an Arab minority is shadowy in the minds of most Americans—some say, also in the minds of most Israelis—in spite of the fact that it is over one-tenth of the nation, like the Negro minority in the United States.

When the Israeli Arabs are not ignored, they are often labeled en bloc as "fifth-columnists" and suspect agents of the foreign Arabs who are foes of Israel; for they are all Arabs, aren't they. They are spoken of as the "remnant of the enemy defeated in 1948" in spite of the fact that they were not defeated in 1948 since they did not fight against Israel.

Israel's Arab problem, of course, goes back to the beginnings of Zionist colonization. It is not true that the Zionists came into Palestine as "agents of British imperialism" with the creation of the Mandate after the First World War. What is true is that they came as conscious junior partners of British imperialism: they would ensure continued British domination of the country, they proposed, if they were in turn given a free hand to take it over from the indigenous Arabs. Chaim Weizmann, who became Zionism's world leader and later first president of Israel as the shrewd architect of this symbiotic relationship, is quite candid about this in his autobiography.[1] It is not his fault, or that of the Zionists, if this policy foundered after 1945, when the British government under Bevin made a sharp turn to the Arabs.

The Zionist infiltration into Palestine, therefore, took place before Arab eyes as the entrance of an alien and hostile force, under the umbrella of another alien and hostile force. Unfortunately the Zionist movement and the Israel government, despite frequent bows to the ideal of Jewish-Arab friendship, have never ceased to give nourishment to this feeling.

At least ever since Dr. Weizmann blurted out in 1919 that Zionism aimed to make Palestine "as Jewish as England is English," the Arabs have feared that this aim could not be achieved without driving out or otherwise getting rid of the population that was in the way. Zionists countered with arguments supplemented by promises and pledges. Deeds are always more important.

Today we find that, in truth, the setting up of the Zionist state coincided with a process whereby the large majority of the Palestinian Arabs found themselves separated from their land and homes. How did this happen?

1.

And it shall be, when the Lord thy God shall have brought thee into the land which he sware unto thy fathers . . . to give them great and goodly cities, which thou buildedest not, and houses full of good things, which thou filledst not, and wells digged, which thou diggedst not, vineyards and olive trees, which thou plantedst not. Deuteronomy 6:10—11

This is the nearest good starting point for an investigation of the current situation of the Arabs in Israel, as well as of the Arab refugees around Israel. It is a story enveloped in a fog of propaganda on both sides.

On November 29, 1947 the UN General Assembly adopted its resolution for the partition of Palestine. When the British Mandate ended next May, the Zionists declared the establishment of the State of Israel, and the Arab states invaded Palestine to forcibly annul the partition by aggression.

When the fighting broke out in 1948, even before May, there began a great flight and displacement of the Palestinian Arab population, a veritable exodus from their homes and farms. Out of 700,000 Arabs, there were only about 170—180,000 left within the enlarged borders of Israel when it was over.

The official Zionist version is that this flight took place in cooperation with the invading armies of the foreign Arab states. The official Israel government pamphlet, The Arabs in Israel, asserts:

It began on the express orders of the Arab commanders and political leaders, who assured the [Palestinian Arab] people that their evacuation to the neighboring

Arab countries would only be of short duration and that they would soon return in the wake of the victorious Arab armies and receive a handsome share of the booty.[2]

In addition, according to the same official version, the Palestinian Arabs had thought the invasion would be a walkaway, but when the Arab armies were defeated, "they panicked and stampeded across the frontiers. ... Knowing what they had intended to do to their neighbors, they now expected the victorious Jews to mete out similar treatment to them."[3] A mass guilty conscience. The Jews, on the other hand, according to this same account, vainly tried to convince these Arabs to stay and keep the peace.

The official version, therefore, provides the moral and even juridical justification for three aspects of Israel policy:

(1) Israel claims little responsibility for or to the hundreds of thousands of Arab refugees from its territory who are now living across its borders in misery and seething hatred.

(2) The government used the Arab flight to justify a series of laws which have stripped these refugees, as well as many Arabs who never left Israel, or are still in Israel, of their lands, groves and property.

(3) The version of the Arab flight, with its accompanying view of Arab disloyalty, is also the justification for the maintenance, up to today and for the indefinite future, of military-government rule over the large majority of Arabs still in Israel. Eighty-five per cent of the Arab minority in Israel live under political conditions which often resemble that of a conquered enemy under army occupation by its foe. This is not exactly a help to Jewish-Arab friendship.

How important this version of the Arab flight is to the Zionists can be realized only by indicating its economic meaning. In the following summary, the legal terms "absentee property" or "abandoned" property refer to property seized from Arabs who had left their homes during the fighting for any reason:

Of the 370 new Jewish settlements established between 1948 and the beginning of 1953, 350 were on absentee property. In 1954 more than one-third of Israel's Jewish population lived on absentee property and nearly a third of the new immigrants (250,000 people) settled in urban areas abandoned by Arabs. ... Most of the Arab groves were taken over by the Israel Custodian of Absentee Property. ... In 1951-52, former Arab groves produced one and a quarter million boxes of fruit, of which 400,000 were exported. Arab fruit sent abroad provided nearly 10 per cent of the country's foreign currency earnings from exports in 1951. In 1949 the olive produce from abandoned Arab groves was Israel's third largest export ranking after citrus and diamonds.

The CCP [UN's Conciliation Commission for Palestine] estimated that the amount of Israel's cultivable abandoned Arab land was nearly two and a half times the total area of Jewish-owned property at the end of the mandate [1948].

In 1951 abandoned cultivable land included nearly 95 percent of all Israel's olive groves.[4]

The government's Custodian of Absentee Property was in 1953 "one of the largest employers in Israel, and perhaps the largest single landlord, renting over 65,000 housing and business units of Arab absentee property."[5]

This will give a preliminary idea of the role played by the flight of the Palestinian Arabs in the establishment of the State of Israel. Much is at stake when the Zionists insist that the flight represented an act of hostility to the State of Israel.

But suppose it was only the normal reaction of people trying to get out of the way of flying bullets? Suppose it was not in cooperation with the Arab invaders, but out of fear of them? Suppose it was also out of fear of Israeli atrocities? Suppose it was also due in part to the ouster of peaceful Arabs by Israeli troops?

Let us investigate three forces at work in precipitating the flight: the Arab states' invasion; the Zionist forces, regular and irregular troops; and the British who were departing the country in bitterness in the twilight of their power.

2.

Two nations are in thy womb, and two manner of people shall be separated from thy bowels. Genesis 25:23

A couple of things about the social structure of the Arab community in Palestine should be mentioned for background.

When the British ended the mandate and withdrew, the Jewish communities had a whole quasi-government, or shadow government, ready to take its place and carry on all essential government functions and social services. Not so the Arabs.

> When the British administration evacuated . . . there was no organized Arab body to manage the services of government essential for communal organization. With the breakdown of all functions of government necessary to maintain public law, order, and well-being—water, electricity, posts, police, education, health, sanitation, and the like—Arab morale collapsed. [6]

This provided the context, not the cause, for the flight.

Besides, mass flight was not uncommon in the history of the Middle East, in similar cases where a population had reason to fear the waging of a war over their soil.

It was not only governmental services that collapsed, but also the social structure. As we shall see, it was the Arab upper class which fled first.

> The upper class consists, as a rule, of a few great families whose members occupy key positions in the economic, professional and other occupational fields in the country. ...

> It was this small but extremely wealthy and influential class which represented Arab Palestine in practically every manifestation of social, civic, economic and political life. ... It was common knowledge that their interests were often diametrically opposed to those of the fellahin who constituted three-quarters of the Arab population of Palestine but were illiterate, inarticulate and unable to voice any opinion.[7]

This thin upper-class layer was highly nationalistic but also socially and politically reactionary. Though it did not represent the interests of the peasant masses, yet when it fled, the whole Arab community became structurally unstable. This was even more true in the Arab urban communities, like Jaffa and Haifa.

According to the official Zionist and Israeli version (for example, the government propaganda pamphlet Arabs in Israel) not only did the Palestine Arabs support the invasion by the foreign Arab states but, even before the May invasion, Palestine Arabs formed the majority of the bands of Arab irregulars who harassed Jewish settlements in the first months of 1948.[8] This may or may not be so, but how many such Palestine Arabs were there? On the other hand, what was the attitude of the mass of Palestine Arabs?

Arthur Koestler, a lifelong Zionist (Revisionist) who was then in Palestine as a correspondent, writing of this early-1948 period, reports:

Ragged strangers kept appearing in increasing numbers in Arab villages and towns. ... As the Palestine Arabs shows little willingness to fight, most of the sniping, ambushing and guerilla warfare was done by the foreign volunteers ... after the first serious clashes had occurred between Arabs and Jews in Tiberias ... the heads of the two communities arranged a truce, the Arab delegates stating that the attackers of the Jewish quarter were 'strangers who had forced their way into the town.'[9]

The Jewish ethnologist Raphael Patai writes:

The majority of the Israeli Moslem Arabs, however, chose not to become involved in the Arab-Jewish fights. On the Jewish side there was never any pressure exercised on them to take up arms against their own brethren; and they themselves tried hard to escape the demands of the Arab armies and guerrillas for active help or financial support.[10]

David Ben-Gurion himself, in a magazine article published at the beginning of 1948,[11] testified that

Indeed, the vast majority of the Palestinian Arabs still refuse to join in this war despite the combined pressure of the Mufti and his gangs, of the Arab rulers and potentates who support him and of the Mandatory Power [Britain] whose policy aids and abets Arab aggression.

... The Arab villages have in their overwhelming majority kept aloof from the struggle. Were it not for the terrorization by the Arab bands and the incitement of their British supporters, the Arab people of Palestine would have soon resumed peaceful relations with the Jewish neighbors.

This was written before the land-grab had begun. It was only later that Israeli propagandists started putting forth a different version—i.e., after the land-grab was under way.

In the same issue of the same Zionist organ from which we have quoted Ben-Gurion, the same picture was drawn by another Arab expert of the Zionists, Yaakov Shimoni.[12] Among other things he stresses that

the fact remains that the bulk of the Arab population has so far kept aloof from attacks on the Jews. Up to the present, the instigators of the disorders have been unable to enlist the mass of either the fellahin or the urban Arabs. . . .

And after a detailed account of the people's reaction, he concludes:

The hopes of the Mufti and the AHE [Arab Higher Executive] have thus far been disappointed because although they instigated and initiated the attack, they have been unable to deliver the goods: the mass of the Arab people of Palestine have failed to rise at their orders and have proved reluctant and incapable of fighting the Jews.

The interested reader can find testimony to the same effect in several other Zionist sources.[13]

Now, as mentioned, the Zionist story is that the Arab Higher Executive called on the Palestine Arabs to flee their homes, come over the border, and wait till they could return in triumph to a conquered land.[14] If we assume for the sake of argument that it was indeed the policy of the AHE to issue this call, it still does not tell us whether or not the Palestinian Arabs did in fact heed the call. For that, the testimony we have just cited is more relevant.

3.

What mean ye that ye beat my people to pieces, and grind the faces of the poor? Isaiah 3:15.

What is agreed upon by virtually all sides, however, is the class differentiation in the flight. This may also serve to explain a kernel of truth in the Zionist version of the flight.

It is to the well-to-do Arab upper class (a small minority) that part of the Zionist story does apply, not to the Arab masses. In the first phase of the flight—i.e., before the start of heavy fighting, also before the Deir Yassin massacre, for example—it was these elements, the rich leaders of Arab society, who fled of their own free will.

Even the Israel government propaganda pamphlet takes note of the class distinction:

> During the earlier phases of the fighting, the movement [of mass exodus] was on a small scale. Approximately 30,000 Arabs, mostly of the well-to-do classes, left for the neighboring states to await the outcome of the struggle, as they had done during the troubles of 1936—39.[15]

But this is relatively grudging admission compared to the abundant evidence on this point from Zionist sources. The Israel Digest in April 1949 said that "the well-to-do ones departed before May 14th in pursuance of a deliberate plan" (the plan being the AHE strategy previously quoted from the Zionist story, but the significant thing to note is that it is here ascribed only to the few rich Arabs), but "The poorer classes did not flee until the first month of Israel's existence. . . ."[16] According to this, the "poorer classes" did not join in the flight until after the Deir Yassin massacre and many other things had happened. What then happens to the now-official Zionist story of an AHE plot for a mass exodus as the justification for Israel's refugee policy, land policy, and military government over the Arab minority?

Exactly the same statement is made in the January 1949 issue of the Tel-Aviv journal Israel & Middle East.[17]

Yaakov Shimoni wrote a few months later that "the educated and wealthier people ... were among the first to run away, in contrast to the poorer strata of the community."[18] As early as February 4, 1948, the British High Commissioner reported that "panic continues to increase ... throughout the Arab middle classes, and there is a steady exodus of those who can afford to leave the country."[19]

A Zionist writer reported: "in the town it was the workers and the poor who remained, together with a thin layer of middle-class families."[20] The well-known journalist Hal Lehrman, writing in Commentary for December 1949, summed up:

> The imams fled from the mosques, the kadis from the courts, the doctors, the teachers, practically all the intellectuals. Only workers and peasants remained.[21]

22

A great understanding can be gained if one remembers that
the Israeli Arab minority problem as we know it today concerns the
treatment of these workers and peasants who remained, in spite of it all.

4.

For they fled from the swords, from the drawn sword, and from the
bent bow, and from the grievousness of war.
Isaiah 21:15.

"In spite of all" covers a great deal. Even if the Arab invaders'
contribution to the flight was not that given in the Zionist version (the call
to an exodus, etc.), still it played a bit role. This role, however, was usually
just the opposite of that which is commonly used to justify Israeli policy.

The Palestine Arab population did not flee out of sympathy with and in
cooperation with the Arab invaders, but out of fear of them and of the war.
This is easy to understand, but for the Zionists to admit this is to stamp their
subsequent Arab minority policy with a certain brand.

Yet it creeps into even the Israel propaganda pamphlet which puts
forward the official story; there we learn incidentally that time and again the
foreign Arab commanders had to use force to prevent the local Arabs from
making truces with the Israel forces.[22] It creeps into the book by the
Revisionist leader Schechtman where, as a matter of fact, we get the theory
(by Schechtman) that the very reason why the AHE called for a mass exodus
was "to prevent the possibility of establishing normal relations between the
Jewish authorities and the Arab minority; for once this occurred, it might
lead to Jewish-Arab cooperation and ultimately to Arab acquiescence in the
existence of Israel."[23] For a chauvinist like Schechtman, this already
confesses a great deal.

Pierre van Paassen, a well-known pro-Zionist of the Christian-mystic
fellow-traveling type, is anxious to prove in his book[24] that the Arabs did not
flee out of fear of Israeli atrocities. No, he argues, they fled out of fear of
being murdered by the Mufti's henchmen if they stayed and refused to
cooperate. He seems quite unaware that he is giving the lie to the official
Zionist version and condemning its policy.

The ardent Zionist historian Harry Sacher likewise gives us this truth: he
remarks that "the Arab commandants ordered the Arabs on the fringes to
evacuate their villages" [italics added].[25]

An Israeli writer told in 1949 of the village of Tarshiha, whose Arabs did
not flee. The villagers described how Kaukji, the Syrian leader of the Arab

irregulars who had undertaken guerilla operations even before the formal invasion,

> ruled this district for several months and quickly brought it towards destruction and death. ... One hears the same story throughout the whole of Western Galilee, in dozens of villages along the Lebanese frontier, the same tale of the despotic rule of Kaukji's brigands. They would carry people from their homes in the darkness of the night—never any questions asked. It was enough to "be on the list" on the slightest suspicion, a single word from one of the brigands. They removed them from their families to places outside the village, a few shots were heard in the darkness, and once more the population was reduced by a couple of villagers.[26]

This is hardly the description of a population which was so sympathetic to the invader that it deserves, today, to be robbed, discriminated against, and slandered as "fifth columnists" en masse.

Chaim Weizmann, speaking to U.S. Ambassador McDonald in 1948, talked "of the flight of the Arab population from Israel—a flight at times so panicky that coins were left on the tables of huts in the Arab villages. "[27] This also scarcely fits the official story about a planned exodus at the call of the foreign Arabs.

5.

> But this is a people robbed and spoiled, but they are all of them snared in holes, and they are hid in prison houses: they are for a prey, and none delivereth; for a spoil, and none saith. Restore. Who among you will give eat to this? Who will hearken and hear for the time to come?
>
> Isaiah 42:22—23

A similar picture emerges from war-news items of the time in the Palestine Post, semi-official Zionist English-language daily in Jerusalem. When Iraqi invading forces took over the Ramallah area, which was and is Arab, they had to proclaim martial law and a curfew—

> and the population was warned that violators would be shot at by the Iraqis. Houses of Arabs who try to run away in the future will be blown up, the P.B.S. [radio] announced. Mukhtars and elders of

24

villages in the Ramallah area were ... threatened with severe punishment in the event of panic or chaos. [May 7, 1948.]

This is a population under foreign occupation, not a population cooperating with invaders. Or take the report on Tiberias, quoting a Jewish Agency spokesman, which appeared in the Palestine Post on April 21, 1948: the local Arab leaders there had always been friendly, opposed to the anti-jewish policies of the AHE; Kaukji's irregulars had occupied their houses "against the wishes of the inhabitants"—

A number of clashes occurred between the local and foreign Arabs, and local Arabs asked the British authorities for help to get rid of the invaders, but none was given.

Then, when the invaders were defeated by Jewish forces, they forced the local Arab families to evacuate. "This measure was meant to rouse the neighboring Arab States and induce them to send help."

In the same issue, the Zionist daily editorializes on the fact that the entire Arab population of Tiberias "were forced to leave by the Arab command. ... In fact, the gangs were resisted as far as possible by those whose interests they had come to 'protect.'"

The nearly five months of fighting in Palestine has proven that the Arabs of the country—the ordinary townsmen, the fellahin and the Bedu [Bedouins] of the South—have no heart in the struggle. They did not want it to begin and they have no wish for it to continue."

But many of these Arabs, forced to abandon their land, were later robbed of it through the "abandoned land" and "absentee property" laws rigged up for the purpose by the Israelis.

Or if they wound up across the border in refugee camps, they became willy-nilly part of the hapless hundreds of thousands who were reviled as "enemies" and "fifth-columnists" while their property was being stolen.

How could non-hostile Arabs wind up across the border? Read, for example, a feature article in the Palestine Post on May 12, 1948, written sympathetically by Dorothy Bar-Adon: she describes how

the "displaced" Arabs seeking refuge in the Emek unburden their hearts to the Jews whom they meet at roadblocks or in the fields. It is the familiar, time-worn complaint—"they," the outsiders, are responsible for all this.

And she describes how "The refugees are driven from pillar to post. There is simply no room and no food." They go to Nazareth; then despairingly have to move on to Jenin; to Beisan; nowhere can they be provided for.

So the refugee crosses to Trans-Jordan. From here he may be deported back again. And where does one go then?

Dorothy Bar-Adon prefaces this account with the appealing remark: "And who can understand this bewildered running better than the Jew who has been doing it on and off for a few thousand years?"

A Revisionist-Zionist writer who minces no words about his aim of squeezing all the Arabs out of Palestine—even this chauvinist found it possible to report honestly in 1950:

> I truly sympathize with the great pain of those tens of thousands of Arabs who fled from Israel under pressure of the Mufti's bands, although they themselves wished to continue to live in neighborliness with the Jews and find work and their livelihood among them. I know of villages which defended themselves with arms against the forced entry of hired Mufti soldiers, and subsequently "evacuated" the villages for fear of military courts which threatened them.[28]

He mentions about a dozen that he knows of "personally."

Or take the case of the Jawarish (or Arab el-Guarish) tribe, as it came to light after they were finally resettled. This tribe had been such firm allies of the Zionist colonizers that they had been trusted to guard the Jewish settlements at Gedera; they had helped Jews get around British regulations and Arab hostility against Jewish purchase of land by lending their own names for the deals. Yet, when the fighting began, they had to flee simply to live, winding up in one of the refugee camps of the Gaza strip.[29]

They were not repatriated until years later—even these Arabs, who were quislings from the point of view of the nationalists—and even they never got their own land back, but were resettled on new land provided by the state with a well-publicized ceremony in 1953.

Perhaps the most notable case of a tribe that was friendly to and supported the Jews, but which fled across the border during the fighting, was that of the village of Abu Gosh, which we will not document here since it is a longer and more important story which will fit better into a subsequent article on Israel's Arabs since 1948.

But in most cases it did not matter whether Arabs were friendly or hostile; it did not matter why they had to flee; it did not matter whether their flight was due to fear of the foreign Arab "liberators" or of Israeli atrocities like Deir Yassin; many were impartially stripped of their land and property, or relegated to the miserable refugee camps if that was where they landed, or subjected to military rule inside Israel—on the pretext that they had fled in order to answer the call of Israel's enemies!

6.

Thou makest us a byword among the heathen, a shaking of the head among the people. Psalms 44:14.

If the foreign Arab invaders are the first force to be considered that precipitated the flight, then the second that must be taken up is the British.

The attitude of the British imperial power in giving up the mandate was a vicious snarl of spite: "We wash our hands of this mess, and may you all bog down in it." And if the resulting disordered tangle were to become bad enough, who knows but that the British might be called back? They were not sorry to see themselves followed by chaos. And more than one observer has charged that they helped chaos along a bit.

The sharpest indictment of the British role as a precipitant of the Arab flight was made by E.N. Koussa, a prominent Israeli Arab attorney, in a letter to the Palestine Post of February 2, 1949.[30] Koussa testifies how the British authorities, before departure, encouraged and often initiated Arab evacuation, worked "to create an atmosphere permeated with fear and alarm,"etc.

When conditions in Tiberias, where the friendly relations between Arabs and Jews formed a bright illustration of the possibility of the two communities cooperating, became acute, the British authorities forcibly transported the Arab inhabitants en masse to Transjordan, he charged (as quoted by Schechtman).

The Greek Catholic bishop of Haifa, Msgr. Hakim, also ascribed much responsibility to the British.[31] A World Jewish Congress leader, N. Barou, wrote that the British helped the flight along "by spreading atrocity stories. ... They also provided transport, convoys, etc."[32] and he repeats the accusation about Tiberias. When British authorities told Arabs (in Haifa, for example) that the Jews would cut them to pieces if they stayed,[33] some may really have thought so or they may have been motivated by guile, but in either case our own investigation has only the following question before it:

Insofar as the British role was a factor in causing the flight, how can one justify the draconic punishments imposed by Israel on the Arab minority as well as the refugees for what was not their own doing? How in good conscience can even the paid Israeli propagandists claim that the harsh refugee policy, or the land-grab, or the military government, is justified because these Arabs who were displaced were "enemies of Israel"?

7.

Now go and smite Amalek, and utterly destroy all that they have, and spare them not; but slay both man and woman, infant and suckling, ox and sheep, camel and ass.

1 Samuel 15:3.

All this might be enough in itself to confute the Zionist version; but when we find further that the Zionist-Israeli forces themselves played a prominent role in causing and intensifying the flight, then a darker and more sinister shadow falls over the harsh penalties which they later imposed on the Arab victims of their own actions.

The first sector of this question concerns the Zionist terrorist group, the Irgun Zvei Leumi, the military outgrowth of the Revisionist wing of Zionism—i.e., the most chauvinistic, most anti-Arab, most reactionary wing, which shaded into fascist tendencies (today organized in Israel in the Herut party, now the second strongest in the country). These extreme chauvinists always had, as compared with the other Zionists, the most consistent perspective of a Palestine which would not only be "as Jewish as England is English," but which would also be as Araberein as Hitler wanted Germany to be Judenrein.

From early in the fighting, it seems clear, the Irgun oriented toward utilizing the war to achieve this objective, well in advance of the official Zionists' uneasy drift toward this same end. They struck their big blow on

April 9, 1948 against Deir Yassin, an Arab village near Jerusalem on the highway to Tel-Aviv.[34]

Why against Deir Yassin? the distinguished British Zionist editor Jon Kimche writes:

> Deir Yassin was one of the few Arab villages whose inhabitants had refused permission for foreign Arab volunteers to use it as a base of operations against the Jewish life-line into Jerusalem; they had on occasions collaborated with the Jewish Agency."[35]

Deir Yassin had to be the victim because its Arabs were friendly with the Jews. In Labor Action, Al and Ed Findley gave more details culled from the Jewish press:

> It was the only village in the Jerusalem area that had not appealed to any Arab authority as being in danger from the Jews. The villagers lived under an agreement of non-aggression with Jewish settlements surrounding it. In the winter of 1947 (long before the Deir Yassin massacre in April 1948) Abba Hushi, Jewish labor leader, cited a number of Arab villages in which the villagers had fought off Arab bands attempting to infiltrate and occupy them as positions against the Jews. Deir Yassin was prominently noted. Its villagers had successfully repelled an armed Arab band which attempted to entrench itself in the village mill. These Arab villagers ... faithfully carried out their obligation to exclude strangers and to maintain peaceful relations, despite the partition fighting.[36]

This was the village chosen by the Irgun for their planned massacre of (writes Kimche) "some 250 innocent Arabs, among them more than a hundred women and children."[37] The International Red Cross representative who visited the scene of the outrage, Jacques de Reynier, reported that the bodies of some 150 men, women and children had been thrown down a cistern while some 90 other bodies were scattered about.[38] The houses were destroyed. The few villagers who were not slaughtered were paraded by the Irgun through the streets of Jerusalem—in triumph.

Deir Yassin resounded through the land, indeed through the world, and with the desired effect. Even a record of friendship for the Jews was no protection, no insurance. It was after this that the Arab flight became general.

There is no question about the fact that there were also atrocities committed by the Kaukji and Mufti armed forces against Jews; the invaders had their Deir Yassins too, even if on a smaller scale. There is an abundance of testimony on this. But this would be relevant only in a debate on a subject which is not ours: namely, which side was worse in the Palestine war?

8.

Such is the way of an adulterous woman; she eateth, and wipeth her mouth, and saith, I have done no wickedness.
Proverbs 30:20.

But didn't the Jewish Agency condemn the Deir Yassin massacre and apologize for it? It did. Even if that were the whole story, few people would wonder why the mass of Arabs, already confused and panicked by Arab invaders and British, decided that flight held greater safety than trusting in the regrets of Ben-Gurion. But there are two other facets to this story.

(1) The official-Zionist army, Haganah, repudiated the massacre, undoubtedly sincerely, but also went on to claim that the Irgun had attacked Deir Yassin without any military justification and without the agreement of the official forces. The Irgun countered by releasing the exact text of the letter from the regional Haganah commander agreeing to the attack (not to a massacre, of course).[39] This has not really been refuted. The friendly village was not supposed to be turned into an abattoir, naturally, but it was supposed to be assaulted and invested as a military operation, in cynical violation of any non-aggression obligation to it.[40]

(2) The official-Zionist righteously deplored and condemned—but did absolutely nothing to take any effective steps against the repetition of Irgun atrocities. On the contrary, the relations between the official Zionists and the Irgun were now closer than ever.

Only seven months before, on September 18, 1947, the Haganah had raked the Irgun and Sternists with the denunciation:"these organizations gain their livelihood by gangsterism, smuggling, large-scale drug traffic, armed robbery, organizing the black market, and thefts"; and announced measures to root out terrorism.[41] But partition changed all that in November. By December the Haganah had overcome its moral sensibilities and was negotiating with Irgun for an agreement on cooperation. Such an agreement was reached in April, the very month of the Deir Yassin massacre.

The prominent Zionist historian Harry Sacher uneasily limits his comment on this to:

> ... Much is still obscure as to the relations between the Haganah or the Government and the Irgun. For comprehensible reasons the Government does not think the time yet come to tell its story fully and frankly.[42]

Among the obscure relations is undoubtedly the role of the other official—Zionist armed force, the Palmach. The Palestine Post reported four days after the massacre:

> The Haganah statement denied IZL [Irgun] claims that Palmach units had cooperated in the attack, and pointed out that it was only after urgent appeals for help that the Palmach had provided covering fire, to enable the administration of first aid to the wounded dissidents [Irgunists] in the village [April 13, 1948.]

It is not easy to see what, according to the official story, the Palmach was doing there in the first place.

So it is not quite true that the Deir Yassin massacre was simply the uncontrollable act of mavericks for whom the official Zionists were not responsible, as it is represented by all good Zionist writers who duly express their horror at it. They do not express any horror at the idea that the government and Haganah at this time made their alliance with these perpetrators of this "Lidice," and continued it. (It was not Arab-extermination which moved them to break with the terrorists; it was the assassination five months later of the UN mediator, Count Bernadotte, by Sternists.)

9.

Is there yet any portion or inheritance for us in our father's house?
Genesis 31:14

The Deir Yassin massacre "was a turning point," says Sacher quite accurately. The foreign Arab invaders trumpeted its horror far and wide, no doubt with the aim of stimulating anti-Israel militancy on the part of the anti-war Palestine population; the actual result of their propaganda

31

was to convince all strata, poor as well as rich Arabs, that the best thing to do was to get out of the war zone—to flee until the hostilities were over.

The massive effect of Deir Yassin on the flight is testified to from all sides.[43] The flight for the first time became general. The matter of chronology is very important; for it proves that the flight cannot be explained away as due to some previous call by the Arab invaders, as is done by Zionist party-liners and the official history-rewriters of Israel.

Another thing has to be noted about the impact of Deir Yassin. Like others we have used the term "official Zionists" as distinct from the terrorists. But this was the month before the establishment of the state. As far as the Arab people knew, was the Irgun really less "official" than the Haganah?

Jon Kimche's book provides an important bit of background here. He explains at length how the Irgun set about convincing the British, the world press and the Arabs that it, not Haganah, was the decisive power in the Zionist community, that it was "taking over," etc. The British passed this on to the Arab governments.

> It had the desired effect among the Arabs. It swayed many who had been hesitating on the brink of decision, whether to flout the United Nations and go to war against the Palestine Zionists or not. For though it has become a habit among Israelis and pro-Zionists to assume that there was nothing but evil hatred behind the Arab decision to go to war against Israel, and that the Arab explanation that they came to save their brethren from attack by the terrorists was a cheap excuse. For the benefit of those who cared to believe it, it must be stressed that there was great and very real Arab concern for the fate of the Palestine Arabs. This concern reached fever-heat when the British information was passed on that the terrorists were becoming the decisive factor in the Jewish armed forces.[44]

Kimche notes that this belief was reinforced when the Irgun took it upon itself in April to attack Jaffa, the Arab twin city to Tel-Aviv.

10.

Woe to him that buildeth a town with blood, and establisheth a city
by iniquity!   Habukkuk 2:12.

Deir Yassin was fresh in the minds of all when later in April the Zionist
forces got ready to attack the Arab city and port of Haifa in anticipation
of the withdrawal of the British troops. The Haifa situation requires
special attention because it is the big show piece for the Zionist contention
that, far from pushing the Arabs out, the Jews pleaded with them to stay.
As in some other cases, there is a kernel of truth here which the Zionist
apologists pretend is the whole story.

Menachem Begin, the Irgun commander, stresses in his book that the
effect of Deir Yassin was decisive for the flight from Haifa:

> The legend of Dir Yassin helped us in particular in the saving of
> Tiberias and the conquest of Haifa. ... [And after describing the
> assault on Haifa:] All the Jewish forces proceeded to advance
> through Haifa like a knife through butter. The Arabs began fleeing
> in panic, shouting: 'Deir Yassin!'[45]

In this period there were indeed cases where official Zionists tried to
persuade the Arabs not to flee. Haifa was one of these;[46] in this
commercial city Jewish-Arab relations had been particularly friendly. It
was the terrorists and their chauvinist ilk who realized earlier than the
others that the Zionists had an exceptional opportunity to "solve the Arab
problem" within the Jewish state-to-be by the expedient of getting rid of
the Arabs themselves. Friendly relations stood in the way of this aim.
Hence the year before, in this very port city, the Irgun had tried out a
"Deir Yassin" on a small scale:

> The Irgun picked an area in Haifa that was known for friendly
> Jewish-Arab relations and threw a bomb at the entrance of a
> factory employing 1800 Arabs and 400 Jews, killing six Arabs and
> three British workers. Their provocative act resulted in the
> massacre of 42 Jews.[47]

As we have seen, the Arab Higher Executive too reserved its choicest
hatred for those Arabs who tried to maintain friendly relations with the
Jews. In the middle was the Arab leadership of the Haifa community, who

opposed the AHE and wanted to make a truce with the Zionist authorities.[48]

If there was an Arab community in Palestine that had no sympathy at all for the war against Israel, it was the Haifa Arabs, who stood to lose—were indeed losing—their whole livelihood and existence. Their evacuation of the city was due to threats from the Arab invaders and panic fear evoked by the Irgun atrocity, reinforced and encouraged by the British.[49]

This feeling of panic was also reinforced by the tactics of the beleaguering Haganah, in spite of the fact that Zionist authorities urged the populace to stay. This was a species of psychological warfare waged against the population with the intention of producing demoralization. Koestler insists that this demoralization was an important reason for the Haifa flight, and furthermore:

> By that time, Haganah was using not only its radio station, but also loudspeaker vans which blared their sinister news from the vicinity of the Arab shuks. They warned the Arab population to keep clear of the billets of the foreign mercenaries who had infiltrated into the town, warned them to send their women and children away before the new contingents of savage Iraqis arrived, promised them safe conducts and escorts to Arab territory, and hinted at terrible consequences if their warnings were disregarded. [Italics added.][50]

Kimche, who was there, also describes the "psychological blitz" launched on the Arab quarters, and concludes: "The Arab nerve broke shortly after dark, and the flight from the town assumed panic proportions even before general fighting had started."[51] (He does not say anything about a warning to send away the women and children.) It was particularly after this that the Jews tried to persuade the remaining Arabs to stay. The latter were anxious to agree and come to a truce, but, according to Kimche's personal account, it was the threats of the Arab League authorities which finally convinced the Haifa Arabs that flight would be safer. Only 5,000 remained out of the 65,000.

> But though they had left in a panic, there was a strangely unpanicky atmosphere in the port area. The departing Arabs meekly allowed themselves to be searched by the Haganah. They exchanged greetings and farewells with Jewish port workers, with many of whom they had worked for years.[52]

These are among the Arabs whose flight, according to the latter-day Zionist hack version, was due to sinister enmity against the Jews.

Whatever weight anyone chooses to give to the various cruel pressures on these Arabs pushing them toward flight, not one of the real reasons for the flight justifies the later merciless Israeli punishment of these victims, for the "crime" of fleeing.

Moreover, in the case of Jaffa, there were two additional factors: (1) As mentioned, this attack was launched by the Irgun itself, the very perpetrators of Deir Yassin; and (2) "The desire to get out of the range of Arab bombs which were soon to fall on Tel-Aviv was as potent an incentive as the fear of the Jews," explains a Zionist writer.[53]

11.

By little and little I will drive them out before thee, until thou be increased, and inherit the land ... for I will deliver the inhabitants of the land into your hand; and thou shalt drive them out before thee. ... They shall not dwell in thy land.
Exodus 23:30—33.

But the blackest part of the true story is still to come. It was only in the first period that it was official Zionist policy to frown on the flight. They were still under the influence of the lip-service which they had been used to giving to the idea of Jewish-Arab friendship; the flight had been unexpected; but they were not too slow in reorienting. Within three months after Deir Yassin, the official Haganah forces themselves were driving the Palestine Arab population out of their native villages, towns and cities, like cattle.

Referring to the flight, "Dr. Weizmann ... spoke to me emotionally of this 'miraculous simplification of Israel's tasks'" reported U.S. Ambassador McDonald (an active Zionist propagandist) in his book.[54] The flight was greeted as a "miracle" by more than Weizmann; and like other pious people, they had no objection to helping the miracle along.

By August 1, Foreign Minister Sharett was saying that "the Palestinian Arab exodus of 1948 is one of those cataclysmic phenomena which, according to the experience of other countries, changes the course of history." While Israeli soldiers were driving innocent Arabs out of their homes, the government was already making clear that it would be a long while before any of the refugees were allowed back.

The New York Herald Tribune's war correspondent Kenneth Bilby, in a book remarkable for the general impartiality of its tone, says, after relating that at Haifa the Zionists urged the people to stay:

> Not until the war had swung noticeably in favor of the Jews and the pressure of the Jewish immigrant inflow had begun to exert itself did Israeli government policy change. Then those civilian Arabs who fell into the army net were not only permitted to depart: they were encouraged. And the borders of Israel closed to the refugees, except for a few family categories.[55]

Likewise Jon Kimche, in the British Zionist organ which he edits:

> But after the first period of fighting, the Palestine Arabs were no longer encouraged to stay; on the contrary: they were "encouraged" to leave Lydda and Ramleh, and later, towns like Beersheba.[56]

The quote-marks around "encouraged" give way to a franker formulation in Kimche's book:

> Ramleh and Lydda fell on the 13th [July]; and a flood of 60,000 panicky Arabs were compelled to take the road to the nearby Arab lines. This was no Haifa. The Jews no longer hoped the Arabs would stay. They had tasted the benefits which the earlier Arab policy of evacuatioon had bestowed upon them.[57]

Which means that the 60,000 people were expelled. There had not even been a pitched battle with Arab forces (let alone the civilians), because the Arab Legion had withdrawn without a fight. The people were simply driven out, to make the towns Araberein and provide property for incoming Jews to expand into. Among the people expelled were refugees from Haifa and Jaffa. This was done by the Haganah, not by Irgun.[58]

But although the Arab Legion had already withdrawn, here is Bilby's description of how the Israeli troops entered Lydda. It is the only such passage in Bilby's book, which has been favorably cited by Zionists as source to disprove other Arab charges of atrocities.

> The ring around the twin cities [Lydda and Ramleh] was now complete.

At dusk one evening an Israeli jeep column took off from the Lydda airport and raced into Lydda, with rifles, Stens, and submachine guns blazing. It coursed through the main streets, blasting at everything that moved. The town toppled in panic. I went into Lydda the following day with Major Yeruham Cohen, brigade intelligence officer, the corpses of Arab men, women and even children were strewn about the streets in the wake of this ruthlessly brilliant charge. Civilians who had been trapped by the Jewish encirclement cowered behind shuttered windows; white flags were draped from every home.[59]

The reader must keep in mind that many Arab inhabitants who survived the submachine guns, and were merely driven out onto the open road, are among those who were punished for becoming "absentees" by laws which stripped them of their "abandoned" property.

In 1949 Hal Lehrman wrote in Commentary (December):

Now that I've travelled every corner of this country [Israel], it has become clear that the Israeli troops must have been decidedly tough even with non-combatant Arabs during the war. There are, for instance, too many dynamited, desolated native villages where little or no fighting ever occurred. The Jews simply came in and smashed the place, often sparing only the mosques ... it is obvious, too, that the Israelis—themselves surprised by the scope and speed of the Arab exodus—did an extra-thorough job of destruction to make sure that the Arabs would have nothing to come back to. There is no evidence that this was official government policy, but it certainly must have been in the minds of many local commanders. ... Looting was not too zealously repressed either. No less an authority than the present Speaker of the Knesset, Joseph Sprintzak, has been quoted as saying that the looting of Arab homes and shops was a major defeat for the new government of Israel.

Then, after referring to the Deir Yassin massacre, Lehrman asks "Were there other outrages?" and quotes a UN observer as saying yes.[60] And he continues:

I am more shaken by the expressions of grief and shame I have privately received from non-political but prominent Israelis whose personal integrity is beyond question. "The Israeli soldier has looted, burned, and slaughtered," I have been told, "and it is no comfort for us that soldiers of every other army do likewise." It is even hinted that certain officers actually ordered their troops to let themselves go. The best evidence that there were atrocities—and, I suppose, the best apology for them, if such things can be apologized for—came to me from a high-ranking veteran of the Jerusalem siege. "Our soldiers," he said, "were no worse than the Americans or British. They were even better."

But the question we are interested in here is not the moral superiority of the Haganah looters and perpetrators of atrocities over Americans or British, or vice versa, but in a far simpler one: Many Arab peasants against whom the looting and atrocities were committed, and who were driven out or who fled in fright, were later robbed of property and land and had a military government imposed over them because they had fled or were driven out—i.e., because they left their habitations as a result of or in fear of such atrocities—and this was done not by Haganah soldiers but by the parliament and government of Israel. This was the real atrocity.

12.

My father made your yoke heavy, and I will add to your yoke: my father also chastised you with whips, but I will chastise you with scorpions.   1 Kings 12:14.

Besides, the looting was not mere looting for its own sake; at least in part it was committed in the Zionist cause; that is, as a means of driving out the Arabs. Jon Kimche explains with heavy heart, in his book, speaking of the Haganah and the Jewish Agency:

... The Irgun practice of looting Arab homes and shops was soon explained away and later justified as ministering to the needs of Jewish evacuees who had lost their homes and their all as a result of the four months of attack from Jaffa. It was perhaps natural, though it was certainly detestable, that before long the rest of the Jewish soldiers of the Haganah and the Palmach should join in the orgy of looting and wanton destruction which hangs like a black pall over almost all the Jewish military successes. It could have been stopped by firm action at the outset. But it soon became a practice for which there was always a material incentive, a sophisticated justification, and an excuse.[61]

The fact that the "detestable" practice was initiated by the Irgun is significant. Irgun was the arm of a movement which consciously and systematically aimed at making Palestine Araberein. Looting and "wanton destruction" was a political means. As in so many other cases, the Revisionist-Irgun-Herut movement showed the way to consistent Zionist practice, and the official Zionists followed with more or less reluctance, consistency and heartburning.

But it would be a mistake to think that the ousting of Arabs by official Israeli forces was a matter only of massacres or unofficial looting. The strange thing about the official-Zionist version of the flight is that one of the most important contributions of the Israelis to the ousting of Arab peasants was—in 1948—public, overt, and reported in the Zionist press as military news. This was the dynamiting of villages, and evacuation of their population, on grounds or pretext of military necessity, when foreign Arab invaders had used or might use them for a base. There is also involved the barbarous practice, introduced by the British, of collective punishments for a whole village in case of sniping.

Thus Arthur Koestler recorded in his diary of June 6, 1948 as he drove along the road from Haifa to Tel-Aviv, observing some peaceful Arabs still tilling their fields:

> But not for long. A few weeks later some Arab lads will start sniping from these villages at Jewish trucks on the road; the Jewish army will herd the villagers together, dynamite their houses, and put the young men into concentration camps; while the old ones will tie a mattress and a brass coffeepot on the donkey, the old women will walk ahead leading the donkey by the rein and the old man will ride on it.[62]

At this point, the official Zionist apologist will inform us that this is military necessity, and cannot be helped. Before commenting, let us see some more military necessities. We quote from the military news published as a matter of course by the Palestine Post in 1948:

... Kolonia village overlooking Motza was destroyed by a Haganah striking force. ... Most of the house in Kolonia, occupied by Arab gangs [Kaukji's foreign Arab guerrillas] that had been attacking Castel, were blown up on Saturday night, and in a short but sharp fight the Arab unit in the village was wiped out. ... Yesterday, Haganah men completed the destruction of the village by blowing up the remaining houses. ... The village had been evacuated by most of its residents during the past week. [April 12, 1948. Italics added.]

The next day the paper reported, in a similar news item, that three villages had been "pounded into desolation" and "reduced to rubble" after being deserted by their residents and occupied by "Arab gangs." It adds matter-of-factly:

Abu Shusha village ... was recaptured by the Haganah this morning, and is being blow up. [April 13, 1948.]

The fact is, then, that Arab villages were systematically dynamited and razed not, or not merely, in the course of fighting but after capture. The military necessity was presumably to prevent their use by hostile forces. No doubt, the system of destroying these villages down to their foundation stones had a real convenience for the Israeli forces from this point of view, though other civilized armies seem to have gotten along in various wars without this practice. For present purposes we will also assume for a moment that the Zionist authorities never gave a moment's thought to the fact that this convenient custom had the additional advantage of scorching the earth for the Arab inhabitants and contributing to the "purity" of an Araberein Palestine. We only ask readers to remember, once again, that even if we accept the plea of military necessity at face value, the question which is at issue in this study is the subsequent fate of the innocent Arab peasants who were driven out and despoiled out of this alleged military necessity, and not because of their alleged offense in taking flight at the call of the Arab invaders.

But it would take great willpower to convince oneself that military necessity was the answer. Kenneth Bilby wrote, for example, summing up the 1949 picture:

Israel ruled three-quarters of Palestine, and scores of Arab villages deemed uninhabitable had been razed as insurance against their owners' return. [Italics added.][63]

Harry Sacher, a prominent British Zionist leader, is very delicate in the following remarks:

... For strategic purposes the Jews began to blow up the Arab villages, which they occupied. ... The massacre at Deir Yassin by the Irgun on the 9th April, 1948, was a turning point. ... It became the rule that, when the Jewish forces advanced, the Arab inhabitants of the occupied territory fled; nor was the flight always without stimulation or encouragement from the Jews. [Italics added.][64]

An internationally known professor and author at Hebrew University, Norman Bentwich, remarks regarding the injustice of the later Absentee Property Law:

Many [Arab residents of Israel] were driven out for a time from their villages by the Jewish military forces in the course of the campaign, and are now living in adjacent villages, and are prevented from recovering their properties which are vested in the Custodian.[65]

Hal Lehrman—writing about an entirely different topic, the widespread prejudice by Israeli Jews against the new immigrant Oriental Jews—quotes an Israeli friend who complained to him,

not entirely in sour jest, that "we drove out our good Arabs, and now look at what we have in their place!"[66]

The alleged half-jest is about the Oriental Jews; the remark which slips out incidentally about having driven out the Arabs is not part of the sour jest.

And it came to pass, when Joram saw Jehu, that he said, Is it peace, Jehu? And he answered, What peace, so long as the whoredoms of thy mother Jezebel and her witchcrafts are so many? 2 Kings 9:22.

As a matter of fact, the infamous land-grab, which after the war was carried through systematically by special laws and ordinances, got started during the war itself under the umbrella of military operations. Dr. Don Peretz writes:

> When Israel's military and paramilitary forces first occupied abandoned Arab areas military field commanders improvised policy on the spot, often turning property over to the secretaries of Jewish agricultural settlements or local security officers.[67]

In a series of articles on Israel's Arabs which appeared in the leading Israeli paper Haaretz, we read that

> Every piece of land which had been abandoned for any reason whatever—whether in the whirl of war, or during the truces, or soon after the Israeli occupation—was at once seized by the nearby [Jewish] settlement or settlements and attached to their estates.[68]

This grab was not a matter of individual lawlessness merely; it was organized and stimulated by Zionist authorities for Zionist aims. Dr. Don Peretz describes it for this period:

> Squatters [on seized Arab property] often received semi-official sanction for their occupation of empty buildings. Even before the status of the abandoned Arab areas were determined, the Jewish Agency was directing the flow of new immigrants toward the vacant Arab settlements. The military also participated in this unauthorized mass-requisitioning. In one instance, a group of army officers supported by tanks seized large areas of absentee [Arab] property in Jaffa. [Peretz's footnote here refers to the January 9, 1949 issue of Haaretz.].

When the first Custodian of Abandoned Property was appointed, in July 1948, all of Jaffa had been occupied....

In one of his early reports the Custodian claimed that nearly all absentee houses had been occupied and that their seizure by the Jewish Agency for the use of new immigrants would be recognized. Nearly all movables in these houses, which had not been looted or destroyed, were sold to the army before the Custodian arrived.[69]

The role of the Jewish Agency in this grab was attested to in November 1949 when Finance Minister Kaplan (the cabinet member in charge) made a Knesset speech replying to charges of government laxness. He "accused institutions like the Jewish Agency, which were responsible for the settlement of new immigrants, of causing the greatest difficulties in management of absentee property."[70]

At this time, the callous robbery of the Arabs was not yet being justified officially by reference to the needs of the new immigrants. The conception had not yet taken root in all circles that the injustices and crimes committed against European Jewry by bestial anti-Semites were sufficient reason for the wronged Jews in turn to commit injustices and crimes against the native Palestinian Arab population. It was being done, but only officially-unofficially. When the first Custodian made his report to the Knesset, such robbery was condemned at least in words, though nothing whatsoever was done against it. The government washed its hands; so did Haganah.

In his April 18, 1949 report to the Knesset Finance Committee, the Custodian maintained that the "moral feelings" of the Jewish community had "prevented the despoliation of the enemy,"but he did admit this much:

Feelings of revenge, moral justification and material temptation did, however, overcome many.

In such conditions, only extreme measures by the military, civil and legal authorities could have saved, not only the property, but many individuals and institutions from moral degeneration.

Such action was not forthcoming and was, perhaps impossible in the prevailing conditions, and affairs in many areas degenerated without restraint.[71]

Note that this official lists "material temptation"—i.e., looting for the sake of the loot—only third; and note his reference not only to individuals but to "institutions," which means the Zionist agencies and organizations.

The leading newspaper Haaretz—then, as now, a Zionist voice that was deeply conscience-stricken over it all—spoke out. Its columnist, the Hebrew author Moshe Smilanski (of the Ichud), agreed with the Custodian's report that a large part of the public was responsible for the theft of Arab property.[72]

> Towns, villages and agricultural property were robbed without shame, and lawless individuals of the masses as well as the intelligentsia enriched themselves from occupied property.

He called for measures against those responsible, but that was naive.

Smilanski also wrote: "Some time we will have to account for its theft and despoliation not only to our consciences but also to the law." There he was quite wrong. The same people who tolerated the robbery devised a whole series of laws which not only legalized the grab but permitted its systematic extension; but that is for another article on the story of the Israeli Arab minority.

14.

> Now ye may see this, as we have declared, not so much by ancient histories, as ye may if ye search what hath been wickedly done of late through the pestilent behavior of them that are unworthily placed in authority. Esther (Apocrypha) 16:7.

While the robbery could always be reconciled with law, given the power of a state, it could not be reconciled with conscience by those Israelis who hold out against the tide of chauvinism in the little country. The intellectuals of Ichud or Haaretz are wont to lament the moral degeneration exhibited when a people, themselves so recently persecuted and despoiled in Europe, visit such wrongs upon a minority which is under their own newly acquired power.

Without in the least derogating this moral indignation at the treatment of the Arab minority, which is richly justified, one aspect of the denunciation misses the mark. The moral indignation should not be visited in the first place against the miserable, harassed, driven Jewish DPs from Europe who, in their fear and need, were used as pawns to grab the

44

land and property of the dispossessed Arabs. They were steered and pushed into this position by those who knew what they were doing—Zionist arms like the Jewish Agency, Zionist authorities in the armed forces and government, both by design and by toleration.

Zionism—the ideology of Jewish chauvinism—showed that it was and is one of the deeply reactionary conceptions of the political world. The child of anti-Semitism, it became the father of another form of ethnic oppression; if genocide means the murder of a people as such, then there should be a word for the robbery of a people as such.

What Zionism created in Palestine in 1948 was the first act of the tragedy.

New International Summer 1956

Chapter IV
ISRAEL'S ARAB MINORITY:
THE GREAT LAND ROBBERY

But the discussion of Zionism is beset with the additional difficulty that clear and honest thinking is subtly hindered by the fact that really honest speaking is almost unattainable. An exceptionally long history of struggle and suffering has left many sore and sensitive spots in the body of Israel, and the thoughtful Gentile feels the necessity of excessive caution lest he touch any of these tender spots; while the Jew, no matter how emancipated, cannot completely overcome the effects of a traditional attitude which puts group loyalty above devotion to the simple truth, and regards it as the most deadly sin to tell the truth in the hearing of the hereditary enemy. Self-respecting Jews also cannot help leaning backward in expressions which may endanger their being identified with those who for their belly's sake creep out of the Jewish fold. The discussion of Zionism has thus been largely left to those who are more zealous about the triumph of their righteous cause than scrupulous about the justice of their arguments.
Morris Raphael Cohen

As a result of the mass flight of the Palestinian Arab population during the 1948 war, there were only about 170,000 Arabs left within the expanded borders of Israel's territory after the armistices, as compared with 700,000 Arabs in this area before the start of the war.

This was a tremendous reduction from the proportions envisioned in the Partition Plan adopted by the UN in 1947. In the smaller Israel marked out by the partition, about 45 per cent would have been Arab (not even counting in the Bedouin); though it was expected that Jewish immigration would soon change the figure.

So Israel virtually began with an Arab minority of only 10 to 11 per cent, about the same as the Negro minority in the United States.

Today, according to government figures, the whole non-Jewish population is about 192,000, out of a total population of about 1,720,000. If we eliminate the 17,500 Druzes from this non-Jewish figure, then of the remaining 174,000 Arabs there are 131,500 Moslems and 42,800 Christians.

The proportion of Christians among the Arabs, as against Moslems, is now over twice as high as it was before the war—20 to 25 per cent as against the pre-war 10 per cent. This means an added barrier against the automatic identification of the Arab minority with most foreign Arab regimes.

The largest Arab concentration, the all-Arab town of Nazareth, is predominantly Christian. It has over 20,000 Arabs, as against the remnant of 7,000 in Haifa and 5,500 in Jaffa. All together, 51,000 Arabs live in towns (according to government figures) as against about 70 per cent who live in the 102 Arab villages.

A basic fact to keep in mind, too often obscured in both Zionist and Arab propaganda, is that this Arab minority as it presently exists consists largely of those Arabs who succeeded in resisting all of the considerable pressures to take part in the wartime flight, both from the foreign Arab aggressors and their irregulars and from the Zionist forces. They withstood a great deal and did not become refugees.

Even if one accepts the standard Zionist tale that the Palestinian refugees fled the country out of support to the foreign Arab invaders, still surely those people who did not become refugees thereby proved doubly and trebly that they were far from being "fifth-columnists." While the Zionist agencies seized the opportunity afforded by the flight to despoil the displaced Arabs of their land and property, surely there could be no question of dispossessing these Arabs who had not fled over the borders?

There was question indeed. While much of the story of the land-grab concerns the refugees, who are now outside Israel's borders, we shall be presently concerned with the treatment of the Arab minority who remained inside.

In our preceding article on the flight, we referred to the un-official looting, property-snatching and land-grabbing which went on in the course of the fighting, directed against Palestinian Arab civilians. This, to be sure, was the start of the land-grab but it was still unofficial in the sense of being unsanctioned by explicit law and official government action, however deliberately it was carried through by official Zionist bodies like the Jewish Agency, or furthered by the military commanders. This was bad enough, but the story that has to be told now is of a different order: the robbery of a people carried through in planned, deliberate, "legal" action by the formal action of the Israel government over a period of years, and not in the heat or turmoil of war.

The extent of this robbery, in terms of its economic importance to Israel, has already been partially sketched:
over a third of Israel's Jewish population lives on property stolen from displaced Arabs; most Arab-owned citrus groves were taken, plus almost

all of the olive groves; etc. Let us now fill out this picture, keeping in mind that the entire area of Israel is not much over five million acres or 23 million dunams in the Palestinian measure, of which less than a quarter are under cultivation. (A dunam equals one-fourth of an acre for rough estimate.)

Just before the war, the total amount of Jewish-owned land in all of Palestine was only 1,850,000 dunams. The total amount of cultivable land taken from the Arabs after that was 4,574,000 dunams, or nearly 2 1/2 times as much[73]—a fifth of the total area of the country. As for the total land taken—

> The CCP [UN's Conciliation Commission for Palestine] estimated that although only a little more than a quarter was considered cultivable, more than 80 per cent of Israel's total area ... represented land abandoned by the Arab refugees.[74] [The 80% figure includes areas, such as Bedouin lands in the Negev, that had been held by Arabs traditionally with virtually all rights except juridical ownership, which was retained by the British colonial government.—H.D.]

Furthermore:

> ...They left whole cities like Jaffa, Acre, Lydda, Ramleh, Baysan, Migdal-Gad; 388 towns and villages; and large parts of 94 other cities and towns, containing nearly a quarter of all the buildings in Israel. Ten thousand shops, businesses and stores were left in Jewish hands.[75]

> Twenty-thousand dunams of absentee property were leased by the Custodian [Israel government official in charge] in 1952 for industrial purposes. A third of Israel's stone production was supplied by 52 Arab quarries under his jurisdiction.[76]

> The Custodian was also responsible for four million Palestine pounds in Arab bank accounts blocked in Israel,* and an

---

* The money in these blocked bank accounts was one of the few items of Arab property largely released later—four-fifths by the October 1956 report of the UN's CCP. Of course, this benefited mainly better-off Arabs, not the fellahin. The problem involved only 6050
(continued...)

undetermined amount of shares in businesses, corporations, companies and partnerships. In 1953 his office was one of the largest employers in Israel, and perhaps the largest single employer of new immigrants.[77]

According to the CCP (UN) estimate, the total value of the lands taken from the Arabs was over 100 million Palestine pounds, to which should be added another 20 million pounds for movable property appropriated.[78] (In 1950, this total of 120 million Palestine pounds was worth $336 million.) Arab estimates went up to 10 or 20 times this amount. The Israel government has refused to give its own estimate.*

Of course the above inventory applies to all the displaced Arabs, most of whom are now refugees and not in the country. But how much was stolen from Arabs who are still in the country and who did not flee?

---

* (...continued)
Arab refugee accounts.

* In general the Israel government has cloaked many details of the land-grab in secrecy. Dr. Peretz writes:
"Much information concerning the use, amounts, and distribution of abandoned Arab property and the government's policy toward it was secret. Records and most reports of the Custodian of Absentee Property were secret. . . . Even the United Nations, in spite of frequent requests, was unable to obtain adequate information about Israel's disposition of Arab property."—Peretz (ref. n. 4), vol. II, p. 230.
Israel consistently refused to participate in UN attempts to set up mixed commissions "to administer conservation of existing properties including orange groves; to determine property ownership; and to evaluate property damages, including those to orange groves." The Arab states accepted these proposals. (Ibid., p. 262.)
The Israel agency in charge, the Custodian of Absentee Property, wasn't telling anybody: "The decision [of the government in 1953 to sell Custodian-held urban property] caused great concern to the Israeli Arabs who feared that their absentee property would also be sold. At a meeting in Nazareth called to clarify the situation, absentee Arab citizens were told to send their questions in writing to the Custodian's office for study. A year later they had still received no reply." (Ibid., p. 303.)
In the 1958 Knesset debate on a new land-grab law, when opposition parties made angry charges that the government was favoring the ruling Mapai party in distributing this acquired land, "One General Zionist member attacked the Custodian's office as 'a secret organization' which operated free of parliamentary control." (Ibid., p. 285.)
The UN agency (Conciliation Commission for Palestine) therefore had to work out its own estimates with considerable
effort; Peretz's book explains at great length the bases and methods it used in arriving at its conclusions, which he gives.

50

The leading Israeli daily Haaretz wrote in a survey of the Arab minority problem:

Individual DPs may be found in virtually every Arab village in Israel. 15,000 is the estimated number of fellahin [peasants] who have been dislodged from their homes and farms and left utterly destitute. About 15,000 more have been only partially hurt, some more and some less. The area of land seized under the Land Acquisition Law from the Arabs who did not flee from Israel—not counting those who did flee, from whom much more was taken away—amounts to over a million dunams, at least one half of which represents fertile and easily cultivable level country, the balance being stony mountainous terrain capable of cultivation only with the fellah's primitive plow.[79]

On the basis of a different estimate,* Dr. Don Peretz writes that

Approximately 40 per cent of the land owned by legal Arab residents of Israel was confiscated by the authorities as part of their absentee-property policy.[80]

Forty per cent of the land owned by presently legal Arab residents of the country, not even counting the other Palestinian Arabs who were driven out, or helped out, or kept out of the country by the Israeli refugee policy!

Let us now see how all this was done, from 1948 to the present.

1

The day we lick the Arabs, that is the day, I think, when we shall be sowing the seed of an eternal hatred of such dimensions that Jews will not be able to live in that part of the world for centuries to come. Judah L. Magnes 1946

---

* Of the 4 million-plus dunams taken from Arabs, "approximately 300,000 dunams belonged to Arab residents of Israel who had fled from one section of the state to another during the fighting, or had been moved from their villages by the Jewish authorities for 'security reasons.'" (Peretz, "The Arab Minority of Israel," *Middle East Journal,* Washington D.C. Spring. 1954.) And in his book (ref. n. 1) Peretz also mentions 30,000 such Arabs, adding, "as well as much of their urban property."

We have already seen how the land-grab and property-steal began in the course of the 1948 war itself under the initiative particularly of the Jewish Agency (an arm of the World Zionist Organization executive) and of the military commanders on the spot, who of course were formally the agencies of the new Israel government, as well as of less official looters and pillagers; while "affairs in many areas degenerated without any restraint."*

Almost a month after the Deir Yassin massacre, when the Arab flight was reaching a flood, the Zionist daily Palestine Post (May 5) already announced that a "Custodian of Arab Property" had been appointed in the Jerusalem area, and that similar authorities had been set up in other sections. This Custodian, said the paper, was a Haganah officer, name a secret, appointed by the Jewish Agency. In view of the role being played by the army and the Jewish Agency itself with respect to the grab of Arab property, one may wonder whether the appointment of an officer as Custodian was meant to restrain the grab, or merely to regulate and channelize it. (This, of course, was still over a week before the State of Israel and its government were formally set up by the declaration on May 15.)

> In the early days of the war, the ad hoc decisions of various field commanders substituted for a unified, preconceived plan of operation [regarding Arab property] ...

> ...From April until the Custodian's appointment [in July], the army had primary responsibility for occupied Arab property. Because it conquered the property, the military considered itself the rightful owner. When the time came for the Custodian to take over from the army, military authorities often placed obstructions in his way. Sometimes for days and weeks, the army prevented the Custodian from entering cities to take charge of absentee property.[81]

(In studying the fate of the Arab minority in Israel we will often find that the military authorities, representing the most chauvinist elements in Zionism, bucked the government or its courts for a more reactionary policy, perhaps the most spectacular case being the razing of the Arab town of Ikrit in 1951. This pattern began early.)

---

* NI, Summer 1956, p. 103–4.

Once the state came into existence and the provisional government took over, bits of emergency legislation were improvised to give a color of legal sanction to what was actually being done. The first was on June 24, an Abandoned Areas Ordinance which gave a most peculiar definition of an "abandoned area":

> 1. (a) "Abandoned area" means any area or place conquered by or surrendered to armed forces or deserted by all or part of its inhabitants, and which has been declared by order to be an abandoned area.[82]

This law was made retroactive to the creation of the state, and in it the government gave itself the power to make all regulations for the "abandoned areas."

The definition of "abandoned area" was deliberately made so wide-open that it applied to virtually any Arab village or town or section, whether it had been abandoned or not. Even where the population had really "abandoned" a village, they may have merely gone a few miles away to wait out the shooting before coming back; or only some of the inhabitants may have fled; and indeed nobody at all need have fled anywhere, according to the carefully expansive formulation of the definition.

The ordinance therefore did not have to use ethnic terms to pinpoint its objective as Arab property. Actually many a Jewish area became "abandoned" by this definition too, but this is purely academic in view of the fact that the sharp edge of the ordinance was intended to be wielded solely in one direction.

The government set up a "Custodian of Abandoned Property"— a change of label from the previously designated Custodian of Arab Property in order not to formalize the fact of ethnic robbery. The first Custodian was appointed on July 15.

Since he naturally was not going to work the land himself—

> ...therefore steps were taken to legalize its use by the Jewish agricultural settlements which had occupied much of it. The Ministry of Agriculture was given power to assign this land to cultivators whom it could designate for a period of up to one year.[83]

It is clear, then, that the government did not aim its ordinance only against "bad" Arabs who had fled to help the invaders, as the Zionist story goes. No such criterion is involved in this ordinance in any way.

This ordinance was only the beginning.

Dr. Peretz relates:

> Long-term policy in the latter half of 1948 was to present the Arabs with the fact that a large part of their property no longer existed and that areas for their resettlement in Israel would be determined by security and political factors. As yet there was no government plan for the use of refugee property, but due to security reasons, their immediate return was not permitted.

> By the end of the year, government policy concerning use of the property also began to assume long-term aspects .[84]

In December 1948 the Ministry of Finance issued its first Absentee Property Regulations. A "Custodian of Absentee Property" replaced the Custodian of Abandoned Property. This had the effect of transferring the label from the land to the person affected, but the change in terminology didn't help much. Just as "abandoned" property had been defined to include land that was never abandoned, so "absentee" was defined to include Arabs who were not only present in Israel but who had never been absent. According to Haaretz, "there is even a special label devised for these people, 'present absentees.'"[85]

The key definition of "absentee" in these regulations was: a Palestine citizen who had left his normal or habitual place of residence.[86] There was no pretense at limiting it to Arabs who had fled over the border or even to the other side of the fighting lines. Dr. Peretz explains:

> Every Arab in Palestine who had left his town or village after November 29, 1947 [date of UN partition decision] was liable to be classified as an absentee under the regulations. All Arabs who held property in the New City of Acre, regardless of the fact that they may never have traveled farther than the few meters to the Old City, were classified as absentees. The 30,000 Arabs who fled from one place to another within Israel, but who never left the country, were also liable to have their property declared absentee. Any individual who may have gone to Beirut or Bethlehem for a one-

day visit during the latter days of the Mandate was automatically an absentee.[87]

Naturally, this formula was so broad that it could also net Jews who might come under the extended definition of "absentee." This danger was mainly academic, since those who administered the regulations knew well enough against whom it was aimed. But there were safeguards just in case:

> The Custodian could issue a certificate stating that anyone was not an absentee if "in his opinion" such a person left his residence from fear of Israel's enemies, or if the Custodian believed that he was capable of managing his properties efficiently, without giving aid to Israel's enemies.

There is no case where the provisions of the various land-grab laws (this one, or any subsequent one) were ever enforced against a Jew, even though they may have applied, and even though the laws were never ethnically formulated so as to be applicable to Arabs only.

Here are some of the other remarkable provisions of these regulations:

(1) The Custodian "could take over all property which might be obtained in the future by an individual whom he certified to be absentee."[88] (Italics added.)

(2) The Arab is guilty till he proves himself innocent:

> The Custodian could take over most Arab property in Israel on the strength of his own judgement by certifying in writing that any person or body of persons, and that any property was absentee. The burden of proof that any property was not absentee fell upon its owner, but the Custodian could not be questioned concerning the source of information on the grounds of which he had declared a person or property absentee.[89]

(3) The Custodian could expropriate business associates of "absentee" Arabs, even though the associates themselves were not absentee:

> All businesses in which at least one-half of the number of persons, partners, shareholders, directors or managers were absentees, or in which absentees were dominant or controlled at least half of the capital, were turned over in whole to the Custodian. [Italics added.][90]

55

(4) Even where the Custodian might decide to release "absentee" property to its rightful owner, the game was not finished:

> The Custodian could require the owner to deliver other property in exchange for his released property. ... The Custodian could withhold the certificates to release property until he received a maintenance payment not to exceed five per cent per annum of the property's value, to be determined by the price which could have been obtained had the property been sold on the market. ... In addition, the Custodian was entitled to receive payment for all expenses incurred in holding the property, together with interest at the rate of six per cent per annum from the date he took over.[91]

(5) The Custodian could do no wrong:

> Any person carrying out an order given by the Custodian was not held responsible if it was later proved that the property was not absentees'.[92]

When this legal atrocity was discussed in the Knesset, some of the truth about it was told by the Arab deputy Sayf al-Din al-Zabi, who represented a Mapai-affiliated "Arab" list.*

> [He] challenged the seizure by the Custodian of property belonging to Arabs who were legal residents of Israel, who had participated in the first elections and who held government-issued identity cards. Many were absent from their residence for a few days only during the fighting which overtook their villages, but did not leave the country. Al-Zabi pointed out that many residents of Turan and Nazareth who were gone only a few hours also lost their property to the Custodian. The majority of the villagers of Maalul, Andor [Eindor] and Al-Mujidal who took refuge in Nazareth when

---

* That is, this Arab notable represented an "Arab party" created by the Mapai, which is the ruling Zionist party, to corral Arab votes. In general, these men are regarded as turncoats by most Arabs, and rightly so; but on Arab questions in the Knesset they usually make the record in speeches of complaint and in their vote. At any rate, it is evident, such men as Al-Zabi are not "anti-Israel demagogues" or "agitators" but quite the reverse: the very tamest specimens the Zionists can find. The only point that is relevant here is whether they tell the minimum truth in their speeches of complaint in the Knesset, while still remaining affiliated with the Mapai.

fighting occurred near their homes were declared absentees although they never left Israel's territory. Half the Arab inhabitants of Kafr Elut remained in their village during the fighting. The other half took refuge in Nazareth, but all the villagers became absentees, and even those who remained in their homes were required to pay rent to the Custodian for the use of their own lands. In Acre and Shafa Amr many Arabs were not permitted to cultivate their lands which were used by surrounding Jewish collectives under the authority of the Custodian and the Ministry of Agriculture. Villagers of Baysan and Zippori were moved from their villages by the army long after the end of active hostilities, and their property was turned over to the Custodian. Arabs of Al-Qitna were also moved by the army to Al-Ghabsiya and those of Al-Halhala were moved to Akbara for "security reasons," and their property declared absentee.[93]

So said Al-Zabi; and since he is Arab, perhaps convinced Zionists can persuade themselves that he must be exaggerating, in spite of the fact that he is the Mapai's own domesticated Arab.

But the provisions of these regulations speak eloquently enough of the aims which animated the men who thought them up.

The following month, January, 1949, a new legal instrument came into being in the form of an amendment to the Cultivation of Wastelands emergency ordinance. This empowered the Ministry of Agriculture to grant longer leases to Jewish settlers who were working "absentee" lands. It was a step on the road to their complete alienation; for at this point, it should be remembered, the "absentee" Arabs still owned the land in theory; the Custodian was simply ... taking care of it in their theoretical absence.

> The ordinance enabled the government to begin settling absentee [Arab] villages with [Jewish] farmers who would work the surrounding land. Government organizations were formed to manage the property and to rent land to individual farmers or contracting companies. Settlers were given the opportunity to choose lands near their villages through the Jewish National Fund.[94]

This Cultivation of Wastelands ordinance was also the basis of a land-grab method which did not depend on the "absentee" gimmick, and therefore could be used against those Arab landholders who could not be fitted into the absentee category even with stretching. It

> empowers the Minister of Agriculture to seize any plot of land lying waste, regardless of the reason—the land might even be located in an area not accessible without a special permit, which the Military Governor might refuse to issue—and hand it to anyone for "temporary" cultivation. The only condition was that the Minister send a prior notice to the owner warning him to resume the cultivation of his land—and the warning could be in the form of a written notice displayed in a conspicuous place on his land, which, as we have said, was not at all accessible to the owner—and the owner took no heed of the warning. since the Arab landowners concerned "took no heed" of the warning and proceeded to "keep their lands waste," those lands were leased by the Minister for a nominal sum to Jewish settlements and contractors, who in many instances employed the landowners themselves in the cultivation of those lands, in return for a portion of the corps. And for this purpose the Military Governor was not at all averse to granting them entry permits into the closed areas.[95]

In other words, it utilized what Mordechai Stein has aptly called "a sort of double-play of two laws."[96] One, which permits the government to seize any land in Military Government areas "in the interests of the public safety" and declare it a "security zone," is based on the Emergency Regulations of 1945—i.e., of the British Mandate. The Israeli government has taken over these hated laws, which were originally set up in good measure as a colonialist's means of repressing the Zionist underground, and are equally suited as the Zionists' means to despoil the Arab minority.

When this ordinance is applied to an area, and its Arab owners ejected, the second ordinance comes in to play. Since the land is not being cultivated by its Arab owners any longer, it can be taken over by the state as "wasteland" and handed over to Jewish settlers who will cultivate it—i.e., who will be allowed to cultivate it.[97]

The land-robbery based on this "double play" is also aimed against Israeli Arabs who never fled.* But, as explained at the end of this article,

---

* M. Stein, in the article quoted above (ref. n. 96), writing as a socialist anti-Zionist, says: "With the help of this legal double-play, dozens of Arab villages have been confiscated

(continued...)

this phase of the land robbery will be detailed in a future study dealing with Israel's military rule over its Arab minority.

2

It used to be said in the liberal first quarter of our century that a country was judged by the manner in which it treated its Jews. It is, therefore, understandably natural that the converse proposition should be suggested, and the question asked: how does the Jewish State treat its Arabs? John Kimche

By 1950, with the relative stabilization that followed the victory in the 1948 war, the government felt that a firmer juridical basis for the land-grab was necessary, and so it had the Knesset pass a law to legalize what had been done. Up to this time, the land-grab had been carried through via the ordinances of the provisional government.

This was the Absentee Property Law of March 1950. Dr. Peretz sums it up:

Actually the Absentee Property Law defined no new procedure. It merely legalized the de facto situation which grew out of improvisation under wartime emergency conditions.[98]

But...

Minor changes somewhat curtailed the Custodian's power and improved the status of absentees.[99]

One change was to narrow somewhat the definition of an absentee:
The new definition made an absentee of any Palestinian who, at any time since the UN partition decision of November, 1947, had "left his place of habitual residence ... for a place in Palestine held ... by forces which sought to prevent the establishment of the State of Israel or which fought against it after its establishment" So—

---

* (...continued)
(Ghabslye, Ikrit, Kfar Anan, Ferradie, Birim, Seffurie, Mejdel, Manscura, Berwe, Damun, Um-el-Faraj, etc.)."

It did not include Arabs who remained in areas controlled by Jewish forces after November 29, 1947 [the partition decision], provided they had not left such areas after that date ... the number of Arabs who benefited from the change was not large.[100]

Besides, a good deal of the land-grab had already proceeded according to the wide-open provisions of the preceding ordinances, and the Arabs did not automatically get their land back just because the new law did not apply to them. On the contrary; we shall see that in 1953 the Knesset had to pass another law precisely to legalize (once more) the retention of land stolen from Arabs outside the framework of any law or ordinance.

Other changes introduced by the 1950 law were: the Custodian could take over a business only when all the members, partners, shareholders, etc. were absentees, rather than half; the Custodian was no longer exempt from answering a court about the source of his knowledge about the status of an absentee; his maintenance payment was reduced from 5 per cent to 4. In addition, notes Schechtman,[101] the new law "required the Custodian to pay debts owed by absentees whose property they controlled, and to obey court orders for attachments"—a change which did not do the absentees any good.

Such minor changes did little to effect either the status of absentee property, most of which was already distributed, or the status of its original owners. Presentation of absentee property cases in the courts by Arabs, however, was facilitated.[102]

Dr. Peretz, in an outstanding magazine article, described the effect of this law in terms similar to those we have seen above in connection with the December, 1948 regulations. After noting its definition of absentee, he said:

Consequently, any Arab of Nazareth who might have visited the Old City of Jerusalem or Bethlehem on Christmas 1948 automatically became an "absentee" under the law. Nearly all Arab refugees in Israel, as well as the 30,000 inhabitants of the Little Triangle which became part of the state under the armistice agreements with Jordan, were classified as "absentees." Many Israeli Arabs who, during the battle of Acre, fled from their homes in the new to the old city lost their property under the provisions of this law.

...All of the new city of Acre was turned over to recent [Jewish] immigrants despite the fact that many of its Arab "absentee" home owners were living a few yards away.[103]

The pro-Zionist journalist Hal Lehrman has also remarked that "It was further charged that Israel authorities tended to treat any Arab owner, ipso facto, as an absentee unless he obtained, on his own considerable time and at his own expense, a certificate to the contrary."[104]

In the Knesset at the time of its passage, a series of amendments (offered mainly by the Arab deputies) were turned down, even though many of them proposed only an elementary measure of fair dealing. Among these were amendments to protect the land of Arabs (1) who were legal citizens of Israel, with an identity card, and had not aided the enemy; (2) who had never fled the country; (3) who had been expelled from their villages when these were conquered by the Israeli troops; etc.[105] In defiance of conscience, these Arabs were specifically voted into the "absentee" category.

Another proposed amendment wanted to set up a special authority, instead of the Custodian's say-so, to decide on the property of those Arabs who were legally in Israel. As Haaretz put it on March 20 after the law was passed, "Elementary feelings of justice demand that an Arab who legally returns to Israel should not continue to be an absentee. ... We are not at war with the Arabs who are established citizens of the state. ... A law which automatically makes them absentee is insufferable. ... This is a matter of conscience and political understanding."

But it was the insufferable that was passed; and it seemed that the state of Israel was indeed "at war with the Arabs who are established citizens of the state."

The popular columnist Courtney of the pro-government Jerusalem Post attacked the law as "perhaps the most serious factor creating embitterment among all Arabs."

He pointed out that in Galilee twenty villages had been deprived of their property by Jewish collectives, which "arrogated to themselves, through long-term leases granted by the Minister of Agriculture, lands of Arabs who were free of any guilt or wrongdoing."[106]

The Israeli Arab spokesman E.N. Koussa, writing in the Ichud's organ Ner (January 1951), pointed out there was even a member of the Knesset who enjoyed all the privileges of a deputy and yet, because he was an Arab, "is under a legal disability to control his properties. Such is the actual condition of Mr. Tufiq Tubi, the Arab Knesset member."

Incidentally, Tubi is a Communist Party deputy, but this is hardly relevant to the fact that there exists a peculiar Israeli institution of "absentee" deputies voting on the country's laws.

One aspect of the Absentee Property Law precipitated a fight among the Jewish deputies themselves. Opposition parties criticized the great power vested in the Custodian, who was appointed by the Mapai's minister of Finance. "Control of a quarter of Israel's wealth and most of its land was a plum they hesitated to let fall to Israel's largest party,"[107] though they had not hesitated to steal this plum from the Arabs. Opponents accused the Custodian of giving 90 per cent of absentee property to Mapai-controlled institutions, cooperatives, etc., at half of its market value, and of selling absentee property to a favored few.

As mentioned above, one advantage gained by the Arabs was that it was easier to bring the government robbers to court, for an accounting. On this whole issue of the land-robbery the Israeli courts have often been a prominent bright spot as defenders of justice,* but their remedial power has been too limited to make any considerable difference in the outcome. Court cases, however, have been particularly useful as documentable illustrations of what was going on, though one must bear in mind how few Arabs could even think of going through the court procedures.

Thus Dr. Peretz cites the "claim of Tanus Ilyas al-Askar against the Custodian" as "typical of many cases which reached the courts and thousands that did not." Let us take a look at this "typical" case.

Askar was a legal resident of Haifa, with an Israeli identity card; he had in fact voted in the national elections. In January 1948 he had gone to a village near Israel's northern frontier but had returned to Haifa in March.

He then obtained permission from the Custodian to receive rent from his home in Haifa and to lease a shop. Shortly thereafter he

---

* For example, Oscar Kraines of NYU writes in his book that under the 1950 land law, "the Custodian of absentee owners' property was authorized to exempt Arabs who had left their residence for valid reasons. In a number of appeals, the Supreme Court, to its credit for judicial integrity and impartiality, upheld the Arabs and severely reprimanded the Custodian and his staff for arbitrary, capricious, and harsh action in excess of their authority." (*Israel, the Emergence of a New Nation*, 1954, p. 27.)

was denounced as an absentee who had procured his contract under false pretenses. The Custodian certified that he was an absentee and ordered him to evacuate his shop.[108]

Askar went to court in self-defense. The High Court found in his favor on the ground that he had in fact exercised de jure citizenship rights and that this "automatically exempted him from the Custodian's arbitrary authority."

The court expressed the opinion in this case that, in the light of the evidence, Askar had been classified an absentee in order to force his removal from his shop. "It can be said," stated the court, "that the certificate [classifying him as absentee] was issued only to deprive the claimant of elementary rights and of legal assistance and defense, and in this respect the Custodian acted in an untoward manner."[109]

Another case is summarized by Judd Teller, a professional Zionist journalist who was UN correspondent in New York for Davar, the Histadrut organ. This is from a 1951 article of his:

There is the case, still pending in the courts, of Abed il Al and his family, who live in Om il Faraj, a Galilee village, and whom the military authorities had ordered deported as infiltrees. Al, admitting that he had fled the village at the outset of Arab-Israeli hostilities, claims that he has lived there all his life, that it is ridiculous to brand him an infiltree, that his troubles in fact started only after he had refused to agree to a proposal by the military that he exchange his rich land in Galilee for an inferior parcel in another part of the country, and that if he lost his case all other Arabs in that village soon would face a similar choice because a nearby kibbutz was determined to increase its own holdings by annexing Arab lands. In a somewhat similar case, the Israel claim and nullified an evacuation order.[110]

On the role of the courts in tempering the land-robbery law in some cases, the pro-Zionist journalist Hal Lehrman remarked:

Mistreated Arabs could appeal successfully to the Supreme Court for redress. But the very frequency of such appeals showed the extent of the abuses, and many Arab fellaheen lacked the sophistication, the funds or the daring to go over the head of the official controlling their areas. The Court itself found occasion severely to reprimand the Custodian's office for its unjust interpretation of the law.[111]

Now in general, as we have noted, the Absentee Property Law of 1950 only legalized the de facto robbery that had already gone on, though in some minor respects (which we have noted) the status of absentees was a bit improved. Outside of the issue of Arab rights, however, "The fundamental change introduced by the law was the Custodian's privilege to sell property."[112]

Up to this time, theoretically the Custodian was simply holding the land on behalf of its owners. The new provision in the law "was the first step toward legally implementing the new policy of absorbing Arab holdings through development,"[113] that is, of permanently and juridically alienating the land from its Arab owners. A Development Authority was set up which had the right to buy absentee property from the Custodian. The Jewish National Fund was specifically authorized to purchase such land.

The Hebrew University professor Norman Bentwich states in his book Israel, published in 1952:

The [Jewish National] Fund has now become an indispensable adjunct of the State for both rural and urban development. It buys from the Custodian of Absentee Property, appointed by the State, the land and houses of the fugitive Arabs, and makes them available to the State Development Board for occupation, the purchase-price, in whole or part, being held as compensation for the former Arab owners. Till 1947 it has acquired 250,000 acres—1,000,000 dunams in the Palestine measure; by 1951 it had trebled that holding. The programme for the next five years is to acquire another 500,000 acres, and for that the Fund hopes to collect 250,000,000 dollars. [Italics added.][114]

It should be remembered that the purchase-price, which is referred to, was set by one Zionist official for sale to another Zionist official for the purpose of integrating the land into the Zionist scheme of development. The "former" Arab owners had nothing to say about it, least of all about whether they wanted to sell in the first place. In addition, as Bentwich indicates, the Arab owner might be allocated only a "part" of the purchase-price which is thus set for his own land.

The expectations of which Bentwich wrote were indeed realized. On July 3, 1953 the Jerusalem Post reported that

The Government signed an agreement with the Jewish national Fund this week for the sale of two million dunams, mostly abandoned land, it was announced yesterday.

The agreement was concluded in accordance with Government decisions in 1949 and in 1951.

The land in question is in all sectors of the country and is mostly agricultural. About 400 new [Jewish] settlements have in the meantime been established on it by the Jewish Agency.

After the mass flight of the Arabs the Government took over the custody of their holdings. In order to normalize [sic] the land situation, abandoned land is being transferred to the Jewish National Fund in a series of land transactions.

The significance of the latest land transaction may be measured from the fact that the entire area of Israel is a little over 20 million dunams, of which only 5 million dunams are under cultivation.

Thus the deed was consummated.

A little ease-up on one point took place in 1951 under the pressure of the election campaign for the Knesset. After all, the Arabs had 10 per cent of the votes, and the Mapai-affiliated "Arab" parties had to have some reason for asking for these votes; the Communist Party was getting the support of up to a third of the Arab minority and the government parties were worried. It is remarkable that even under these circumstances the paltry concession that was made was only such as to point up to the nature of the whole operation.

The amendment that was passed allowed Arabs who were legal residents to keep any property which they might obtain in the future; they were not to be robbed of any property which they did not yet possess. The change did not affect the steal that had already gone on and was still going on. Such was its magnanimity.

According to Dr. Peretz' account, even this great-hearted gesture was first initiated in the Knesset, late in 1950, by a Mapainik, David Ha-

Cohen, who had to break party discipline in order to do so. But the following year, under the spotlight of the election campaign getting under way, the Knesset passed it.

Even Arabs who were not absentees were liable to be affected by the [Absentee Property] law without Ha-cohen's amendment. If a non-absentee Arab citizen willed property to his wife or child or to another member of his family who returned to Israel [from refuge abroad] under the plan to reunite families, their inheritance would be insecure. The Custodian could immediately seize it under the present law.[115]

That much was vouchsafed to justice. Other things were promised with an eye on the vote. The Custodian, and also Moshe Sharett, talked about loosening up on some of the stolen property. Haaretz commented (June 2, 1951):

Is it not strange that only now... measures are promised on behalf of the Arab minority? So far no steps have been taken. It seems hardly likely that the policy will change after the elections.

It was a safe prediction.

3

And it came to pass after these things, that Naboth the Jezreelite had a vineyard, which was in Jezreel, hard by the palace of Ahab king of Samaria.

And Ahab spake unto Naboth, saying, Give me thy vineyard, that I may have it for a garden of herbs, because it is near unto my house: and I will give thee for it a better vineyard than it; or, if it seem good to thee, I will give thee the worth of it in money.

And Naboth said to Ahab, The Lord forbid it me, that I should give the inheritance of my fathers unto thee.

1 Kings 21:1-3

The Juridical completion of the land-robbery was, however, not quite accomplished yet. One loose end had to be gathered up. There were still tracts of land that had been taken away from Arab peasants, during the war or right after it, whose robbery could still not be justified under any law, in spite of the wide-open character of the measures already passed. Besides, the whole operation could scarcely be considered cleaned up till a show had been made of offering some compensation.*

The task was met handily by the Land Acquisition Law of March 1953. It did not bother with any niggling piecemeal pretexts for stealing land from Arabs. In one fell swoop it came out with a formula which automatically legalized any and all land-robberies that had already taken place.

The way this is done is surely a juridical curiosity. The heart of the law is in Paragraph 2: land "will become the property of the Development Authority ... free of any encumbrance" if the minister in charge certifies "by signed document" that it fulfills the following three provisions:

(1) On April 1, 1952, was not in the possession of its owners;

(2) Was used or earmarked within the period from May 4, 1948 to April 1, 1952, for purposes of essential development, settlement, or security;

(3) Is still required for one of these purposes. [116]

The crux is in point (1), which carefully applies the law to any land that "was not in the possession of its owners" for any reason whatsoever—the important reason being, of course, the simple fact that the owner had been illegally kicked off.

The law is being wrongly interpreted by Israel's Arabs, wrote a Zionist journalist from Haifa to the London Jewish Chronicle. They are in "panic" because they think it means all Arab-owned land can be "confiscated at will." That is not so, he assures; the law's main aim "is to grant legal status to an already existing situation."[117] It seems he expects his readers to heave a sigh of relief.

Haaretz related, in its January 1955 issue:

Since the publication of the law in the Official Gazette, up to the end of 1954 the Government Printer had his hands full with the job

---

* For the question of Israel's offers of compensation to Arab refugees outside the state, which is outside the purview of this study, see Dr. Peretz's work (ref. n. 4).

of issuing official brochures crammed with announcements to the effect that "I, the Minister of Finance ... acting under the powers granted me in the law... hereby affirm that the lands specified below are covered by the following conditions... and therefore I order that they be transferred to the ownership of the Development Agency." This short announcement would always be followed by long lists of Arab villages, numbers of land parcels and series of coordinates sufficient to construct an entire map of Israel. When the work was concluded about two months ago,* the Development Agency of the State of Israel found itself the richer by over a million dunams.[118]

Before its passage by the Knesset, the 1953 law was strongly criticized as unjust by a number of liberal and socialist Jewish deputies and spokesmen, but when it came to a vote not a single vote was cast against it by any Jewish deputy. At a protest rally of liberal Jewish and Arab notables, it was stressed that—

> ...the reason why not a single Jewish member of parliament voted against the bill, although many members of the Mapai and Mapam parties strongly criticized it before it was adopted, is that a number of powerful kibbutzim (collective farms) belonging to both Mapai and Mapam parties benefited directly from the law by acquiring the land requisitioned from the Arabs. The Left-wing [Mapam] kibbutzim Hamishmar and Kfar Masaryk were the chief beneficiaries. They acquired so much of the requisitioned Arab land that they now rented out parcels of it to some of the Arabs who previously owned it.[119]

In the Knesset a forceful speech against the law was made by Masad Qasis, a deputy of a Mapai-affiliated "Arab" party. Among other things he complained that Jewish collectives were given land in some villages still legally inhabited by Arabs, for example Shafa Amr, al-Hamma, Evron; talk of development and security was "sheer deception."[120]

Haaretz openly said that the purpose of the law was to legalize the seizure of Arab land by Jewish settlements that wanted to expand. "There is no reason to legalize the fact that certain farms exploited the victory of

---

* The Israel government propaganda booklet *The Arabs in Israel* (p. 27) says, "The transfer of such land to the Development Authority was completed by March 1954."

the State in the defense war against invaders, to seize for their own benefit the lands of their neighbors," it said (March 10, 1953). Being politically conservative, Haaretz also thought it worthwhile arguing that "seizure of the [Arab] minority's property is liable to undermine the foundations of private property rights."

The Ichud, the only wing of the Zionist movement with a consistent conscience on the subject, naturally spoke out with burning indignation. Here is a good sample from Dr. Shereshevsky, the associate editor of the Ichud organ Ner, entitled "We Accuse," addressed to a responsible leader of the Knesset:

[The law's] true meaning is robbery of land from people, inhabitants, of the State. They are agricultural people, like you; they are citizens of Israel, like you. There exists only one difference between them and you: they are Arabs and you are a Jew. This difference seemed to you so great and decisive that you were ready to trespass for it all that is required by the Law of Israel and its tradition.

The name given to this "Law" is but a lie to conceal what has truly been fixed by it so that the public may not realize and know that not the "acquisition" of land—by a mutual spontaneous agreement on either side—is meant, but an expropriation of lands that have been seized in an arbitrary and illegal way since 1948. This "Law" puts a stamp of legality on criminal actions, "the taking over of land by kibbutzim and settlements from Arab citizens only because these settlements wanted to enlarge their property" (Haaretz). One village of 7,000 inhabitants, Um-el-Fahm, has thus lost 110,000 dunams and will remain with only 30,000 dunams. The village of Jatt, of 1,450 inhabitants, remains with 1,600 dunams. The village of Tireh (4,000 inhabitants) is left with 9,000 dunams...

It is not on behalf of the Arabs that I am writing this letter. They will know how to defend themselves and their rights ... It is not on their behalf that I am writing but on our behalf, for God's sake "whose name you have profaned among the nations,"for the name of the people of Israel, on behalf of our sons and daughters "who have not sinned"![121]

In the course of a series of articles in the liberal Haaretz, Moshe Keren summed up in January 1954, under a subhead which said "Robbery With a Legal Coating":

> We consider it our bounden duty to spell this subject out in unequivocal terms; for what occurred here was a case of wholesale robbery with a legal coating. Hundreds of thousands of dunams of land were taken away from the Arab minority—I am not talking here of the refugees—through a whole variety of legal devices. The future student of legal devices. The future student of ethnology will wonder how it came to pass that it was the Jewish people, striving to build their state on the foundations of justice and righteousness and having themselves been the victims of unparalleled acts of robbery and expropriation, that should have been capable of doing this to a helpless minority. But the fact remains that they were, and even more depressing is the fact that it was precisely those groups who presume to establish a new society free from injustice and exploitation—the kibbutzim, in other words—who marched in the vanguard of the seizure campaign, and that foremost among them were the self-styled fighters for the idea of absolute justice—the kibbutzim affiliated with Mapam—whose representatives in the Knesset are now missing no opportunity to condemn the government for is discriminatory policy towards the Arabs.[122]

Although the main objective of the 1953 Land Acquisition Law was to provide a sweeping legalization of all land-robberies committed up to date against Arabs, it formally presented itself also as a law to provide compensation for the lands that had been and were being stolen.* On the one hand, this allowed the government to present the operation as a respectable financial transaction; on the other, it enabled Zionist

---

* The UN's Partition Resolution of 1947, which provided the juridical basis for the creation of the state, had had something to say about land expropriation and compensation, in anticipation of such attempts to take away the minority's land. It provided that the constitution of the new state must embody certain provisions which could not be abrogated by any law or official act, and which were "under the guarantee of the UN" itself. Among these was the following (Chap. 2, Art. 8):

"No expropriation of land owned by an Arab in the Jewish State (by a Jew in the Arab State) shall be allowed except for public purposes. In all cases of expropriation full compensation as fixed by the Supreme Court shall be paid *previous to dispossession*." (Emphasis added.)

propagandists to invent a picture of the law as a veritable boon for the Arabs and another clinching "proof" of the happy life which the Arabs led under the Zionist state.

The law did indeed offer a compensation system, and a number of Arabs did get some compensation. A close look at this compensation system, however, will raise the question whether the measure was designed to ensure fair payment to despoiled Israeli Arabs or to get around making such payment.

One point is basic, before any such consideration is made at all. This is the fact that even a scrupulously fair compensation system could possibly make up for the injustice that was done to this people by separating them from their land in any way at all. The land was not only the economic sustenance of these Israeli Arab peasants; it was also the root of their family life, social life, culture and identification with their ancestral mores. Stealing their land meant, literally, destroying their way of life, even if a certain number of pieces of gold and silver were place in their hands. And it must be borne in mind that the Arab could not simply take the money and buy any other land he might want—land was able to go in one direction only, ethnically speaking.

Pieces of money could no more take the place of land in their culture than, say, a refugee Jewish diamond merchant settling in Lhassa could be compensated for the theft of his cutting tools and precious stock by an equivalent value in stocks of Tibetan rancid yak butter, a Himalayan delicacy.

It is important to emphasize this because, otherwise, an unwary reader may absorb the notion that the justice or injustice of the entire land-grab operation stands or falls with the adequacy or inadequacy of the compensation which may be the final outcome for some. It would be better not even to discuss this aspect of the question at all than to further this notion by getting into the financial argument involved. With this warning, however, a few points about the compensation offered by the law are in order.

It should be borne in mind, too, that the compensation offered by the law was only to Arab peasants who were legally in Israel, and did not refer at all to any who were refugees outside the country. It was therefore an offer of payment for only 300,000 dunams* out of the millions of dunams

---

* This figure is Dr. Peretz's estimate. The government says, "The total of Arab-owned land involved is estimated at 250,000 dunams,"in its propaganda pamphlet, *The Arabs in*
(continued...)

that had been taken. According to Dr. Peretz's account, "The law was also an attempt to appease the growing sentiments which favored payment to the country's Arab citizens for their requisitioned property."[123]

According to the compensation provisions of the law, the Arab owner will be indemnified in money, "if not otherwise agreed" between him and the government. What about his getting land in return for the land taken from him? This was spelled out in the following paragraph of the law:

> If the acquired property was used for agriculture, and was the main source of livelihood of its owner, who owns no other land from which he can derive a livelihood, the Development Authority is obliged to offer him, on his demand, other property, either in ownership or in lease, as full or as part indemnity. A competent authority, to be appointed by the Minister, will determine the kind of property to be offered, its location, area, and in the case of lease, the term of the lease (provided it is not less than 49 years) and the value of the property for the purpose of satisfying his requirements for livelihood, all in accordance with rules to be laid down in regulations.[124]

So the Arab owner is not to be given as much land as was robbed from him; he is to be given only as much as befits "his requirements for livelihood," the difference to be made up in money. Who will determine how much he needs for his livelihood? Naturally, those who are engaged in robbing him. In any case, whether this determination is made fairly or not, it is written into the law that these Arab peasants shall be deprived of all land except a subsistence tract, even if the land is legally admitted to be theirs.*

---

* (...continued)
Israel, p. 27—Incidentally, the next sentence in this propaganda booklet is a good example of the slickly misleading statements which fill it: "The other 1,020,000 dunams transferred to the Development Authority under the Act was either Government-owned or Jewish-owned land." Thus the disingenuous author distinguishes it from the "Arab-owned land." But all of this land was equally stolen originally from Arab holders.

* The aforementioned government pamphlet *The Arabs in Israel* falsely states on p. 25 that the law aims "to provide for appropriate compensation either in land or in cash *as desired by the claimant*" (emphasis added), even though some details given on the very next page would indicate the falsity of the statement to close inspection.

The government decides, subject to court review, what land shall be given in compensation, what kind, where, how much and whether it is to be granted outright or merely leased to the peasant.[125]

In case of money compensation, all cash payments are based by the law on the value which the land had in 1950, three years before the law was passed; namely, before the devaluation of Israel's currency. Surely a most unusual provision! How could it be justified? In the Knesset debate, spokesmen for the law argued that

> The Committee [of the Knesset] had fixed the date to prevent owners from benefiting by any rise in value caused by improvements of the Development Authority.[126]

This might be considered legitimate if it referred to improvements like new buildings, etc. on the land in question,* but if that were really the consideration involved, it would have been much more straightforward and simple to write into the law the requirement that this deduction was to be made for the purposes enumerated.

But this would not have suited the intentions of the lawmakers since it would have failed to take advantage of the currency devaluation that took place between 1950 and 1953. "In January 1950 the average official value of the Israel pound was $2.80. At the time of the Knesset debate on compensation, the average official value of the Israel pound was $1.00."[127] A piece of land price-tagged 100 pounds in 1950 would have been tagged somewhere near 280 in 1953; but the Arab would be given little more than a third of what it was worth.

Now just to show that it understood this, the Knesset specifically voted into the law a provision which, it claimed, made up for this currency devaluation: the 1950 value, for purposes of compensation, was to be increased by an amount equal to three per cent for each year since then. Only three per cent!

---

* But in a discussion with a New York representative of Israel's Histadrut, I got this interpretation of what is meant by "improvements" from which the Arab must not benefit: e.g., if a new road is built and raises land values around it, including an Arab's land, the latter's land should be evaluated without taking the change into account, for why should "they" benefit from what "we" do? Israeli Arabs are here thought of as "they" (aliens) while only "we" (Jews) are truly of the country; for is it not a "Jewish State"? This is the authentic ethnocentrism of the Israeli Zionist climate. So the Arab is to be compensated on the basis of what land values were at the time he was robbed, just as if he legally ceased to own the land by virtue of being robbed.

In the Knesset, the Arab deputy Masad Qasis (of a Mapai-affiliated "Arab" party) made another point about the 1950 date:

> In 1950 Arabs were permitted to sell land exclusively to the JNF [Jewish National Fund, the Zionist agency]. They received no more than £I 25 per dunam and in some places as little as £I 15, whereas the present price was nearer to £I 250 or £I 350 per dunam. Qasis proposed to give the courts power to fix the kind and amount of compensation.[128]

So much for the fairness of the law's provision that three-year-old values, not current ones, were to be used as the basis of compensation.

But this is only one of the factors involved in the reluctance of the despoiled Arabs to settle their claims in accordance with this unjust law. Here is a review of the situation in the January 7, 1955 issue of Haaretz:

> The least that might have been expected from the perpetrators of this draconic law is that the one constructive paragraph of the law would be implemented with fairness and decency. Official figures disclose, however, that to date, two years after the passage of the law, no more than one thousand compensation claims have been filed, of which only a few hundred have been settled—and that these are mostly the claims of townsmen whose confiscated lands have been merely a small and subsidiary source of their income, and who are only too glad to receive the money offered them by way of compensation and some rich farmers who suffer from no lack of land and for whom compensation constituted no problem at all. But not one single fellah, among the thousands of DPs concentrated for the most part in the Galilee has so far been the beneficiary of any measure of agricultural rehabilitation. Why?[129]

This is certainly a very striking fact, particularly given the class differentiation which the Haaretz writer stresses.* It is precisely the poor

---

* As for the fact itself, note that the *Haaretz* statement quoted above says "not one single fellah"; and other sources indicate that, even if all Arabs are counted, the overwhelming majority were unwilling to settle or held out for quite some time. Thus in an article in *Haaretz* on January 14, 1955 by Moshe Keren (ref. n. 122) the writer notes that "a certain improvement in the disposition of the land problem has been taking place in this year, the seventh after the establishment of the State of Israel. Some 500 out of the total 2000

(continued...)

peasants who find the law most unjust and unacceptable; the richer have substantially less difficulty in coming to terms with the masters—hence, incidentally, the very existence of those Mapai-affiliated Arab deputies whom we have had occasion to mention, and who are widely regarded as turncoats; but that is another story.

The Haaretz writer asked "Why?" Here is his answer:

The officials entrusted with the administration of the Land Acquisition Law reply that the bulk of the DPs refuse to listen to any offer of compensation and insist on being allowed to return to their lands and villages, and that the few who desire rehabilitation in some other locality are only willing to take strictly Jewish lands, that is, they refuse to resettle on the property of absentees appropriated by the Development Agency,which is the only category of land the Government is prepared to grant them.

This is quite true, and in unofficial talks with DPs' representatives they freely admit that they would not think of "soiling their hands with the plundered property of their brethren who fled across the border." And those familiar with the mentality of the Israeli Arabs add that the DPs fear—or maybe hope—that the present situation may be reversed, either through a "second round" or through the detachment of the Galilee from Israel in a peace treaty, as a result of Israel's eventual agreement to readmit the Arab refugees.

In other words, the Israeli Arab DPs who are in Israel are asked by the government not only to condone the robbery of land from their brothers the refugees, but as a matter of fact to become accomplices to the theft by themselves becoming the recipients of stolen property. One cannot

---

gainsay the cleverness of the scheme from the Zionists' viewpoint: by settling Israeli Arabs on the refugees' property, these will be made willy-nilly into defenders of the robbery against their people, Arabs against Arabs. But of course the Israeli Arabs regard the stolen property as stolen property, and their disinclination to take it is not hard to understand.

From this point, the rest of the script is acted out: The government can now point to the recalcitrants as holding up that measure of Justice which the land-robbery law as designed to vouchsafe, and Zionists can inspire articles everywhere to the effect that this shows, does it not, that the Israeli Arabs are all fifth-columnists who are waiting bloodthirstily for another round of foreign invasion.

In this connection, Dr. Peretz mentions that "The military discovered that often Arabs within Israel, after agreeing to use land of refugees who fled to the Arab States, made illegal payments to the former property owners across the border."[130] One sees that the Israeli Arabs even tried to square it in their own way, at their own expense; but of course such "treasonous" goings-on could not be permitted by the state.

To come back to our Haaretz writer, his discussion of the situation continues with two other facets of the picture:

> But it is doubtful whether this reason alone, which the authorities are powerless to remove, would have prevented the DPs for any length of time from agreeing to resettle even on absentee lands, were it not for some additional delaying factors for which the Government alone is responsible: the endless procrastination, the lack of good will on the part of the responsible officials, the multiplicity of administrative agencies, the bureaucratic confusion which baffles the Arab fellah.
>
> And even when he had finally overcome all these difficulties, the fellah finds out that the Development Agency would grant him no more than 25 dunams of non-irrigated land, the balance of the compensation being paid in money—a few tens of pounds per dunam. So he asks: The money will be spent pretty soon, and how am I supposed to feed my large family from 25 dunams of barren soil?
>
> And thus the ugly affair drags on month after month, year in year out, to this very day, the ominous challenge it poses to the moral character of Israel.

With regard to "the lack of good will" mentioned by Haaretz, we may also note the statement by Dr. Peretz that "Most Israeli Arabs declare that even after winning court cases against the Custodian, they failed to receive adequate compensation for their losses."[131]

Dr. Peretz goes on to mention, like others, that the government explains Arab reluctance to take land on the ground that they fear reprisals in a "second round," and then he adds:

A more plausible explanation might be that farms offered in exchange for "absentee" property are usually granted on short-term leases and in more or less standard-sized holdings which do not necessarily correspond to the amount of land requisitioned.

This point about leasing rather than giving the land is, then, still another reason for the Arabs' reluctance to accept the law's settlement. (A little more on this question below.)

And finally, as another reason, not quite covered in all that we have given so far, is this one, perhaps the simplest of all: "Many of them avoid filing their claims on the ground that this would be tantamount to signing away their lands ..."[132] as indeed it would; and so they hope against hope for real justice.

In this way the above-mentioned law achieved three aims at one time: It established order at home; there are no more illegal land-grabs in Israel; everything is now legal. In addition, the Israel government can now make a show to the world of its decency and justice toward the Arab owners of land which was stolen for "development and settlement." And in addition to all this, the state retains the entire compensation, both the money and the land.[133]

That is a harsh summary from the pen of an Israeli anti-Zionist, M. Stein, but it is conformity with the facts in the case of the uncompensated "present absentees."

4

"It gives you a queer turn," said one of the [UN] officials who visited the DP camps in Germany and who now works in the steaming, unsanitary camps into which these sorrowful victims of the Palestinian conflict [the Arab refugees] are herded. "If you close your eyes and listen to them, you believe you are back in Bavaria. You ask them where they want to settle, Transjordan, Egypt, Syria, just the way we used to ask the Jews in Germany if they wanted to go to the United States or to South America or to England, and the answer is always the same—'Palestine ... Palestine ... Palestine,' exactly as it was in Germany." He shook his head at the overlapping and repetitive quality of agony in our century.

Irwin Shaw: Report on Israel

These remain a few aspects of the land-robbery still to be noted.

The 1950 law provided certain circumstances under which absentee property could be released back to its Arab owner. Did this ever happen? In some cases, but then mostly in the case of urban property like houses—rather than agricultural land, which was the main prize desired from the spoliation of the Arabs.

Hal Lehrman writes, discussing serious criticisms made not only by Arabs but also by Israeli Jews whom he talked to:

> The Custodian of Arab Property was empowered by law to exempt absentees who had left their residences for valid reasons, but such exemption, it was asserted, was sparingly given and only in exchange for large fees.[134]

Dr. Peretz writes, referring to the time in November 1949 when Finance Minister Eliezer Kaplan answered charges in a Knesset debate:

> The government classified tens of thousands of Israel Arabs as absentee. But in urban areas only 400 residents of Jaffa, Haifa and Jerusalem who had never left the country recovered some of their property, according to Kaplan. The non-urban property of "several score" Arabs was also released. The Custodian issued a total of 209 certificates releasing property to its Arab owners. Maintenance grants from the income of absentee property were made by the Custodian to "several families of absentees in Jaffa, Haifa, and Jerusalem." There were also a few instances in which merchandise was returned to Arabs after they proved their ownership.[135]

And later:

In urban areas the Custodian returned over 2,000 dwellings to their Arab owners who had been classified as "absentees" by 1953.[136]

The Jerusalem Post reported on October 10, 1952 that, as of August 1, 828 houses, 276 plots, 22,127 dunams of land were returned upon the recommendation of the Committee.[137]

And in those cases where a house was returned to an Arab owner, he might find himself stuck with a tenant in that house whose rent had been fixed by the Custodian, because it was "absentee"-owned, at a specially low level. The Jerusalem Rent Court handed down a ruling that the restored Arab owner could not raise that rent, even if only to the prevailing level.[138] One can have no quarrel with measures designed to keep rents down, especially for the benefit of arrivals from Europe's DP camps, but this was a measure which automatically discriminated against Arabs only, and did not affect Jewish landlords.

Next: we have already mentioned that the government, in allocating compensatory land, tended to give it to Arabs only on lease, rather than outright. In fact—

In many areas the paradoxical situation arose in which the Custodian rented "absentee" property to its original owners. All the Arabs of Kfar Ilit near Nazareth were declared "absentees," although half of them had never left, not even during the fighting which occurred in the village. After the war, those who remained were forced to pay rent to the Custodian for the use of their own lands.[139]

Truly a fantastic situation, in which "absentees" are so thoroughly present that they are kindly permitted to rent their own land from those who stole it, and where the land itself is so far from being urgently needed for "development and settlement" that, indeed, there is no one to cultivate it except the very Arabs who have been dispossessed of it... As Dr. Peretz explains when he mentions that the Custodian at one point leased 100,000 dunams to Arabs:

The move resulted from pressure by the Arab minority, Jewish political groups sympathetic to the minority, and government failure to recruit enough Jewish settlers to farm all cultivable absentee land. About 5,000 Arab families—between 25,000 and 30,000 people—in nearly 100 villages were each granted yearly leases of 20 dunams. In most cases the land was leased in exchange for property commandeered by the Custodian.[140][Italics added.]

If it is a matter of compensating for property "commandeered" by the Custodian, why then isn't the land given outright, rather than leased? The answer suggests itself: as long as the land is only leased, the Arab protest is temporarily stilled but the land itself still belongs to Jews and the Arab tillers can always be eventually squeezed out. Thus the authorities reason, for the land-grab is not over; but meanwhile the state badly needs the food and crops which will be raised by these Arab lease-holders.

The Mapai-affiliated Arab deputy Masad Qasis, in his complaints against the 1953 law in the Knesset,

> strongly opposed compensation in the form of leases for land previously owned by Arabs on the grounds that it would give the government unusual powers over former Arab landowners...

> He accused the government and various institutions of holding property illegally and unjustly for other than security or development reasons and wanted to confine their power to requisition of Arab lands which were either actually settled, or used for security purposes. Although the government prevented Arabs from securing ownership of their land, in many places it permitted them to lease their own holdings from the Custodian. Jewish collectives, on the other hand, were given land in some villages still legally inhabited by Arabs. This occurred in Shafa Amr, al-Hamma, and Evron. In such cases talk of development and security was "sheer deception." Qasis, therefore, proposed an unconditional return of the lands to their rightful owners.[141]

But it is not the objective motive of "development and settlement" that governs the over-all policy of the authorities. The question is: development and settlement by whom? all citizens of Israel without discrimination, or Jews only? What governs the real policy of the government is an ethnic chauvinism derived from the Zionist ideology. Hence every foot of ground owned by an Arab citizen of Israel has a question-mark over it. Cutting down the amount of land under Arab holding becomes an end in itself, even apart from the fact that the "Jewish State" is not going move Jewish settlers who are squatting on stolen land. Thus Qasis' complaints went on:

Despite their large agricultural contribution, the government refused to restore the untilled land which belonged to the 30,000 Arab refugees who legally resided in Israel. The government often prevented Arab farmers from cultivating unoccupied land near their own villages. Much of the 300,000 dunams requisitioned under the Land Acquisition Law was uncultivated. If the government wanted these lands developed, Qasis thought it should return them to their owners. [Italics added.][142]

Restrictions on Arab land-holding point toward an eventually Araberrein Israel. In February 1953 the Ichud raised this question of restriction, among others, in a sharp attack on the government, in which it linked it with the leasing practices of the authorities:

Why did he [a government spokesman] announce to Arab "refugees" who wanted to set up a village in order to bring waste land under cultivation, that "no new Arab villages were to be established in Israel?" Why are lands leased to Arabs for only a one-year period? Does this not prevent capital investments for long-term cultivation and improvements? Do such acts not cause damage to an excellent agricultural area which supplies a considerable proportion of the products so much needed by our population and which save us large amounts of foreign currency? [Italics added.] [143]

The last remarks do indeed indicate economic motives which come into play to counter the Zionist-chauvinist ones. Arab agriculture is badly needed; Arab-owned or -cultivated land still has to be put up with, at least for the present. So Arab farmers even have to be aided to produce, today (as we intend to discuss in a future article). But no Arab can feel secure in this atmosphere.*

For the land-grab did not end with the 1953 legalization of all previous land-grabs. We have not even discussed—only barely mentioned, on page 58— one whole sector of this subject of how the Arab minority has been

---

* An American liberal critic of Zionism, *Christian Century* editor Harold Fey, reported from Israel that "It is common practice to establish a Jewish land settlement close to an Arab village. If an Arab's sheep strays to land used by the Israelis, the Arab is arrested and may be fined 50 pounds. Encroachments on Arab land are frequent, beginning with the commons owned by the Arab village and extending now to privately owned land. Many Arab villages sit like a duck in a freezing pond, in the midst of a shrinking circle." (Fey, "Israeli Citizen, Class B," *Christian Century*, Jan. 13, 1954.)

despoiled of its heritage. That is the method of the "double-play" which depends on expropriation by the military—the proclamation of certain lands as "security areas" for border defense and the mass eviction of the Arab population from these lands, so that they can be replaced with Jewish settlers.

But this fact raises a larger question—the military occupation under which 85 per cent of the Israeli Arab minority live. This military occupation and the land-grab are the two great and overshadowing realities under which the Israeli Arabs exist, beside which everything else is secondary. The military sector of the land-grab, therefore, will be considered as part of a future article on the military occupation as a whole.

Some readers may wonder: What possible justification do Zionists give for this wholesale robbery of a people? The question is an idle one, for the most part, since virtually all of Zionist literature, with few exceptions, is designed to deny and falsify the fact of the robbery itself. Zionist accounts of the land laws, while dissembling their real meaning and contents, repeat endlessly that the only losers are those fifth-columnist Arabs who fled to the enemy out of frothing hatred of the Jews and who are now only whooping it up for war against the state of Israel, etc., etc., etc.

It is therefore enough to establish the facts, as we have done here, to cut through these myths.

But another approach needs a word, since it is given considerable space in the book by the World Zionist-Revisionist leader Joseph B. Schechtman, The Arab Refugee Problem, which is a down-the-line propaganda production for the Israel government position:

Israel's Finance Minister, Eliezer Kaplan, stressed in the Knesset on November 23, 1949, that the Israel legislation on Arab abandoned property was patterned on that of India and Pakistan, who were confronted with similar problems growing out of the partition of India in 1947. That resulted in vast exchanges of population with the abandoning of enormous quantities of land and other property. Some 7,900,000 Moslems left India for Pakistan and simultaneously some 5,000,000 destitute Hindu and Sikh refugees arrived in India from Pakistan. ...

These problems were substantially the same on the Indian subcontinent and in Israel. The legislation dealing with the matter was bound to be construed along similar lines.[144]

This attempt to establish an analogy with the India-Pakistan exchange of population requires a certain kind of boldness which one can admire. We can note first the question of the voluntary character of the exchange, though that will only get us into the official Zionist claim that all the Arab "absentees" fled voluntarily, etc.—a claim which we have already considered. More to the point, there was no exchange at all in the Palestine case, of any kind, voluntary or involuntary. The Israeli Arabs who are now refugees in the Arab states did not get—and are not offered—the property of Jews in those states who move into Israel. This exchange-analogy is a grim jest, quite apart from any criticism of what actually happened in the India-Pakistan operation.

The cream of the jest, however, is to be found a few pages ahead in Schechtman's book,[145] in a passage entirely unrelated to the exchange-analogy. There we find Schechtman echoing the indignant Israeli complaints against the action taken by Iraq in 1951 when that Arab state confiscated the property left behind by Jews leaving for Israel in a mass exodus of over 120,000. Tel-Aviv protested vigorously, and quite rightly. But according to the terms of the exchange-analogy, this was sort of the other half of the "exchange"!

But attempts at propagandist justification like this are exceptional. For the most part it is simply a question of burying the truth. In his burning denunciation of the 1953 land law which we have quoted in its place, Dr. Shereshevsky of the Ichud proclaimed that "The Jewish people in the whole world" will know the truth and "will not put up with it ..." Unfortunately, he was wrong. Most particularly in the United States, not only the Zionist press but the general Jewish press, with the general press mostly going along, has performed prodigies in propaganda and public relations to falsify and suppress any part of the truth, thus keeping it from the Jewish people and all other people.

But would "the Jewish people" put up with it if they knew the truth? Dr. Shereshevsky raises the question. It reminds us that the Ichud people, though sterling liberals and honest democrats, are still enmeshed in the Zionist ideology. "The Jewish people" is no monolithic entity that will or will not put up with it; it spreads over the political spectrum.

This is also what is disturbing about one of the constant refrains of those Israeli liberals who do tell the truth about the Arab minority. They tend to pass the guilt off onto the backs of "the Jewish people." The reader can see a typical example of this in the quotation from Haaretz's Moshe Keren on page 70: how could "the Jewish people" do this to "a helpless minority" when it has itself been the victim of robbery and exploitation and has so often vowed itself to righteousness and justice?

One must respect the motives of this breast-beating, but the content is distressing. In other mouths, such a sweepingly false and slanderous accusation would sound sinister indeed. It was not "the Jewish people" but the Zionist authorities, the Zionist movement, and the Zionist government that bear the responsibility; and the difference is enormous.

Such sweeping attribution of guilt to a whole people, for crimes committed by some among them, is more familiar as a methodological habit of anti-Semites and other racists. It is dangerous. In the present case the conscientious Zionist liberals apply it to their own people, whom they love, whereas the anti-Semites apply it to an alien people whom they hate. This great difference bespeaks the virtues of the liberals, but the dangerous similarity bespeaks the pitfalls of the Zionist identification of all Jews as one nation and of world Jewry with the state of Israel. Here we touch upon that common axis from which Zionism and anti-Semitism branch off in opposite directions as bisymmetric phenomena.

A NOTE ON SOURCES

As before, it is the aim to document all important statements from sources which Zionists would recognize as being pro-Jewish rather than pro-Arab. Exceptions to this are clearly labeled in the text or references notes, wherever necessary.

More than before, the present article refers most often to a basic work which is unfortunately still unpublished, though it has no near rival as the authoritative and scholarly work on the subjects covered. This is the Ph.D. thesis (Columbia, 1954) by Don Peretz, "Israel and the Arab Refugees," in two mimeographed volumes.

Since we lean so heavily on it, and on the same author's magazine articles, an introduction is in order. In viewpoint Dr. Peretz is a disciple of, and dedicates his book to, Judah L. Magnes, founder of the Ichud, a small group in Israel which is the only wing of the Zionist movement which still consistently stands for justice to the Arab people.

Peretz studied at the Hebrew University in Jerusalem till 1948; during the Palestine war, he was a correspondent for NBC; in 1949 he returned to Palestine as Quaker representative with the UN agency in the field; later he was Middle East media evaluator for the Voice of America. In 1952 he studied Israel and the Middle East on a Ford Foundation grant, leading to his thesis. More recently he has been an expert on Middle East affairs for the American Jewish Committee.

Thanks are also due to Mr. David I. Marmor, director of research of the Israel Office of Information (N.Y.), for his cooperation in checking matters of fact and expressing his differences in matters of opinion and interpretation.

The Tel-Aviv newspaper Haaretz which is mentioned several times is the leading daily in Israel, sometimes called the "Times" of Israel, liberal in viewpoint. Its record of relative frankness on the Arab question is very exceptional.

New International Winter 1957

Chapter V
THE SUEZ INVASION:
ISRAEL'S ALLIANCE WITH IMPERIALISM

The joint attack on Egypt by the British, French, and Israeli forces is as gross an imperialist aggression against a small country as any in the history of colonialism.

Led by Britain and France, with Israel acting as their catspaw and junior partner in behalf of its own aims, the attack by the Western allies is a continuation of their three-month-old drive to blackjack Egypt over possession of the Suez Canal and reverse the nationalization of the Canal Company, to put the waterway under "international" (i.e., imperialist) control.

But Egypt had and has a sovereign right to take control of this piece of Egyptian territory.

Cairo was willing to, and proposed to, concede various guarantees of free shipping through the canal, of compensation of the Canal Company coupon-clippers, etc. But Britain is really concerned that any victory for Egyptian rights would inspire other Arab and Middle East countries to make difficulties about the foreign exploitation of their oil resources and European domination of their affairs; the French government hates Nasser's support to the Algerian fighters for national freedom; both are deathly afraid in the first place that any backdown before Egypt's rights on the Suez will inspire the whole region to defy the European colonialists and encourage resistance to their power.

This, the irrepressible revolt against colonialism that has swept the world since the Second World War weakened the old colonial empires, is the background and context of the Middle East war that has been unleashed with the decision by London and Paris to settle affairs with the defiant Egyptian regime by the same methods and instruments as Russia is using to settle with the defiant Hungarian revolutionaries.

They are not attacking Egypt because Nasser is a despotic military dictator. They are not attacking Egypt because Nasser's regime rules over an oppressed and poverty-stricken people who need domestic reforms instead of an expensive army buildup. They are not attacking Egypt because Nasser has been keeping Israeli ships out of the Suez Canal in violation of Israel's rights ever since 1949–50. They would be glad to prop up this same oppressive dictator if he would play ball with their power-play.

Their aims converged with a different set of aims in the minds of the leaders of the Israel government, who had their own accounts to settle with Egypt.

Up to the day before yesterday, figuratively speaking, the main open advocate of Israel's starting a "preventive war" by initiating aggression against its Arab enemies was the Herut party, second largest in Israel, which shades from extreme reaction into fascism. With the outbreak of the Suez dispute, Herut leader Beigin openly proposed backing Britain and France in their assault on Egypt. Prime Minister Ben-Gurion ruled it out, at least in public.

All over the world, and most particularly in America, Zionist leaders held up their hands in horror at the very idea that Israel ("the democratic bastion in the Middle East") could even be thought to be capable of such an offense against peace, international morality and simple good sense.

As we remarked on August 20: "If one wishes to conjure up an appalling prospect that would finish off Israel in the Middle East, then one can take seriously a suggestion made by the Franco-fascist organ Arriba (Madrid) that Britain use Israeli troops as 'Sepoys' to reoccupy the Suez Canal." In this article, however, we refused to take this seriously, and instead gave credence to Ben-Gurion's proclaimed intention of keeping out of the British-French line-up.

The "unthinkable" is now a fact on both counts—launching of "preventive war" and open alignment with the brutal colonialist aggression—and the result is bound to be an historic tragedy for the people of Israel and the Jewish people generally, regardless of military victory and regardless of how much added real estate the Israeli leaders may be able to grab.

The strategic timing of the attack may well have been determined of the Israeli leaders by three considerations,

(1) The Suez affair, as we explained above, seemed to be petering out; yet the Israeli leaders had undoubtedly hoped that, without their having to take a hand themselves, Britain and France would "take care" of Nasser.

(2) November 6 was a deadline set by the U.S. election; till that date, they expected, Washington would be hamstrung by vote-getting considerations from taking too strenuous action against them.

(3) Then, when Russia became unexpectedly embroiled in revolts against its rule in Poland and Hungary, and therefore also seemed immobilized, the plotters may well have decided that their cup was overbrimming.

It was the Israeli partner which triggered off the events by sending its armies across the border into Egypt, to seize the Sinai peninsula. It was the British and French partners who moved in to seize Suez, cynically using as pretext their benign desire to stop the fighting between their partner and their intended prey. To this end they issued their farcical ultimatum to "both sides," which invited the Israelis to move up to 10 miles from the Suez Canal while their victim moved away from the canal so that the outside imperialists could step in and seize it just as they had been threatening to do all along.

This little piece of play-acting was no less and no more ham-handed than the equally benign consent of the Moscow murderers to bring the blessings of peace to Hungary by rolling tanks over the bodies of the Freedom Fighters.

The primary character of the present war, therefore is determined by the British-French colonialists' aggression on Egypt, which is a continuation by guns and jetplanes of its three-months-old drive to punish that country for asserting its national rights over Suez. it is an outright imperialist attack against which the Egyptian people have every right to defend themselves.

The defense of Egypt will not be helped by the oppressive dictatorship under which they resist imperialism; it will not be helped by the social backwardness in which this regime has kept the country. Above all, it will not be helped by the fact that Nasser has forfeited great sectors of sympathy in the world by his own (and the other Arab states') reactionary and provocative declamations about destroying Israel as a state, their militaristic threats to go with this, and refusal to consider a peace settlement with Israel; and by the Egyptians' share of responsibility for the tension by organizing, stimulating and encouraging border raids and fedayeen forays into Israeli territory.

It is in spite of this, and only because of their socialist abhorrence of the colonialist politics behind the aggression, that the British Labor movement, both on top and in the ranks, is unlimbering such fighting spirit and fiery opposition to the war-mongering of the Eden government, as shown in the great Trafalgar Square demonstration and in Labor speeches and press attacks on the crime in the Middle East.

We hail British Labor's fight all the more in contrast to the heinous role being played by the two self-styled "socialist" premiers who, with the Tory Eden, plotted this outrage against national freedom.

The role of Guy Mollet's France against Egypt is a continuation of the frenzied persecution of nationalist freedom fighters in Algeria. In Algeria,

French colonialism is bogged down in a hopeless struggle to suppress North Africa. Floundering in its crisis, the jingos in Paris drive themselves to try to break out of the North African impasse by "teaching Nasser a lesson." They hope that a crashing success in Egypt will restore European supremacy all around the Mediterranean. Thus they try to break out of one trap by a desperate dash into another.

The role of Ben-Gurion's Israel is at once more complex and more tragic.

It is in the first place, a subordinate partner in this imperialist enterprise, as we have been pointing out; and so also is its armed struggle subordinated to the over-all colonialist character of the war. Yet, at the same time, it must be recognized that the politics of which its attack was a continuation, from its own side, are different from that of Britain-France.

The question leads us to the current apologies being offered wholesale in the press for Israel's disgraceful decision to launch that very "preventive war" which its leaders and spokesman had so often sworn was the Unthinkable.

In this connection we have naturally been hearing a great deal about that share of responsibility for the border tension which is Egypt's, and which we took up above. This is one side of the truth.

The other side of the truth consists of the Israel government's contributions, since the 1948 war, toward provoking border incidents, embittering relations, and refusing concessions indicated by simple justice.

This side of the truth would have to tell that the majority of the so-called border "infiltrators" are Palestinian Arabs who had been cruelly driven out or kept out of their native homes by Israeli force and laws, and that a good part of their "infiltrations" consist of attempts to recover some of their own property; that the Arab refugee problem, which is in very substantial part the creation of and responsibility of the Israelis, has been spurned by the government and all concessions refused; that in reply to the "infiltrations" the Israel regime has steadily, since the Kibya massacre, taken the initiative in raising the ante and heightening the savagery of the border fighting, up to and including the recent provocative shelling of Gaza by Israeli cannon; that the hatred of the Arab world has been wooed by the Zionists through the indefensible, discriminatory and second-class position in which even Israeli Arabs are place by law and practice, including military rule over most of them.

It is a story which would explain why Israel, through its reactionary chauvinist policies, has been working itself into an inextricable trap in its part of the world—a trap which closes in both economically and

90

politically—as long as it sets a course which fails to integrate it into the Middle East of which it is a natural part and without which it cannot exist healthily. Its reactionary chauvinist policies have made it easy for the Nassers to isolate it (just as, we explained, Nasser's reactionary regime makes it easier for world sentiment to be mobilized against Egypt's rights).

Israel's tumble into the pit of "preventive war" is a desperate attempt to extricate itself from the consequences of its chauvinism—by resorting to more of the same, and worse. It is like an alcoholic who is trying to cure the jitters with more drink, except this time the shot must be stiffer and the alcohol rawer. It is a classic pattern of the consequences of reactionary politics.

Labor Action, November 12, 1956

Chapter VI
THE TRUTH ABOUT THE FEDAYEEN

The finger was put on a tell-tale weak point in Nasser's case for blockading Israeli shipping when it was demanded that the Egypt regime say whether or no it considers itself in a state of war with Israel. The Cairo dictator has refused to say because either a yes or a no exposes his hand.

To be sure, no one can dream of unraveling the Middle East mess by simply threading a way through the tangle of juridical rights involved, but this question of belligerence is a bit more than juridical. If Nasser said yes, then he could hardly object if Israel also considered itself at war (though others could); if he said no, then he would deprive himself of his formal basis for excluding Israeli ships from the Suez Canal and probably also from the Gulf of Aqaba.

As earlier articles have brought out, the Arab socialists (specifically, the Baath Socialist Party) unfortunately support Nasser's blockade on the ground that it is an alternative to war. This hardly makes sense. A rock-bottom prerequisite in the Middle East, for the operation of any solution whatever, is a firm cease-fire. Anyone who breaks the cease-fire or provokes its breach deserves the condemnation of all people.

In the past week the Egyptian dictator has let it be known that he is ready to give the blockade up if Israel concedes on the Arab refugee issue. In reply, the Israelis say they are ready to talk about it. Anything fruitful that emerges, of course, would be a fine thing, but realism obliges one to fear that both sides are simply playing with that tragic issue as they have been doing for over eight years.

If Israel is responsible for cruelly keeping the Palestinian Arab refugees from their lands and homes, which it grabbed, then it is also true that Egypt (like most of the other Arab states) has shown little desire to do what it can to alleviate the refugees' sad lot. Among the Gaza refugees, there is a reservoir of hatred not only for Israel but also for the Egyptians who have kept them herded in the Strip as in a concentration camp without allowing them to taint Egyptian soil by entering on it, while using them callously as fodder for fedayeen raids.

This anti-Egyptian feeling and potentiality in the Strip is not as well publicized in this country as the resentment against Israel that fills the refugees, for the simple reason that it does not fit very well into the propaganda which seeks to justify Israel's October aggression by putting the spotlight solely on one side of the total picture. But it is very important, among other reasons, because it is one of the facts which points to the possibility of a peaceful political solution by Israel of its "Arab problem." But it is a solution which would require a fundamental reversal of current Zionist policy.

The Gaza Strip could have been used as a demonstration-ground to show the Arab masses (in all the states) that Israel means justice to them. That is, a different kind of Israeli regime could have demonstrated this, on the basis of a different policy, for the Ben-Gurion team of chauvinists, who regrettably head Israel had no such intentions.

This has been well brought out in A.J. Liebling's "Letter from Gaza" in the March 16 New Yorker:

> The Israelis, during their four-month occupation of the Strip, which began when they captured it last November 1st and is ending as I write, did nothing to reduce this human edema on their borders beyond shooting a disputed number of civilians when their troops entered and removing twenty-five families compromised by overfriendliness when they left. Their renewed contact with the refugees seemingly offered an opportunity to begin negotiations for the return of some and the compensation of others, but the chance was neglected, and the popular Israeli line on Gaza following the withdrawal may be gleaned from a piece, signed Diplomatic Correspondent, on the front page of last Tuesday's Jerusalem Post: 'To continue to administer this island of misery and hate would be a tiresome and costly undertaking for such a small country as this. The best thing for the refugees themselves is, probably, the way chosen by nearly a million Jews—emigration.' Diplomatic Correspondent's advice to people trapped in a submarine is to call a taxi.

While on the subject of Liebling's report from Gaza, another section of it demands quotation as giving one of the rare balanced views of how the Gaza refugees have been bedeviled on both sides. It is a good thing to keep in mind:

> The Egyptians, when they were here, tried to strengthen this romanticism [of revenge] by precluding the hope of any other solution; it was a species of treason, for example, for an individual to admit that he might accept compensation from the Israelis for his land if compensation were offered. Egyptian security agents kept excellent tabs on the interminable public conversations, and there

was no temptation to depart from the official doctrine of all or nothing, since there was no possibility of getting past the barrier up the road. In the Egyptian days, no refugee could be found who would say even that he would take his own land back if it meant returning to Israel as an individual and living among Jews. (There is no record, of course, of any such offer's having ever been made.) This legend of the monolithic intransigence of the exiles—not the Gaza lot alone but all the diaspora, in Lebanon, Syria, and Jordan—was in its time useful to Israel, too, because it barred any payments to anybody. The Israeli argument when visitors raise the question of the possibility of piecemeal compensation is that conditions have changed since the Arabs went away—and besides Israel can't spare the money. On the piecemeal resettlement of the refugees in Israel, it is 'We need the land for a hundred thousand Jews we expect from Portugal'—or Pimlico or Guatemala; details are unessential. Many Israelis are not only incapable of thinking that this is a paradox but unable to believe that it seems odd to a foreigner. Yet there are Palestinians on the Gaza beach who say, 'My land is five miles from here, and they have taken it to give it to men from ten thousand miles away.' The difference of opinion is irreconcilable. The degree of intransigence expressed varies, however, with the known political views of your interpreter, who is usually a camp official, and the men among the refugees who have the most substance and education, and who themselves speak English or French, are generally the most reasonable of all. 'I would go back and see if I could live happily in the new environment,' one such said to me—I had been warned against him as a hothead—and then see if I couldn't sell out and go where I felt I had more freedom.'

Yes, there would be plenty of ground for a progressive political appeal by the people of Israel to the Arab masses. That road exists, in spite of the too often repeated sentiment that the only way to teach Arabs any sense is to knock 'em on the head, etc.—which is a lineal descendant of the notorious MacArthur theory of how to deal with Orientals, of the dictum that "the only good Indian is a dead Indian," and of many related maxims of chauvinism and the military mind.

That road exists, and well-wishers of Israel can help it best by pushing it to take that road, instead of threatening to teach the Egyptians a lesson (all over again) by shooting its way through the Gulf of Aqaba in the name of Justice.

○ ○ ○ ○

One doesn't often go to the New Yorker for serious political issues, as we did last week, but here we go again. The occasion is a second dispatch from embattled Palestine by A.J. Liebling; this time (March 30) a "Letter from Tel Aviv" which wends its way through the back-of-the-book cartoons, ads, and clippings for the Raised Eyebrows Dept.

In spite of the title Liebling is again writing about what he found in Gaza. Here, in a no-man's-land between the Israelis and Egyptians, he saw both contestants quite plain, and, more than that, dares to say so. The result is unusual reportage.

There are two things he does very well. The first continues a theme in his "Letter from Gaza." He goes in to it again, and we do too now, since there is nothing more important than this point in any discussion of the Middle East conflict.

It is the opportunity that was not taken by Israel.

Parenthetically, Liebling thinks an opportunity was also lost by the UN, for he seems to favor the UN's forcible internationalization of Gaza, as the least evil. We can go along with him a certain distance, for, as we explained March 4, we favored a free plebiscite by the people of Gaza and would hope in such a plebiscite that the choice be for internationalization under UN administration. But unfortunately Liebling simply takes for granted that this solution should be imposed on Israel and Egypt by foreigners, just as both of the rivals yell for UN imposition of their own desires on the other fellow.

But the conditions which Liebling describes are very relevant to the line of policy for Israel which socialists should favor—and which has shown itself to be so impossible for the chauvinist Israeli regime.

There was plenty of potentiality in Gaza—even in the hell-hole of Gaza!—for a genuinely socialist Israeli government to appeal to the people of Gaza themselves as against the Egyptian enemy.

This fact is the starting-point of a program for Israel-Arab relations which turns a sharp edge against both the provocative chauvinism of Ben-Gurion and the reactionary dictatorship of Nasser. It undercuts the propaganda of both sides, which is about the only reading fare one usually has.

As mentioned, Liebling goes back to the theme of his previous dispatch: "The state of belligerency between Israel and Egypt gave both countries an excuse for ignoring the refugees. The two governments were, in a sense, allies against the Gazans, just as Israel and Jordan, though belligerent, are tacit allies against the internationalization of Jerusalem ..."

"Egypt," writes Liebling, who does not suffer from even a smidgen of pro-Nasserism, "which has steadily refused to offer the refugees Egyptian citizenship or to permit them to immigrate, has profited by their presence as an excuse for holding her Calais [i.e., a bridgehead on foreign territory] and at the same time refusing to accept any surcease of their woes short of what she knows to be impossible—mass return to their precise points of departure." Israel too has put on the subject of compensation.

Liebling puts no stock in the pro-Egyptian demonstrations held in the Strip after the Israeli departure; he derides their "spontaneity" and reports they were organized by Egyptian henchmen. For background on this and other points, by the way, Liebling is very good in conveying the atmosphere of idleness and despair which is forced on the Gazans and crowded refugees by conditions for which not they have the responsibility but the Egyptians and Israelis together.

> The Egyptians had built up a big reservoir of resentment against themselves because they treated both the long-time Gaza residents and the refugees as subject peoples... I heard several spontaneous testimonials to the former occupants, among them, 'The Egyptian soldiers took off their shoes so they could run faster. ... Only the Palestine Regiment [recruited from refugees] fought—that's why it had all the casualties', and even (if the speaker was sure his inter-locutor wasn't an Israeli) 'All the fedayeen were refugees. Do you think an Egyptian would dare go across that line?' On the night of the Egyptian surrender, a mob looted the enormous, hideous new palace of the Egyptian governor. ... While there was a prospect that the United Nations would take the Strip over for an appreciable period, a good deal of anti-Egyptian sentiment—even in the presence of known Egyptian informers—was audible.

The fact is, then, that hatred, militancy and despair were forces that boiled up in the Gazan population against both the Egyptian and Israelis. The Egyptians were able to channelize this elemental force against Israel for obvious reasons: the country right across the border was one that had robbed the refugees of their land and property. This Israel was their enemy.

The thought that obviously haunts Liebling is that a different Israeli government, one of justice and mercy, could and should have made friends and allies of the Palestinian Arabs of Gaza.

In February–March, says Liebling (who was there at this time), "there were a great many people who, for disparate reasons, had become approachable by an honest broker." But Israel took no steps; plainly didn't want to. "And from the moment when the Israeli leaders recognized that they would not be there long—which must have been indeed early in their negotiations with the Americans and the UN—they did nothing to lay a foundation for future reconciliation."

Like the Egyptians, Israel treated the Gazans as simple pawns, objects that were in the way, deplorable encumbrances on the scenery; the attitude was the callous one of the colonialist. (One notes that Lt. Col. Gaon, the Israeli military conqueror and then military governor of Gaza, had gained his military experience "with the Dutch army in the Far East.")

Here the remarks Liebling made in his first dispatch would come in; but in the present article he does something additional that is interesting. For from a distance it is only on the big issues that one can concretize what it would mean for a new Israel to make an appeal-from-below to the Arab masses. And from a distance this is no doubt enough.

Being right on the spot, however, Liebling goes into some detail on two very immediate things that the Israelis could have done during their occupation if they had really wanted to use Gaza as a model to show that Israel intended justice and friendship to the Arab people, as against the Arab kings, colonels, and dictators.

He explains how Israel could have helped the Gazans save their orange crop this year—true, at some expense of generosity on their part but not really very much. And secondly, there had been a plan to rebuild the jetty at Gaza's fishing port, which was a wreck when Liebling saw it after four months of Israeli occupation. Nothing was done, for: "I fear that the Israeli occupation authorities wanted to put nothing into Gaza that they couldn't take out with them."

These are only two examples; but they open a door; for otherwise how can one, in New York, possibly detail all the things it would mean if Israel were to come to the Arab people not as conquerors or threats but as friends and allies of theirs against their Arab overlords?—that is, if Israel were really to be that "bastion of democracy" in the Middle East that its admirers pretend?

Of course, this is not just a question of Gaza; this applies to the whole gamut of Israel's relations to the Arab peoples in the surrounding states, to the Palestinian Arab refugees outside the borders, to the Israeli Arab minority inside the borders. In Gaza, the Israel-Arab problem is only synopsized and heightened in dramatic quality.

Are there people in Israel who see the problem this way, who can see through the miasma of chauvinist feeling which lies over that country like a chilling fog? Liebling has shown that he is quite sensitive to this aspect of the ideological climate of Israel; so he has no illusions. But he sees at least one chink of hope.

If the Israeli occupation had remained, he thinks, maybe personal contact with the people of the Strip would have influenced Israelis' thinking. Maybe. In any case, he takes heart in meeting a young Israeli paratrooper, who is also a writer of sorts, a sabra (native-born) though his parents had come from Europe.

"I looked at those people sitting there so sad," the young soldier-intellectual told him. "Having been born here, I speak Arabic, of course, and I talked to some. I thought, they are Palestinians like me. I felt ashamed. I thought, we have driven our neighbors from their land and we are giving it to Europeans—we are begging Europeans to come here and take our neighbors' land. But we must live with our neighbors if we are to stay here. The old men who run the government don't understand this, because they are Europeans, too."

Liebling adds, as his final word: "I wonder how broad and deep this current runs."

It is a good question, and a moot one. The current represented by the young soldier has often been noted among the youth, but no one really knows.

o o o

The second big point made by A.J. Liebling in his dispatch to the New Yorker entitled "Letter from Tel Aviv" concerns the tale that Israel's primary consideration in invading Egypt was the need to stop the attacks by Egyptian fedayeen from the Gaza Strip.

To go by Abba Eban's much-praised elocutions in the UN, or N.Y. Post editorials and columnists, or other apologists for the Ben-Gurion regime, the Israeli leaders were simply forced into the invasion by this pressure.

This is a complete myth, and one of Liebling's services is that he shows it up. This is what he writes, and it is worth quoting at length.

> The question of whether or not raids and reprisals are resumed—and of who raids and who reprises—is not a matter of such dramatic import as the press here contends. During the two years of scraggly border warfare that preceded the Israelis' decision to raise the ante last October [the invasion of Egypt], the 'crimes of the fedayeen' claimed considerably fewer victims in Israel than the Israelis bagged on the Egyptian side of the line. The score kept by the UN observers of the Egypt-Israel Mixed Armistice Commission shows that between Jan. 1, 1955 and Sept. 30, 1956 the Israelis killed 239 Egyptian soldiers and 91 civilians, while the Egyptians killed 42 Israeli soldiers and 24 civilians—a ration of just under 6 to 1 in the first category and of just under 4 to 1 in the second. The discrepancy is a measure not of comparative ill will but of comparative efficiency. ... As for the widely photographed peaceful Israeli settlers of Nahal Oz, who work their fields under the menacing shadow of the fedayeen-haunted Gaza ridge, they are members of a paramilitary farm colony planted there about six years ago to catch raiders. Border kibbutzim, or collective farms, like this one are an institution copied from the Roman coloniae of ex-soldiers, who received land and livestock as an inducement to settle at points on the imperial frontier where they could be of the most utility when war came. The young Israelis go to these kibbutzim straight from army service. It's a good old-fashioned procedure that provides lightly fortified Stutzpunkte along the frontier at minimal expense, since the colonists grow their own vegetables and dig trenches in their recreation time; the czars planted belts of Cossack colonies along the Tatar and Polish borders for the same purpose. The kibbutzim at points where action seems most imminent are favored not only in equipment but in the allocation of farm machinery and livestock; they are like army units being beefed up for action. A young farmer I talked with at Nahal Oz while the Israelis still occupied Gaza said, half regretfully, 'We've been making great progress here, but if the Egyptians don't come back soon, the kibbutzim on the Syrian frontier will be getting the pick of everything.' Recruiting for the more sheltered

kibbutzim is falling away with the waning of the young Israelis romanticism about the land;[146] the persisting attraction of the border establishments is the opportunity to protect the fatherland from attack. (The only genuine romantic enthusiasm in Israel now, it seems to an observer from outside, centers on the armed forces. The popular line is that the army won the victory and the government threw it away—or Eisenhower or Hammarskjold or the oil companies stole it away.) The Israelis are far better qualified than their opponents for an indefinite game of cowboys-and-Indians. It is highly unlikely that the country will bleed to death because of the measly 'incidents' that the local press is already trying to blow up, like the theft of 3,000 dollars' worth of farm machinery, of an unspecified nature, from the Israeli-governed Bedouin tribe named Abu Grab (in this case, more grabbed against than grabbing)."

Now this, of course, is not a rounded account of the fedayeen episode of the last couple of years, but it is a salutary corrective to the one-sided nonsense that has been written about it. Liebling is on solid ground in taking a fall out of the inflation of the fedayeen problem for purposes of justificatory propaganda, to which it lends itself so easily.

Thus, in its issue dated just one month before the invasion of Egypt, Commentary magazine carried an article on Israel by Benno Weiser, who reported with emphasis that the Israelis themselves shrug off the fedayeen raids and don't take it as seriously as do foreign visitors. Among other things he quotes an "old friend" of his:

"'Look', he said, while we sipped coffee 'there have been about three thousand casualties among both Arabs and Jews in border incidents since the conclusion of the armistice in 1949. That means roughly a yearly average of two hundred Jewish casualties. Every other day a Jew is wounded or killed because of the absence of peace. Compare this with the average number of casualties from our traffic accidents. What the Arabs take is perhaps 5 per cent of the toll of the Fords, Kaisers, Hillmans, and Chevrolets. Does it occur to anyone not to walk on the streets or not to use cars? ...'"

This sort of thing, which sounds callous, was all very well before the invasion, when it was a question of protesting that Israel could never, never even think of starting a preventive war—except for bad people like the Herut gang; it was mainly after the aggression that the fedayeen attrition was converted into a matter of life and death for Israel.

Or take the Reporter magazine, whose staff writer Claire Sterling, like its editor and publisher, is violently pro-Israel. In the May 17 issue of that magazine last year, Miss Sterling revealed from Jerusalem that, fortunately, it was now definite and irrevocable that Ben-Gurion would never, never invade Egypt: "The Israelis will not invade Egypt, now or a year from now." So overwhelming was her relief at this intelligence that she found it possible to reveal, as a moment of aberration happily long passed, that the preceding November "Ben-Gurion was strongly tempted to embark on such a war" and "he might well have tried it" except for warnings from Britain and the U.S.

(In that November of 1955, Israeli troops had forcibly moved into the demilitarized zone of El Auja on the Sinai frontier. Many believed at the time that Ben-Gurion was hoping to provoke the Egyptians into official military retaliation so as to be able to claim that it was the Egyptians who had started the war.)

The point is that Miss Sterling discusses in the very same article how the fedayeen raids had just been intensified in April; indeed they had reached a climax on April 11 when three children and a teacher were killed at evening prayers in a synagogue in Shafrir. Yet it does not occur to her, not even to her, that there is a connection worth discussion between this and the pressure on Israel to attack Egypt.

After the invasion, Miss Sterling's equally authoritative article in the Reporter could have been esthetically appreciated only by staff writers for the Daily Worker before and after the Hitler-Stalin Pact.

But there is much more to the fedayeen story than simply the question of its mythical role in forcing Israel to its aggression.

What is not controversial, but indisputable and well publicized, is the viciously reactionary character of the fedayeen policy of the Egyptian regime—i.e., murderous sneak attacks by kamikaze raiders on Israeli civilians as well as soldiers. What is concealed by so many of the gentlemen who make heart-rending denunciations of these crimes is the equally reprehensible policy of the Ben-Gurion regime which, in point of fact, eventually elicited the fedayeen as a reactionary riposte.

The story of the border fighting begins with the very establishment of the borders—which are not national borders in many places, anyway, but simply the armistice lines established after the 1948 war to end the shooting. These lines were drawn higgledy-piggledy right through many a Palestinian Arab village, frequently separating the peasants' homes from the land which gave them their sustenance.

Israel proceeded to implement a grab of every inch of territory on its side of the temporary line, outside the territory allotted by the UN partition plan. Palestinian Arab villagers found themselves stripped of their ancestral fields and reduced to seeing their property worked by the occupiers under their noses.

At the same time tens of thousands of Palestine Arabs had fled the war as refugees—partly in fear of the fighting and of the invading foreign-Arab forces, partly stimulated by the departing but bitter British, and last but not least, partly driven out of villages or terrorized out by Israeli forces. The Israelis grabbed their property and land wholesale and then, not illogically, refused to let them come back to their homes.

These too piled up behind the barrier of the "armistice lines" which Israel was converting into hard frontiers while their lands, crops, houses, and livestock were expropriated by the occupiers.

Thus began the chapter of the "infiltrators."

The infiltrators were—overwhelmingly—some of these Palestinian Arab refugees or expropriated villagers who, living in seething misery and frustration slipped over the lines now and then for various reasons.

Often the reason was simply to visit friends or relatives still there. Not infrequently it was to secretly continue tilling fields which belonged to them and were lying fallow. Or it might be to "steal" back from one of the settlements some piece of property which they still considered to be theirs. Or, working up the scale, to harass out of simple reprisal a settlement that was now planted on their own land, say, by dismantling a pipe ...

So it started, a process that jacked itself up automatically.

The paramilitary colonies that Israel started feverishly planting along the "armistice lines" were in the first place designed to prevent such infiltration. Infiltrators could be and were shot on sight. The toll mounted.

This was a "war" between the Israeli regime and the Palestinian Arabs who had been robbed. The Egyptian or Jordanian regimes were not at first involved—except of course that the infiltrators came from across the line, in their territory.

But even as far as this is concerned, the evidence piled up by the UN agencies established to supervise the armistice is that both of these governments made sincere efforts during this chapter of the story in order to police the infiltrators and put a stop to the border harassment of Israel by its victims.[147]

The response that emerged from the Israeli government to the problem was the old one of "Teach 'em a lesson." Out-of-hand shooting of infiltrators when they were caught was not enough. Paramilitary squads from the border coloniae began to make terror-raids across the lines at refugee centers and Arab villages in order to "teach 'em a lesson," by shooting them up.

The Arabs thus killed (as "lessons") were, of course, chance-selected by bullets; they themselves were not infiltrators, necessarily. The theory was that of collective punishment (well known to the Israelis from the former British rule.)

These paramilitary raiders cannot be called Israeli fedayeen because that word means "self-sacrificers" and implies a suicide operation.

Thus the jacking-up process on both sides reached a new level. Or, to change the metaphor, the Israelis raised the ante again. The war was still with the Palestinian Arabs, not with Egyptian or Jordanian forces.

It is this chapter of the story that reached its climax with the infmaous Kibya massacre in 1953, when a well-organized and efficient Israeli military operation struck at the Arab village across the Jordan border, sprayed machine-gun bullets around, blew up houses wholesale, indiscriminately slaughtering over 50 men, women and children in the streets and in their homes. This was supposed to be an "answer" to the preceding murder of three people in an Israeli village, presumably by infiltrators. The ante was now being raised to near "Lidice" proportions. There were many smaller "Kibyas."

By 1955, the spotlight focused on the Egyptian border.

In the Gaza sector, the infiltration problem was complicated also by raids into Israel by Bedouin tribes which had been driven out of Israel into the Sinai area. In February, the Israelis pulled off a military raid inside the Gaza Strip, killing about 40 Arabs. (This turn was heralded by the immediately preceding return to the defense ministry of Ben-Gurion, who had been in "retirement" since the outcry over Kibya.)

The jacking-up process was under way along the Gaza border. On August 31 it reached a climax with an Israeli strike against Khan Yunis, in the southern end of the Strip. This became a turning-point.

Another focal point was the El Auja demilitarized zone on the Sinai frontier. Israel established a military camp there under the guise of a kibbutz; Egypt protested the presence of soldiers. Israel rebutted that the Egyptian check-post just outside El Auja was in fact a few yards inside the lines. Clashes started. In October an Israeli force destroyed an Egyptian post on the border further south. Then in November (as we have already mentioned) Israeli troops moved in force against the Egyptian position and took over the demilitarized area in open battle.

This is where, as Claire Sterling later admitted, Ben-Gurion was ready to provoke a war. There were no fedayeen as yet.

To quote from the Jewish Agency's Digest of Nov. 22, 1956 on "The Fedayeen—Nasser's Secret Weapon":

"Some time last year the prestige of the Egyptian occupation authorities in the Gaza Strip and in Egypt proper was at a low ebb because of their apparent inactivity against Israel. The public demanded military action. Fearful, however, that an all-out offensive by the regular Egyptian army may meet with failure, the Egyptian dictator hit upon an ingenious scheme ..." [i.e., the Fedayeen, H.D.][148]

This makes crystal-clear from unimpeachable sources what has been treated as a well-known truth by many other observers: it was at this time, after at least seven years of Israeli ante-raising, that the Egyptian regime riposted by organizing the fedayeen forays in response to what "the public demanded."

(The long-sufferance of Cairo should not be ascribed to overweening kindliness. As Liebling observed in a similar connection, it was basically due to disinclination to risk another military debacle.)

The "teach 'em a lesson" policy had been raising the ante in order to bring the Arabs to their knees with pleas to the conquerors to kindly stop murdering them. The chauvinist-militarist mentality of its protagonists (spearheaded by Ben-Gurion) saw it as the way to make impudent aborigines grovel before their masters. Although it was initially directed against the Palestinian Arabs, it could naturally be carried through only in complete contempt of the Egyptian and the Jordanian states.

The monster that this monstrous policy created is called the fedayeen. It was sired by Israeli chauvinism upon the body of Egypt's reactionary Nasserism. The fedayeen themselves were recruited from desperate Palestinian Arab refugees.

When Israel invaded Egypt last October, it was raising the ante again. There is a line that goes straight from Kibya to the Sinai aggression, and that goes, in the other direction, back to the expropriation of the Palestinian Arabs.

It is not the only line that delineates the politics of the Middle East mess, but it is the one most often left out of the picture. It is also a line which serves to cross out the pretense that the Israeli regime's role in that shameful aggression was basically a defensive one against intolerable harassment.

Labor Action, April 22, 1957.

Chapter VII
THE ORIGINS OF THE MIDDLE EAST CRISIS

This article is a somewhat condensed and edited version of a talk given in Berkeley shortly after the outbreak of the Third Arab-Israeli War, dealing with the historical background of the conflict but not with the current situation, which was discussed separately.
H.D.

We have just seen War No. 3 in the tragedy known as the Israel-Arab conflict; and we find ourselves in the position of being unable to cheer for either side in this clash of chauvinisms. At this time I am going to devote myself mainly to the myths and illusions about the Israeli side of the story, for the simple reason that it is these myths and illusions that you mainly read and hear about.

It is not possible to understand what has happened merely by looking at what happened in the last couple of weeks. Behind War No. 3 is a closely connected chain of events and issues going far back. The main link in this chain is the story of a nation that has been destroyed.

That sounds like an echo of what we hear all around, viz. the threat of the Arab states to destroy the state of Israel—the threat which is the hallmark of Arab chauvinism. But while this is a threat, there was a nation that was destroyed in Palestine—already. It is this destroyed nation whose fate has been the crux of the Middle East tragedy, for its fate has been used and is being used as a football by each side.

When I was born, there was an Arab nation in Palestine, in whose midst Jews had lived for 2000 years in relative peace. Where is this nation now, and what has been done to it? The answer is at the heart of the program which we face now.

Today the leaders of the Arab states are saying, "We aim to destroy the nation which inhabits Palestine," and they are rightly denounced for this. But toward the end of the 19th century, a movement arose which did in fact itself the aim of destroying the nation which inhabited Palestine then; and, moreover, it did so. That movement was the Zionist movement.

Everyone talks nowadays about "the Jews" and "the Arabs," with doubtful justice. There are Jews and Jews, as there are Arabs and Arabs; and right now I am talking not about "the Jews," but about the Zionist movement. Israel today is run by the old men of the world Zionist movement, and it is still the Zionist ideology which rules Israeli policy. The European survivors of Hitler's death camps are not the Jews who run Israel; their terrible fate has been a tool used by the men who run Israel, so that the crimes of the Nazis have been used to deflect the attention of world public opinion from the crimes committed in Palestine.

For present purposes, there are three things to understand about this Zionist ideology, which still rules the rulers of Israel. To present the first, I quote a typical example of anti-Semitic literature:

> The converted Jew remains a Jew, no matter how much he objects to it. ... Jews and Jewesses endeavor in vain to obliterate their descent through conversion or intermarriage with the Indo-Germanic and Mongolian races, for the Jewish type is indestructible. ... Jewish noses cannot be reformed, and the black wavy hair of the Jews will not change through conversion into blond, nor can its curves be straightened out by constant combing.

There is more of the same where this comes from. Obviously from the Nazi commentary on the Nuremberg Laws, or from Streicher's Sturmer, or perhaps from Gerald L.K. Smith? Not at all: it is from a classic of Zionism, Moses Hess' Rom und Jerusalem. It is easily possible to quote pages and pages more of this same mystical blood-tribalism from the best Zionist sources, all sounding as if it came from the arsenal of the anti-Semites.

For Zionism is, first of all, a doctrine about a tribal blood-mystique which makes all Jews a single nation no matter whey they live or how. It asserts that Jews are inevitably aliens everywhere, just as the anti-Semites say they are; and that anti-Semitism is correct in feeling this. This is the first element in Zionism.

Secondly: it follows that the Jews must reconstitute their "nation" in a state territory; but not just any state territory. In fact there is a point of view called "territorialism," as distinct from Zionism, which looked for the establishment of a Jewish nation in a land other than Palestine. But Zionism demands that the Jewish "nation" take over Palestine—only Palestine; and by Palestine it means the ancient Jewish state and its boundaries, Eretz Israel, no less. This is what the tribal mystique demands.

Thirdly: the Zionist ideology dictates that this Jewish state must be set up not only by Jews who want to live in such a state. One of the tasks of the Zionist movement is to move all Jews, from all countries of the world, into Palestine, now Israel. In Zionist slang, this is called the "Ingathering of the Exiles"; for it is an article of basic faith that all Jews living outside this territory are living literally in exile, and always will merely be exiles, nothing else. It was not very many years ago that a writer in Davar, the organ of the Israeli ruling party, made the suggestion that a good way of uprooting all those American Jews who declined to go to Israel was to send a gang of anti-Semitic agitators there to make the ground hot under their feet so that they would move. This, of course, is not usually the course recommended on paper, as against persuasion. But how persuasion graduates into denunciation and arm-twisting was seen in the early fifties when David Ben-Gurion, on a visit to the U.S., denounced the Zionist Organization of America as traitors to Zionism because its leaders were not working actively to get the entire Jewish population of the U.S. to move to Israel. It must be understood (though American Zionists systematically obfuscate it to the best of their ability) that the Israeli leaders and world Zionist leaders sincerely believe in their mission to "ingather" all the Jews of the world to the state of Israel, and that they have devoted their lives to this mission.

The Zionists have always been fond of saying that they are tired of the Jews being a "peculiar people," that they have been "peculiar" long enough. They want (they say) the Jews to be a people like any other, and to have a state just like any other state. In Israel. I would tell you, they have succeeded notably in this aim: Israel more and more has become a state like any other state. In this stridently militarist Zionist state, the current of Jewish humanism which was one of the glories of the Jewish people from Maimonides to Spinoza and after, is today represented only by a minority—a minority whose voices are rarely heard abroad, and hardly at all in the U.S.; but it is this minority which represents the only Israel with whom one can identify.

Soon after the creation of Israel the press was full of enthusiastic reports by American Jewish tourists who went to Israel and came back to relate the wonders that they saw there (and there are many to see). One that I remember most vividly was a tourist who was quoted as follows in the course of his burbling: "Why, you walk around Tel-Aviv, and you know what? Even the policemen are Jewish!" That's true, naturally. The cops are Jewish in Israel—and they are still cops. The militarists in Israel are Jewish—and they are militarists. And the people who destroyed the Arab Palestinian nation which I mentioned were, alas, also Jewish—though I do not believe that they will go down in the annals of history alongside Maimonides and Spinoza.

The destruction of that Palestinian nation went through four periods. The first period goes from the beginning of the Zionist movement up to World War I. This was a period of slow immigration of Jews into Palestine

109

and of gradual land-buying. By the time it ended Jews constituted something under 10 percent of the population. Despite Zionism's profession that this was the thin edge of the wedge in its long term aim to establish a Jewish state in the land inhabited by the Arabs, it was not taken seriously enough to occasion much resistance until the second period, inaugurated by the 1917 Balfour Declaration.

It was in this period that British imperialism, taking over the area, started its decades-long policy of playing Zionists against Arabs in order to maintain its imperialist control. The Zionist leadership willingly and knowingly collaborated with the British. They knew that, at this stage, it was not they who could control the Arab people living in the land; only British imperialism could do it for them. To be sure, they were not puppets of the British: they were junior partners, in an enterprise in which each partner considered that it was using the other for its own ends.

This was also the period of the beginning of Arab nationalism, of an Arab national-liberation movement. This movement had every right to fight for liberation from Britain (or in other parts of the Middle East, from France). To supporters of Arab freedom, the Zionist movement could have appeared only as what it actually was: a partner of the European imperialists. It makes no difference whatsoever that the Zionists played this baneful role not out of love for Britain but in pursuit of their own expansion. The fact is that Britain used the Zionist tool to increase the number of Jewish settlers so as to play them off against the indigenous Arab population. Thus it was inevitable that Jewish immigration should appear to the Arabs as a tool of imperialist domination, for it was so.

It was therefore during the 1920s that, for pretty much the first time in Palestine, there began sporadic Arab attacks against Jewish settlers. On the one side, these were the first stirrings of an Arab national liberation movement, directed not only against the British but also against the allies of the British who were at hand, viz. Zionist infiltrators into the country. On the other hand—and here you get the typically tragic element in this story which goes through it from beginning to end—these stirrings took on strong overtones of the backward social and religious aims of the Arab movement; for progressive social elements were weak, working-class formations were incipient. But this hardly can change the fact that there was a legitimate nationalist movement under way.

The third period—which was to prove decisive to the outcome—came with the onset of the Nazis' anti-Jewish drive, first in Germany itself, and then in the course of World War II in the rest of Nazi-occupied Europe, up to the mass extermination campaign and its death camps. It should be added that in the period immediately following the war, there was also the onset of Soviet anti-Semitism on a big scale, thereby boosting the impact of what had happened during the war.

This is the period that everyone knows about; some think it is all one has to know. But there is more to this than meets the myopic eye.

To be sure, for the Jewish remnant Europe represented burning ground: they had to get out—somehow, somewhere, anywhere. This plight of the Jewish refugees—one of the most terrible in the history of man's bestiality to man—was what dramatically captured the sympathy of everyone decent in the world; it is this that is tied up in the public mind with the exodus to Palestine. This is entirely true as far as it goes; but one has to know something else too. This terrible plight and this great world sympathy were not enough to open the gates of a single Western country to those Jewish refugees!

During those years we independent socialists called for opening the doors of the United States to the Jewish victims of Hitlerism, those who were left. I can tell you that in this great "liberal" country, crawling with liberals, there was hardly an echo of such a notion, of opening the doors of this country to the poor Jews for whom everyone's heart bled—in print.

One reason for this is clear and can be easily documented. Morris Ernst, the famous civil liberties layer who was involved at the time, has told the story, among others: about how the leaders of the Zionist movement exerted all the influence they could muster to make sure that the U.S. did not open up immigration to these Jews—for the simple reason that they wanted to herd these same Jews to Palestine. This is what their Zionist ideology demanded. White Christian America was only too glad to go along with this "solution"! Who wanted a few hundred thousand miserable Jewish refugees coming into the country? Not our liberal Americans, who were so heart-stricken by Nazi brutality. Not the British, who took in an inconsequential token number. Nor anyone else. These Jewish victims were people on the planet without a visa. Liberals in this country, as elsewhere, had a convenient way of salving their tender consciences; all they had to do was parrot the line which the Zionists industriously provided them: "They want to go only to Palestine ..."

Now there is no point in anyone's arguing to what extent this was really true or not, or of how many it was true, because no one ever gave them the chance to decide whether they wanted to go to Palestine or to some other country that was open to them The doors were shut against them, with the help of the whole Zionist apparatus and of other "influential" Jews who were no more enthusiastic about "flooding" the country with poor Jews than their WASP neighbors. First it was made damned sure that Palestine was the only possible haven, and then they might possibly be asked where they wanted to go, as if they had a free choice! In my eyes, this is one of the basest crimes committed by the Zionist leadership.

In this way the Jewish survivors of the Hitlerite death camps were herded toward Palestine, to keep the U.S. and other countries from being contaminated by their presence (for some) or to make sure that they were properly "ingathered" (for others). Of course, Palestine was not really open either, being still under the control of the British, but here at least the Zionist movement was willing to go all-out to crash the gates, with heavy financing from many an American Jew who himself had no sympathy for Zionism but could be convinced that Palestine was certainly a more suitable haven than New York.

This turn brought the Zionist movement into conflict with the same British imperialism whose junior partner it had been. The partners' paths now diverged. The Jewish refugees—fleeing from a horror behind them, and rejected on all sides—became the human material the Zionists needed to carry out the goal they had set a half century before: to dispossess the Arab nation of Palestine and install a Jewish state in its stead—and to do this with the sympathy of a good deal of the world.

The Palestinian Arabs, as well as their Arab neighbors, had a very simple comment to make on this situation: "Hitler's extermination program was a great crime, but why does that mean that we have to give up our land to the Jews? It is the world's problem, not just ours." I should like to see someone refute this.

We must note that by this time the Zionist movement had finally come out openly with its proclaimed intention of taking Palestine away as a Jewish state. This had been done in 1942, in the so-called "Biltmore Program." (Up to then, the Zionists had used doubletalk about a "Jewish homeland" to confuse the picture.) Now that the cards were on the table, there were even some Zionists—or at least people who considered themselves to be Zionists—who were outraged. It was around this time that the Ichud was founded in Palestine by Rabbi Judah Magnes. The idea of a bi-national state in Palestine was counterposed to the official Zionist program: instead of a "Jewish state" it meant a state in which both Jews and Arabs could live peacefully and tranquilly together; but it was rejected. Instead, the Zionists said, "We are going to take the whole country"; and they did.

Here I need only sketch how this happened. After a series of doubledealing maneuvers by the great powers (particularly the U.S., Britain, and Russia) which it would take too long to go into, by 1947 the United Nations decided on a partition plan. There were to be two separate states in Palestine, a Jewish state and an Arab Palestinian state. By this time, there was indeed a Jewish majority in the territory assigned to the Jewish state—something like a 60% majority—and therefore one could feel that this majority had the right to invoke the right to self-determination. I might as well mention that, at that time (1948), I did myself believe and write that the Palestinian Jews had the right to make this mistaken choice (for, of course, a right exists only if it includes the right to make a mistake). I mention this only to make clear that I believed and wrote at that time that the attack on the new state of Israel by the Arab states was an aggression and a violation of the right to self-determination.

But at that moment Israel was still new-born, and there were different ways in which it could defend itself—in a progressive and democratic way, and in a racist and expansionist way. The answer to that historical question was not long in coming: it was given right away by the same Zionist leaders who were also the rulers of the new state power. From its first hour the Zionist power took the road of a reactionary and racist purge of the Arabs as such. At this point I am not talking about the foreign Arab states, but of the Arabs of Israel themselves, the great mass of whom never took up arms against Israel or aided the aggressors.

A new act in the Middle East tragedy begins here; although it is a crime smaller in magnitude than Hitler's against the Jews, it is still one of the most shameful in recent history. The Zionist ruler utilized the attack by the foreign Arab states to run the Palestinian Arabs off their land, by means of a series of laws and measures which were taken not only in 1948–49 but which went right on into the 1950s. The forty percent of the population which was Arab in the partitioned territory was reduced to about 10 percent in the new state of Israel. Immense proportions of Arab-owned land were simply robbed from them, by "legal" means. By 1954 over one-third of the Jewish population then in Israel was settled on land that had been stolen from the Palestinian Arabs. And the Arab state of Palestine which had been created by the partition never came into existence; by the end of the war, five sections of it had been grabbed by Israel and were never given up, and the West Jordan area was incorporated into the state of Jordan.

Thus the Arab nation of Palestine was destroyed, except as a discriminated-against remnant in Israel, and even the truncated Arab state of Palestine set up by partition was destroyed. I am entirely willing to denounce anyone who wants to destroy any existing state, including Israel; but some thought should be given to this recent history by those who are willing to denounce only the threat to destroy Israel.

The great land robbery of the Israeli Arabs was the despoiling of a whole people. It was carried out in various ways, but generally speaking the pattern was this: any Arab who had left his village during the war for any reason whatsoever was declared an "absentee" and his land was taken away by Zionist agencies. The Zionist myth has it that all these Palestinian Arabs left at the behest of the foreign Arab invaders and in cahoots with them. This is a big lie. There was a war on, and even if they fled from the Arab invaders and in fear of them, and even if they fled only to a neighboring village, they became "absentees." They also fled from the British; they not only fled from the invading Arabs but also fled from the Zionist troops—the Haganah and the Irgun. This was especially true after the massacre at Deir Yassin.

Deir Yassin was the name of an Arab village in Palestine, whose people were outstandingly hostile to the Arab invaders. In 1948 a battalion of the Irgun (the right-wing Zionist force) attacked the village. There were no armed men in the village, and no arms. Purely for terroristic purposes, the Irgun sacked the village and massacred 250 men, women, and children. One hundred fifty bodies were thrown down a well; 90 were left scattered around. This massacre was deliberately directed by the Irgun against a village known to be friendly to the Jews, as an example. Although the dirty job was done by the Irgun, the official-Zionist Haganah knew of the planned attack; immediately afterward the Irgun, instead of being pilloried in horror by the Zionist movement, was welcomed by the Haganah into a new pact of collaboration. (The Irgun's leader, Begin, by the way, was taken into the Israeli cabinet along with General Dayan just before the outbreak of the recent Third War.)

Of course, the Irgun was able to show the way to the Haganah because it was semi-fascist; but the Haganah leaders learned fast. Before the First War had ended the Haganah too was attacking and ousting unarmed and non-belligerent Arab villagers, although naturally not as brutally as the Irgun (since they were democrats and "socialists"). Especially after the Deir Yassin massacre, it was only necessary that any troops show up, and the Arab peasants got out of the way, as anyone else would do. They thus became "absentees," and their land was taken away by a series of laws

114

over the next several years. All of the Zionist parties, from "left" to right, sanctioned this robbery. There was even a legal category known as "present absentees," who were very much present as Arab citizens of Israel but who were legally accounted to be "absentees" because they had been absent from their village on a certain date—and therefore could be legally robbed of their land. The largest portion of this stolen land went to the kibbutzim—not only the kibbutzim run by the Mapai (right-wing social democrats) but even more went to the kibbutzim of the Mapam (who claimed to be left socialists), whose leaders regularly made clear that their hearts bled for the plight of the Israeli Arabs. However, their hearts also bled for their land, even more.

Along the border areas, Palestinian Arabs were pushed over the line into the Gaza Strip, or into Jordan, and then they were shot on sight as "infiltrators" if they tried to come back. It was in ways like this—which I sketch here only briefly—that Israel's rulers created the massive Arab refugee problem. Literally they surrounded the country with a circle of hatred—hatred which they themselves had caused—the hatred of the despoiled Palestinian Arabs looking over form the other side of the border and seeing their own lands being tilled by strangers whom the Zionists had brought from thousands of miles away to take their place.

This robbery is not transmuted into justice just because some of these strangers were Jewish refugees from Europe against whom another crime had been committed by someone else. The Zionist agencies welcomed these despairing refugees to their new life by putting them on the marches of the hate-encircled state so that they would have to defend themselves, their lives, and their stolen gifts, from the previous Arab owners. (Thus the "exiles" were not only "ingathered" but also very useful.)

Meanwhile in Israel, the 10 percent of the Palestinian Arabs left—who had not taken up arms but had not fled—were placed under military control like an occupied enemy people, and discriminated against in many ways. It is not without reason that they have been called the "niggers of Israel"; but as a matter of fact the American Negroes would not have taken lying down what the Israeli Arabs had to endure for two decades.

On the borders—for example, in the Gaza Strip—the dispossessed and robbed Arabs lived a wretched existence under the control of Egypt, but the Egyptians only used them for their purposes as pawns, while keeping their help to a minimum. They were not admitted into Egypt proper. They were forced to fester there so that their misery and hatred might make them a bone in the throat of the Israelis; at the same time Israel was as little interested as Nasser in arriving at a deal for the settlement of the Arab refugee problem.

Every now and then some of the refugees would "infiltrate"—that is, slip across into Israel to visit his own land or till his own soil or try to take back his own belongings—and would be shot to death by those same Jewish policemen and guards who so delighted the heart of the Jewish tourist mentioned earlier. As a result the Israelis complained bitterly about the "infiltrators" who were so evil as to do this. The terrible situation escalated. Infiltrators began to commit acts of sabotage on the property that had been stolen from them, or struck out more blindly at the robbers. The Israelis began to resort to organized military reprisals to terrorize them into acquiescence. In 1953 there was a massacre organized by Israeli armed forces in the Arab village of Kibya. In 1955—a year that more or less marked a turning-point for the worse—there was a big attack by an organized Israeli military force on Gaza; more and more Israeli leaders oriented toward "preventive" war, since military force was their only answer to the problem created by their own crimes. This was the traditional and classic answer of the militarist and expansionist mentality; it is the same answer as was recommended by General MacArthur on how to treat Koreans and Chinese and other such "gooks"—you show them who's master—that's what they can understand, etc. The answer of the Israeli militarists was, similarly: kill and terrorize the "gooks" and "teach them a lesson" so that they won't do it again.

There were negotiations over the plight of the Arab refugees but neither side was interested in a real settlement—not the Israeli side and not the Egyptian and Arab side. For Nasser, the Arab refugees leading their wretched existence were useful tools to harass the Israelis. As for Israel, at the same time that they argued that they could not restore the land to the Arabs they had robbed, they were industriously bringing in whole Jewish populations, from Yemen and Morocco, for example (not to speak of the whole Jewish population of the U.S. which Ben-Gurion was so vainly anxious to move to Israel). There was plenty of room in Israel for such hundreds of thousands of Jews, but in the negotiations over the Arab refugee problem there was not a dunam of land that could be spared. The decisive thing to remember is that, from the Zionist viewpoint, for every single despoiled Arab who would be readmitted to Israel there was a Jew who could therefore not be "ingathered."

The problem was not how Israel and the Arab states could have made peace; the problem was that neither side wanted to make peace, except of course on capitulatory terms. They did not then, and they do not now.

For Nasser, the Israel issue was a pawn in the inter-Arab struggle for power. It was also a useful distraction from the internal failures of his bureaucratic-military regime, which lacked any progressive domestic program. In both Egypt and Jordan, the pressure of the refugees within the country was relieved only by pointing them outward, against Israel. As for Israel, it must be remembered that Zionism still did not rule the "Land of Israel" as the Zionist program demanded; the "Land of Israel" still included territories outside of the state of Israel. Israeli expansionism was implicit in this, and also in the fact that, if room was going to be made for the millions of "exiles" who were to be ingathered, more land was needed. In 1955 Israeli leaders (some eagerly convinced of the necessity of "preventive" war, some dragging their feet) were looking for some pretext to launch a war against Egypt and the Arab alliance. As it happened, British and French imperialism brought them to launch that aggression themselves. In 1956, openly and in the sight of the whole world, side by side with the two leading European imperialisms (of which it was once again a junior partner), Israeli invaded Egypt as its partners struck at the Suez Canal.

The point is not that Nasser is or was a dove of peace, himself, as has been made clear. One of the reasons why Nasser was not in a position to give warlike substance to his blowhard threats was that he was too preoccupied with internal difficulties and too weak. But if Nasser was no dove, it is still true that Israel exposed itself to the whole world as an open aggressor in alliance with European imperialism. Every dirty expansionist plan it had been accused of turned out to be true. Even after the British and French enterprise failed, Israel fought to retain the land it had grabbed in Egypt and gave it up only after immense international pressure.

This pattern must be remembered in the light also of the way in which the recent Third War was initiated: i.e., with Nasser taking the situation to the brink, talking loudly about destroying Israel, while the Israelis went straight to the business at hand by precipitating the shooting war.

There is one other story to be told for this period—the story of a pogrom. This pogrom was directed against an Arab village in Israel named Kfar Kassem. On the day that Israel attacked Egypt in 1956, the Israeli government declared a new curfew for its Arab citizens (who, remember, were under military control anyway, even without a war). The new decree advanced the curfew from 11 p.m. to 5 p.m. Israeli officers showed up in Kfar Kassem, as well as other places, to make known the change on that day. They were told that the men had already gone out to the fields; the officers' reply was, roughly speaking, "Don't bother us with details." In the evening, when the men of the village returned from working in the fields after the new curfew hour, they were shot down in cold blood by the Israeli soldiers—for violating a curfew that had never been told them. The government admitted that 46 men were thus killed; the number wounded was not made public. The government admission applied only to Kfar Kassem but it was reliably reported that the same thing happened that day at other Arab villages. Even this much was admitted by the government only after a week had passed and the reports could no longer be hushed up. All of Israel was appalled. Some underlings were made the scapegoats.

It was clear, then, that the Zionist program of making Israel a "state like any other state" had come true: it had its own Jewish policemen, it had its own soldiers, it had its own militarists, and now it had its own pogroms.

In 1967, the road that started in Deir Yassin and goes through Kfar Kassem has now reached the bank of the Jordan, where Arab refugees are once again being pushed out and around by the Israelis, as they have been for the last 20 years. It would be useful to go through the whole chapter subsequent to 1956, leading up to the Third War, but, aside from time considerations, we would only find that it is more of the same thing: the tragedy of one reactionary chauvinism versus another reactionary chauvinism.

There is an image that haunts me, about this whole tragic embroilment in the Middle East. Buck deer in the mating season will fight each other, and now and again it has happened that they will entangle their antlers and be unable to disengage. Unable to break loose, unable to win, locked in a static hopeless combat until they die and rot and their bleached bones are found by some hunter in the forest, their skeletons are grisly evidence of a tragedy which destroyed them both, ensnarled.

It may be that, in the Middle East entanglement, the Arabs, or some of the Arabs, can survive this conflict. But it is doubtful whether, in the long run, the Jews of Israel can. What the Zionists have made out of Israel is a new ghetto—a state ghetto, a ghetto with state boundaries. That's not a new life for the Jews; that is more of the old life of which the Jews have had more than their share. This generation of Zionist hawks ruling Israel is a curse. No matter how many more great military victories they win, the sea of Arab peoples ringing them cannot be eliminated from the picture, and hatred grows. It may be another decade or two before the Arab states

118

become modernized enough to wage war effectively; and then it will take more than euphoria over military heroes to point a way for Israel.

There are some in Israel who know and say what has been said here—more who know and fewer who say—and it is to be hoped that the next generation will be more willing to listen to their kind, to the kind of Jews who represent what is best in the history of Jewish humanism and social idealism rather than those who worship the Moloch of a "state like any other state."

New Politics, Winter 1967

Chapter VIII
THE MISTAKES OF THE ARAB SOCIALISTS

In our present discussion of (and argument against) the Arab socialist view, the whole basis of the question will, I think, be quite different from that which Comrade Maksoud and his comrades are accustomed to meet and deal with.

As we see it, for one thing, ours is an attempt to develop a position from a Marxist internationalist standpoint. And above all, we approach the problem as opponents of Zionism and of Zionist ideology and politics.

As I read Comrade Maksoud's article, my feeling is that he has not appreciated the full force and potentialities of a socialist anti-Zionist position like ours, perhaps because of its unfamiliarity; and we will have to devote some space to presenting it as an alternative to the Arab socialists' grievous mistake in calling for the overthrow of the state of Israel.

That is what is in question here, and nothing else; although of course there is a long list of related ideas in dispute that lie behind such a conclusion.

Comrade Maksoud's conclusion is to demand "the emasculation of Israel's sovereignty,"to do away with this state's "sovereign, separate, isolated and independent existence." Instead, the Palestinian Jews are to be given merely "cultural autonomy."

Plainly, it would be simpler to make clear that the state of Israel is to be conquered and crushed, by force of arms in a war, annexed to some Arab state or group of states, and thus wiped out. This is the "solution" to the Israel question of which Maksoud speaks.

We will argue that it is no "solution" at all, since it will solve nothing and mean merely the continuation of the present impasse in a different form. That it cannot bring the peace of which Maksoud speaks. That it will not save the Arab peoples from being pawns of imperialism. That it will not be the key to unlock the revolutionary energies of the Arabs, as Maksoud thinks.

In fact, we have here, I think, a typical example of bisymmetric mistakes. Maksoud has this in common with the Zionist ideology: the insistence that the fate of Israel as a state is inseparable from the fate of Zionism. His insistence that Israel must be forcibly overthrown is the "other side of the coin" of the Zionist-chauvinist concept of the "Jewish state" and policy of persecuting the Arab minority.

At any rate, that's the way we see it, and so will we argue. This bisymmetric pattern has certain inevitable consequences. It is well-nigh inevitable that we will be denounced by Zionists for even printing Maksoud's article. And I'm afraid, under the circumstances, that it was just as inevitable that Maksoud should wind up by charging that we are not really anti-Zionist (because we won't go for the overthrow of Israel); that we may be against Zionist "excesses" but accept "basic Zionist theory."

Thus Maksoud hurls into the same (Zionist) camp all those who would oppose this "solution" of war against Israel.

That is not an advisable thing for him to do.

If the Arab socialists insist that pro-Zionism is the only alternative to their call for war against Israel, they will surely help to convince a great many waverers that the Zionists are the preferable side.

Thus, bisymmetric mistakes always feed on each other. (It works the other way too. When the Arab socialists meet only chauvinistic arguments against them, they are reinforced in their mistake.)

Here then is the central point at which we differ:

We draw a firm line between (1) fighting Zionism, its ideology and politics; fighting against the Zionist politics which are the official policies of the state of Israel, and against the Zionist leadership which is the official government of the state of Israel; and (2) fighting to overthrow the state of Israel as such.

Now, this distinction is simple as ABC. It may be wrong in Maksoud's eyes. It may be a mistake in his opinion. He has a right to argue that we should be against both, both Zionism and the state of Israel as such. But he should not close his eyes to the fact that this distinction must be made.

Yet he insists on doing so. On June 7 last, we had explained the difference by referring to an analogy with Stalinist Russia. We stressed that there was a big difference between being anti-Stalinist and anti-Russian. (Or being anti-Nazi and anti-German). So also, we said, one must not mix up anti-Zionist and anti-Israel, in exactly the same sense.

In each case, it is plain, you have a political movement (with its accompanying ideology, philosophy, program, institutions, "organizational formulas," economic theories, etc.) and at a given time this political movement (Stalinism, Nazism, Zionism) is in control of a state—to the disadvantage of the people of that state.

Everybody knows how easy it has been for reactionary varieties of "anti-Communism" to pass over into anti-Russian fulminations. It was easy for anti-Nazism to mask a chauvinistic anti-Germanism, and it does so to this day all over Britain and France and in the British Labor Party. It was easy for reactionaries, in the U.S. after Pearl Harbor, to whip up lynch sentiment against all Japanese people, even against Japanese-Americans, with filthy phrases like "yellow monkeys."

In the case under discussion, we also have a relationship between a state and a political movement which dominates and controls its government today. As we said, this political movement Zionism (like the analogy of Stalinism) has its own distinctive "philosophy,"program, etc.

Maksoud rejects the comparison. I confess that I cannot even follow his reasoning at that point. With regard to Communism (Stalinism), he agrees that—

> ... the opponents of this system must distinguish between the structural, institutional, and methodological features of Communism, or for that matter, any other system, and the people who live under that system.

But it is "different" for Zionism, he argues—

> Zionism is not an institutional or organizational formula. It is not a theory of how a state ought to be run or the economy organized. It is a movement to create a state for a 'Jewish nation.'

But Stalinism is not an "institutional or organization formula" either—not simply, and not even mainly. To be sure, it has its characteristic "institutions" (like the MVD) and its characteristic "organizational formulas"—but Zionism has its characteristic institutions, etc., also.

Above all, Stalinism arose as a political movement, with a certain political "philosophy," which captured a state. It proceeded to "create" a new state in its own image.

Of course, there are several thousand differences between Stalinism and Zionism which could be mentioned to confuse the analogy; but none of them are relevant to the very, very simple point:

It is possible to be anti-Stalinist without being anti-Russian. It is possible to be anti-Nazi without being anti-German. It is possible to be anti-Zionist without being anti-Israel.

When Comrade Maksoud denies this, then we feel that he is failing to see the very problem, let alone the correct socialist solution to it.

If he denies that it is even possible to be anti-Zionist without being for the overthrow of Israel, then it is indeed difficult for him to grapple with the issues as they present themselves to the minds of most socialists, and not only those with a pro-Zionist bias.*

In our view, this distinction between being anti-Zionist and anti-Israel is the nub; but we must still go on to discuss Comrade Maksoud's positive reasons for being in favor of wiping out Israel as a state. The first of these is bound up with his argument that Israel had no right to existence in the first place.

At this point Comrade Maksoud's article presented a rebuttal to the ISL resolutions, which we had sent him for his information. But his presentation of our position was both inaccurate and inadequate, we think. In any case, it will be useful to sketch our point of view in at this state of the argument. As we see it, Maksoud's error will be most apparent when it is seen on the background of our own approach to the question.

We have always been opposed to the Zionist program of setting up a "Jewish state" by carving it out of an other people's country (Palestine) against the will of the latter.

During most of the history of Zionism, it has sought to become the willing tool of some imperialist exploiter who would foist the Zionist aim upon Palestine for its own imperialist reasons. Zionism began in the 19th century by offering itself to Turkey in that role. After the Balfour Declaration it willingly prostituted itself to British imperialism, in the hope that the lion would set up its "Jewish state" as a fortress for the empire.

---

* In fact, one could raise a question about what Maksoud means by Zionism. In his article in *LA* for June 7, he wrote: "Zionism is a movement which seeks to make religion the rallying factor of a nation. As such it is self-contained, mystical and intolerant of other religions or races (cf. the treatment of Arab minorities in Israel)."

It is just not true that Zionism makes religion the "rallying factor." Surely Maksoud must know that for the majority of Zionists it is a secular movement; many if not most Zionist leaders have even been atheists or agnostics, or at quite unreligious; etc. Here Maksoud misses the whole point about the Zionist mystique and the Zionist form of Jewish nationalism: the Zionist looks on Jewry as being united not by their religion (if any) but by their inherent Jewish "nationality,"and this goes for all Jews everywhere by virtue of birth and "tribal" blood.

And Zionism is just not *necessarily* intolerant of "other religions or races." Within Israel it does not advocate discrimination against Christians, for example. The one religion of which it is most intolerant is—reform-Judaism (and not Islam!) and that basically for reasons of state and not theology. Its disgraceful and criminal persecution of the Arab minority is based on political reasons; it is a political and social persecution, not a religious persecution.

Maksoud here sounds as if he thinks the Zionists are religious fanatics or zealots! Nothing could be further from the mark, or be a grosser misunderstanding of what the fight is all about.

124

During most of its history, what it had to aim at was the setting up of a rule by a Jewish minority over an Arab majority, the Jewish minority coming into power and staying in power as the tool of an outside imperialist force.

Therefore, our resolution spoke of "the criminal policy of Zionism toward the Arabs, a policy which was based on the aim of minority rule by the Jews in Palestine under the wing of British imperialism."

This political character of Zionism was not changed by the events of the last two decades; but at the side of the Zionists' reactionary aspirations there also developed a different, a new, an accompanying factor which did not owe its motive force and impact to Zionism.

Our comrade Maksoud sees only the impact of Zionism. We would like to call his attention to this other explosive development.

This was the exterminationist fate which loomed before a whole people in Europe, the Jewish people.

First, there was the wholesale persecution of the Jews before the war. During the war there took place an event never before seen in the world—at least not in our civilized days—the unprecedented physical extermination of 6 million Jews. This was the Nazi "solution" of the Jewish problem. Not only Germany became untenable: mass anti-Semitic persecution was spreading to Italy and to France under the Nazi occupation. Then after the war, a new wave of anti-Jewish persecution arose in and engulfed the Stalinist empire, the satellites as well as Russia itself.

A whole people was being murdered and driven out of Europe. Driven—where? Where could they go? Even fleeing for their lives, where could they flee?

Why to Palestine? asks Comrade Maksoud in effect. This is a problem for the whole world, not just our responsibility. Why should we have to bear the burden alone?

He is absolutely correct.

The one country that was indicated in the first place as a haven was not Palestine but the United States; not the Arabs' land but ours. Any socialist, any half-decent democrat, who failed to cry this out—Open the doors of the U.S. to the Jewish refugees!—was a fraud. Our resolution said:

The elementary democratic demand of free emigration and immigration, long part of every genuinely democratic program, must be most vigorously fought for in the specific case of the

European Jews. All barriers to immigration to the countries of their choice must be broken down. For socialists in the U.S., the richest country in the world and the one capable of absorbing the largest population, this means the struggle against the exclusion of the Jews from this country. For this reason, independent socialists raised and continue to raise the slogan 'Open the doors of the U.S.!'

We should like Comrade Maksoud to note that it has always been the elementary democratic duty of every genuine socialist to fight for this untrammeled right of free emigration and immigration, by anyone to "the country of his choice." It has been called into question in the socialist movement, historically, only by the extreme chauvinist wing.

The American socialist movement has gone through this. Before World War I, to its everlasting shame and disgrace, the American Socialist Party took the position of supporting the Oriental-exclusion laws. The same socialist leaders who led in this move were those who betrayed socialism in the later war, and who betrayed socialism daily in their reformist politics. They were chauvinists.

At the time the Socialist International repudiated the American SP position and called for the genuine socialist position. We stick with this socialist position.

We had another reason for raising the demand "Open the doors of the U.S." Not only because the U.S. is the richest country: but also because it happens to be the country we live in. Every decent socialist in (say) Britain would be equally duty-bound to demand "Open the doors of Britain," even though Britain is not as rich as the U.S. The same goes for every socialist in the world, bar none.

It is no argument to prove that the influx of such immigration might harm the standards or otherwise impair the situation of native labor. That was the rationale of the American SP chauvinists (mentioned above) and they were right up to a certain point. They were chauvinists nonetheless. If such immigration did not create such problems, then anyone (and not only socialist-internationalists) could easily come out for a humane and internationalist position.

We trust, then that Comrade Maksoud now understands what we (at least) mean by the right of the Jews to go to "the country of their choice." It is a right we would fight for, for anyone, anytime. How much more so in view of the explosive situation we have barely sketched, the extermination of a people?

In this writer's opinion (though it can be mooted) by far the greatest portion of Europe's persecuted Jews would have preferred to come to the U.S. and not to Palestine, given free choice. The influx of Jews to Palestine was not primarily due to a sudden increase in the pro-Zionist sentiments of Jews, out of love for Zionism. But the U.S. banged its doors shut, while pretending to express its horror at the anti-Jewish crimes of others. Other countries banged the door. A steel ring of national boundaries encircled the Jews, while, for many of them, the need for sheer survival forced them or seemed to force them outward.

Something had to give.

International reaction forced the fleeing Jews into the bag set up by the Zionists. Here was one direction in which they could go with some outside help—the help and machinery set up by the Zionist movement. It was the path of least resistance for them, and the pressure could relieve itself (partly) only in this direction.

This is what set up the dynamic push behind the post-war influx of Jewish immigrants to Palestine.

It is in this connection that we come to the passage in our resolution part of which Maksoud quoted, with obvious misunderstanding. The part which Maksoud quoted is italicized:

> The post-war influx of European Jews into Palestine greatly exacerbated Arab-Jewish relations in the country. *The Zionist leaders looked upon this influx of refugees as a means of imposing all-Jewish rule upon the whole country.* The Arab effendis demanded that the Jewish people, hounded in Europe, be deprived of the right to found a new life in the country of their choice.

It should be clear to Comrade Maksoud now that what we are talking about is the right to free immigration. Just as we raised the demand "Open the doors of the U.S.," so also we believe it was the duty of socialists to support the right of Jews to immigrate to Palestine.

In our view, as in Maksoud's, it was a misfortune that the Jewish exodus was channelized into Palestine to the extent it was. That is one of the crimes for which world capitalism and imperialism ought to answer some day. But it was a fact, and not a Zionist plot.

The Zionists were able to take advantage of this anti-Semitic windfall—in general, Zionism has always fed on anti-Semitism—but the problem that was created had to be faced by socialists and everyone else. It could not be faced merely by yelling against Zionism.

We had a program. It was a proposal for a revolutionary solution. It was what we counterposed to the Zionist solution, on the one hand, and to the Arab states' policy on the other.

As concisely summarized in our resolution (directly following the last quotation given), it was:

> The Marxist, firmly opposed to both, advocated a policy which would bring together the Arab and Jewish peoples in a joint fight against British imperialism in the first place, and necessarily bound up with this, against Jewish capital and Arab landlordism, for a Palestine freed from all foreign rule and governed by a democratic Constituent Assembly based upon equal and universal suffrage.

> Such a fight was desired least of all by the Jewish and Arab upper classes. In the course of a joint struggle from below, cemented by common national-revolutionary aims and common social interests, Marxists aimed for a free and independent state of Palestine, based on the coexistence of two equal peoples, with national and cultural rights and autonomy safeguarded for both. This was the only progressive solution of the Palestine question. It looked not only to revolutionary struggles in Palestine but to the upsurge of anti-imperialist and revolutionary strivings in the whole Near East, on the road to a Near East Federation of socialist republics.

This is highly compressed, and we shall have to come back to some points, but certain things should be immediately clear.

In the first place, it should be plain that we oppose, above all, the basic idea of Zionism of building a "Jewish state." The idea, the concept-aim of a "Jewish state" and all that it implies is central to the Zionist ideology. As long as the people and government of Israel, following the Zionist road, continue to try to build Israel as a "Jewish state," there can be no peace between Jew and Arab. So we believe.

For this period when Palestine's imperialist controller was still Britain, which stood over both Jew and Arab, the class-oriented revolutionary proposal which we made was one which would have necessitated freeing the Jewish workers from the bonds of the Zionist ideology as well as mobilizing the Arab masses free from Arab landlordism.

There was an Arab majority in Palestine. A democratic Palestine ruled under universal suffrage meant a Palestine whose Arab majority would decide. This was anathema to every Zionist, and exactly what he would

128

never accept. But on the other hand, it could be accepted by the Jewish masses only in the context of an entirely different relationship between the two peoples. Both sides would have to view the new independent state as the home of two peoples in which both were free.

As we saw it, such a development could come about only through the rise of revolutionary class-consciousness from below. As Maksoud well says in his own article, it is in times of revolutionary stress and uplift that men begin to think differently, and then everything is possible.

Of course, we did not have any illusions about the immediate "practicality" of this program. We knew very well that on both sides the minds of the people were stuffed with chauvinist antagonisms. It was long plain that some reactionary "solution" was more in the cards, and not a revolutionary solution that could have been possible only with the existence of advanced revolutionary-socialist movements in the region.

The "solution" that was pushed through was partition.

We were against the partition as a "solution." Our resolution said on this point:

> For the Marxists, the partition was and is no solution for either the basic problem of Jewish-Arab relations in Palestine, or, still less, for the Jewish problem in the world. As against partition, we advocated a different course ..."[as already discussed above].

> ... As compared with the program we advocated, partition represented a setback on the road to greater understanding and cooperation between the Jewish and Arab peoples: it did indeed lead to a bloody fratricidal war in which and after which national feelings were inflamed even more and state-boundary walls were set up between the two peoples.

And we were right, we believe, in our view that the partition was no solution. Time has shown that. But then our resolution proceeds to make a point which we cannot emphasize too strongly to Maksoud:

> But if partition and the subsequent setting up and consolidation of the new state of Israel did not and could not solve the basic problem, or advance its solution, it did pose entirely new conditions under which that solution had to be sought.

From my point of view, I would repeat that to Maksoud a thousand times:

Partition was no solution. The setting up of Israel was no solution. Your program to destroy Israel would be no solution. The problem is how to bring together the Jewish and Arab peoples on a revolutionary democratic basis, and this problem has to be dealt with on the basis of the conditions that exist. Israel is a fact. Nothing will be gained by an Arab war against it, whether it wins or loses. There is a way to bring peace and a united life to the Near East, but it is not as simple a way as the mere proposal, "war against Israel."

We have outlined the point of view of our resolution as a background for taking up Comrade Maksoud's arguments for war, and as the background for counterposing this other solution of which we speak.

As we see it, then, Comrade Maksoud is reluctant to take a square look at one whole side of the post-war impasse in Palestine. He can see clearly the reactionary contribution which Zionism made to this impasse. But he does not give weight to the force which we emphasized in the first part of this reply: the flight of the Jewish people from Europe, and the channelization of this struggle for sheer survival to Palestine.

An exhausted victim of shipwreck is swimming in burning waters. He tries to climb into a lifeboat. The lifeboat already has its quota. To take on another will not swamp it but it will make the fate of all in it so much the more precarious. "Why pick on our little boat?" say the possessors of the lifeboat indignantly, as they crack the newcomer over the head with an oar and throw him back into the water.

Maybe that picture is not entirely fair, but it will serve to underline a point. The point is that the post-war plight of a desperate mass of Jews brought about a situation around Palestine which could not be met simply with denunciation of Zionism and in which the rights of the Arab peoples were not the only considerations for internationalist socialists.

We have already sketched the revolutionary solution which we proposed, revolutionary in the literal sense that it depended on revolutionary action from below among the Arab and Jewish masses. It was only in the context of such an approach that we had a right to advocate the free immigration of Jews not only to the U.S. and any other "country of their choice" but also to Palestine.

Here Comrade Maksoud does us a grave injustice. He quotes our statement that the Jews (like all other peoples, remember) have a "right" to immigrate ("to found a new life") in "the country of their choice." He then proceeds to transpose this to mean that according to us there is a

"Jewish right to Palestine," and this naturally is exactly the Zionist claim. Therefore, the ISL holds "the concept of a 'Jewish right to Palestine'"and really accepts Zionism.

The right of desperate Jews to find haven in Palestine or anywhere else is not their right to take that country away from its inhabitants. Contrariwise, if Maksoud rightly insists that there is no "Jewish right to Palestine," that does not mean that he must oppose Jewish immigration.

We know well enough why the Arabs link the two questions. It is no mystery. It is because Zionism linked them. The Zionists looked on unrestricted immigration as the means of gaining a formal Jewish majority in the country and thus getting into position to take it away from the Arabs.

The Arab opposition to immigration, and the Zionist calculations on immigration, were the two sides of the same coin. Both sides read: Internecine war and hatred between the peoples—No Exit.

The internationalist socialist attitude on free immigration had to be linked with the revolutionary solution of a bi-national Palestine.

The Arab solution was much simpler: Let the Jews get out and stay out, and go inflict their plight on some other people, who no doubt would feel the same way about it. The Zionist solution was also simple: Take their country away from the Arabs. The Zionist position was not, and never has been, founded on the specific post-war problem of uprooted Jewish masses. They merely demagogically utilized this appeal in order to further their own objective of taking Palestine away from its people. Thus, neither from the Arab side nor from the side of the Zionist leaders of the Jews could a solution be found.

Partition was the UN's attempted compromise between conflicting aims which could lead only to bitter-end war. Sections of Palestine were already inhabited mainly by Jews. Let these Jews have their own territories under their own state, separate from Arab Palestine, and maybe there will be peace.

The calculation was mistaken, and the partition could not bring any real peace or any real solution. As already discussed, we were against partition as a "solution." But being against partition still didn't answer a different question:

Did the Palestinian Jews have a right to self-determination in their territories? We believed that the Palestinian Jews did have a right to decide that they wanted partition, even though in our opinion this was a wrong and bad choice.

Let us try to clear up the following questions about this "right to self-determination."

(1) Simple though it is, it is often important to drive home an easy distinction: there is a big difference between the right to self-determination and the wisdom of exercising that right in any given case.

Sometimes people who have no difficulty in agreeing with this in the abstract have great difficulty in grasping it in a specific case where they are vigorously against the exercise of the right.

Take an American case in point: For a long time the Stalinists raised the demand in the U.S. for "self-determination for the American Negroes" in a certain "black belt" which they drew in maps through the Southern states. The CP made clear that it advocated this breakaway from the union.

Our movement has always ridiculed this demand. Only a handful of Stalinist Negroes have ever been for it. It never struck any response among the Negro people. We could explain why. We opposed the idea.

But that did not stop us from taking up a different question. We said clearly that if the Negro people ever came to favor this move, even against our advice to them, then we recognized their right to self-determination, even though we viewed it as a mistake.

(Is it theoretically possible that the American Negroes might come to such a pass? If the Negroes ever faced in the U.S. the gas-chamber horrors and concentration camps which the Jews passed through in Europe, who can deny the possibility?)

But all we want to do at this point is illustrate the idea of who we recognized the right to a self-determination against which we advised.

(2) "Which Jews have this right? Is it every Jew?" asks Maksoud, and he writes that our resolution did not answer this. This is strange, since our resolution has a specific passage on this very question.

Our resolution said that with regard to this problem of the right to self-determination—

(a) the problem concerns not Jews or people of Jewish descent in the world as a whole, but specifically the Jewish community in given territorial areas of Palestine, and (b) whatever the scientific-theoretical verdict might be for the Jews as a whole, it is obvious that the Palestinian Jewish community has acted and is acting exactly as if it were a national people, and this is enough for the purpose of determining a political program.

132

Isn't that perfectly clear? We (not the Zionists) are talking about a certain peculiar people in a certain territory, the Palestinian Jewish community.

(3) Maksoud asks further: Do the Jews constitute a "national self"? Are they a "national entity"? Also "what Jews belong to this national self?"

Now we are more or less acquainted with many decades of socialist and non-socialist argumentation over the question "Are the Jews a nation (or a race, etc.)?" What our resolution limits itself to pointing out is that this time-honored conundrum does not have to be settled in order to grapple with the question we raised.

For the question always referred to "the Jews" as a whole over the world. Maksoud still does so in his article. I am not at all sure what can be said about "the Jews" of the world collectively; I am not even sure that anything at all can be said that applies to this heterogeneous collectivity called "the Jews." The Zionist line of talk along these lines, in my opinion, boils down to a mystical tribalism, and is of no theoretical value whatsoever.

We were interested in the much more concrete question of the specific Jewish community situated on a certain territory in Palestine, and its right of self-determination not as "Jews" in general but as a certain community in the land.

This community, we pointed out, whatever its origins, had in fact developed to the point where it was demonstrably acting as a national people.

A question of Marxist method is in order here. One can dispute everlastingly whether a certain people constitute a "nation." One can usefully go over various criteria for nationhood, among the varying criteria which have been weighed by Marxists among others. Such theoretical discussion can be very good. But for Marxists above all others, the test of theory comes in life. If "theory" has told us that X is not a nation, but if this people acts historically and collectively in every way that a national people acts, then something is wrong with the theory, or else some important change has taken place which theory has not yet caught up with.

In the case of the Jews, I believe it was especially the latter that was true. On the other hand, a certain Jewish community (however transplanted) had in fact taken root in Palestine and developed a national physiognomy, one which was even different from that of the immigrant Jews. And on the other hand, tens and tens of thousands of European Jews were forcibly turned mentally into the channel of Jewish-national feeling by the simple fact that they were uprooted from every other national soil. Hitler had his victory.

Jewish-national feeling swarmed into the vacuum created in the minds of concentration-campsful of Jews. Hitlerism created Jewish nationalism in a way that Zionism by itself could never do.

In any case, all that our resolution points out (and it limits itself wisely) is that we as Marxists do not impose our schema about "who constitutes a nation" upon facts. It is sheer doctrinairism to counterpose some theory about nationhood, against the fact that the Palestinian Jewish community has acted exactly as if it were a national people.

This is not to derogate theory. I could discuss with Maksoud the theoretical criteria for Israeli nationhood. But I should like to point out that the development of Israeli nationalism (today an indisputable fact, reactionary as it often tends to be) is an historical event which a Marxist has reason to keep in mind in renovating his theory.

(4) Lastly, granted that this specific Jewish community in Palestine may be regarded like other ethnic communities situated in given territories and given the same rights, isn't their case different after all because of the way they got there? That is, since this Palestinian community was established and nourished by Zionism muscling in on Arab territory, aren't they still mere interlopers and invaders?

This is on pretty thin ice, when you start applying it to a whole people, settled in a land, and not merely a military garrison. What might we find out if we dug into the mode of arrival of various minority peoples in many countries?

The whites in South Africa, for example, are invaders and interlopers (in origin); but this undoubted fact hardly points to a solution of the racial problem there. We would not be in favor of throwing the racist whites back into the sea. We are in favor of ending the dictatorship of the white minority over the black and colored majority, and building a thoroughly democratic state where both races could live in harmony. (In South Africa too this objective can be won only through a revolutionary solution.) But if put up against it, we would have to recognize the right of the minority whites to "self-determination" in a sadly partitioned South Africa.

In Palestine the invasion and affront is more recent. The wound is rawer. That is true. It is also one reason for the hellishly difficult dilemma of the region. But we can see no other socialist stand possible.

In summary for this section: this right to self-determination was a right (the exercise of which we disagreed with) of a Palestinian community territorially established and acting as a nation.

Israel has as much "right" to existence as Pakistan. The problem that we see is not whether Israel has a "right" to exist, but how all of the people of the region can live together.

Israel may have a "right" to exist, but its existence will be a hell for the Jews and a thorn in the flesh of the Arabs as long as it insists on being a Jewish ghetto in an Arab world.

Before Israel can find a modus vivendi with its neighbors, it must overcome its Zionist illusions and policies. The Jewish people of Israel must come to the realization that the country must be built as a bi-national state, with cultural autonomy and full equal political and social rights for both peoples. Zionist expansionism must be repudiated. Its anti-Arab measures must be reversed.

All of this requires an internal revolutionary rejection of Zionism's specific politics, whether it consciously takes the form of a repudiation of Zionism or (perhaps more likely) takes the form of a gradual abandonment of all of Zionism's conclusions.

A movement toward this objective, we believe, can be built in Israel, even if only small elements of it are present now. But what will never be built in Israel is any movement or even grouplet which will advocate giving up the country's independence. The "emasculation" of Israel's independence and sovereignty can be accomplished only by war, and then only perpetuated by armed force and terror.

A bi-national Israel is only a first step. We look to a larger aim: an independent federation of the Near East states which constitute an economic and geographical entity. We cannot venture to say whether such a federation can or will include all the Arab states, in line with the aims of Arab nationalism. We are very interested in what our Arab comrades write about this question. But we see the final solution to the Palestine question in federation.

We have written time and again that the genuine socialists in Israel—and we do not mean the hard-bitten Zionist chauvinists, some of whom call themselves socialists, who are betraying socialist principles—can make their great contribution to this end by fighting with such a program for an understanding with the Arab people and for Arab rights, in the first place for the rights of the Arabs in Israel itself. The relative monolithism of Israeli Zionist chauvinism hardens Arab chauvinism.

But now we are addressing ourselves to Arab socialists. We tell them the same thing:

Only insofar as you show fight against the reactionary and chauvinist aims of the Arab governments, can you expect to awake and inflame courage and heart among Jewish socialists who want to break out of the Zionist trap! The responsibility is yours too. It belongs to the genuine socialists on both sides of the line.

You say that the destruction of Israel is necessary to bring peace. Can you really believe that? Do you believe that even if the Israeli armies are crushed in a war by the Arab power, the Jewish population will settle down as Arab citizens? No, as always, the worst will be brought out on both sides, in a permanent state of revolt and war and terrorism. What exactly will be solved, since you insist so strongly on having a "solution" and not only a "settlement"?

Comrade Maksoud wrote on June 7: "The presence of Israel as a state constitutes such a threat to the Arabs that all their attention is diverted away from foreign policy. The true interest of the Arabs in international affairs lies in pursuing a vigorous and positive neutralism, but the local area tensions prevent the effective expression of this interest and block the materialization of a unified Third Force movement in Asia. This movement is the only possible path toward peace. By obstructing it, Israel acts as an agent of war and imperialism."

We beg to submit that this is not socialist thinking, though we can readily believe that it has its appeal to the people. Does it mean, for example, that the existence of Israel leads the Arab regimes to trickle to the West in the hope of winning support against Israel? that this keeps the Arabs from joining some "Third Force movement"? that if Israel were only removed, the Arabs would become Third-Force and peace on earth would be attained?

That is self-delusion at best. In every other country, people have their own reasons for choosing between the war camps and lining up, hoping to gain some advantage, some "lesser evil," some profit. If Israel were to disappear, the Arab rulers would be no more for a real Third Camp than they are now. They would still have much to hope to gain from one side or the other; and in any case, the alternative is not some kind of illusory "neutrality" (even à la Nehru) but a positive dedication to international socialism. A strong Arab socialist movement can do this. But Comrade Maksoud continually keeps identifying the policy of the Arab socialists with that of the Arab regimes as a whole.

We would like to ask Comrade Maksoud and his colleagues: Granted that other Arabs, who are not socialists, are seduced by imperialism because of their hatred of Israel; but you socialists, you the vanguard, is it possible for you to fight for a line which is against every outside imperialism and at the same time extend the hand of friendship to anti-Zionist Israelis on a common program (not war)?

Why do you not swim against the stream and propose an anti-imperialist program for the Arab people, which will stimulate tendencies away from Zionist expansionism within Israel, which will promote revolutionization within Israel—and which will not tell the Israelis that their country has to be crushed in war?

Comrade Maksoud mentions that in the war against Israel it was the reactionary, anti-democratic, sometimes anti-Semitic, non-progressive elements who became vocal, while the "rational democratic forces ... were maneuvered ... to abstention." We did not quite grasp the explanation he gave for this. But it is a development that has been seen before. It often means that the socialists found themselves, in practice, traveling in the train of reaction, because of their lack of an independent revolutionary policy.

Comrade Maksoud's argument seems to say that the existence of Israel is counterrevolutionary in and of itself because the Arab's hatred of it diverts them from settling with their own rulers, diverts their revolutionary energies. But this is exactly the kind of situation in which socialists must act like a vanguard, not as echoes of mass prejudices and fears.

Here in the U.S. hatred and fears of Russia overlay and stifle class-consciousness and socialist aspirations. If the threat of Stalinism could be removed, an enormous weight would be lifted that now weighs down on the socialist movement. In this situation, there are not a few renegades who have concluded that it is wise for socialists to support the drive to World War III in order to settle with Russia.

Arab war against Israel would no more solve the Palestine problem than World War III can solve the world crisis. It is the special task of the socialist vanguard not to go along with majority fears and prejudices but to boldly propose their revolutionary solutions and fight for them against the field. A movement which is seduced by imperialism because of Israel will be seduced in some other way if Israel is removed, for it has lost its socialist moorings.

We propose that the Arab socialists consider the program of a bi-national Palestine in a Near East federation, as the revolutionary alternative to endless war, and to this end organize genuine socialist forces on both sides of the Israeli-Arab border.

Labor Action, August 23, 1954

Chapter IX
THE TRIPLE CRISIS OF ZIONISM

One of the few things about which the Zionist movement in all its sections is pretty unanimously agreed is that the whole movement is today racked from top to bottom by a violent organizational and ideological crisis. The second point, under this, is that the crisis stems from the existence of the state of Israel itself.

Note: it stems from the fact that Israel exists, not from any special difficulties of that state. There is also, to be sure, a much-discussed crisis in Israel itself; but this does not contribute to the crisis of the Zionist movement—if anything, it mitigates its force. The crisis of Zionism is due to that which it hails as its historic success.

This is all very well recognized:

Now the state is established ... and the Zionist organizations are left minus members and without a mass-movement ideology. There has been a great searching for redefinition but so far no new definition has emerged.—E. Katz, president of the Intercollegiate Zionist Federation, in the Student Zionist, February

Perhaps the chief impression [at the convention of the Zionist Organization of America] was one of crisis and also how to explain the crisis. The ZOA now claims a membership of about 164,000. This is a significant drop from the 'quarter million members' which were cited only about a year ago.   —Jewish Frontier, July.

... An intellectual crisis which cuts across parties, but divides Zionists in Israel from Zionist elsewhere. Spokesmen for the divergent viewpoints are trying hard to meet the crisis with the dignity and forbearance becoming to a dilemma so deep and so wounding ... Zionism reached its zenith in the creation of the state. But because of this, Zionism outside Israel has touched its nadir. —Lead article in the Jerusalem Post, Aug. 17.

The rise of the Jewish state brought them [Zionists] a tremendous feeling of elation and triumph, while it also administered a severe jolt to their movement... It is doubtful whether all our friends in Israel realize to the present day the extent and nature of this crisis...

Suddenly and at one stroke, the Zionist Organization was shorn of its political prerogatives and much of its authority... Zionists were not only dejected, but confused, having no clear idea where and how they fitted into the new picture... the Zionist prognosis... doctrine... ideal had triumphed... [Yet] In point of fact its position has tended to deteriorate... This proud position [is] now threatened with collapse.—Emanuel Neumann, in the Zionist Quarterly (ZOA), Summer.

The roots of the Zionist crisis which stems from the setting up of the state of Israel are three. They are quite distinct and with independent effects, though not equally important or fundamental, not equally recognized consciously by the Zionists themselves, and certainly confusingly interlocked in the discussions and struggles within that movement.

(1) The one which the Zionists refer to as "the ideological question" is simply: "What is Zionism now, anyway?" and "What is a Zionist today?" What makes it an ideological crisis is that the answer lies not in providing a definition but in providing a reason for continued existence for the Zionist movement as such, now that Zion itself exists.

(2) With Israel there was born Israeli nationalism as distinct from Jewish nationalism. It has made itself felt in a short space of time, not least within the Zionist movement. Within Israel, of course, there is no conflict between the two simply because the two are identified. For the Zionists outside, they cannot be. The national antagonisms within the Zionist movement are more than visible to the naked eye.

(3) The Zionist movement has always been divided into political parties—"General" Zionist (bourgeois conservative), Labor Zionist (socialistic, further subdivided into reformist and would-be Marxist), Revisionist (chauvinist to fascist), Religious, Stalinoid, etc. As can be seen, its spectrum is that of a state. The struggles were often fierce enough before there was any state power to be the object of the struggle. Now there is. The political antagonisms outside Israel now take on flesh and blood in terms of classes in Israel and their conflict for control of the government, and tend to become as irreconcilable as the class struggle itself.

The World Zionist Congress which was concluded at the end of August in Jerusalem mirrored and focused all the strains and confusions set up within Zionism by these three sources of crisis.

It could not and did not resolve the crisis; it had not really been expected to do so by anyone. But through the struggles at the Congress, as in the discussion which preceded it, the triple crisis of Zionism is quite clear.

1. The Political Antagonism

Zionism has already achieved a remarkable result—something hitherto deemed impossible. I refer to the close union of the most modern with the most conservative elements of Jewry.—Theodor Herzl, at the first World Zionist Congress at Basle, 1897.

That was more or less true (and incidentally an index to the character of Zionism) up to the creation of the state. The union is now strained more and more.

We take it up first not because it is most important but because it is easiest to see. Mainly, at the present stage, it is a complication which serves to embitter and sharpen the crisis.

The power struggle in the movement is largely between the Israeli and American Zionist leaders, but it is not, of course, accidental that the most influential leaders and spokesmen of the Americans (Abba Hillel Silver, Emanuel Neumann, Benjamin Browdy, etc.) and the main organization, the Zionist Organization of America (ZOA), are General-Zionist in politics. Their co-thinkers are the men of Israel's leading bourgeois party, the main opposition to Ben-Gurion's Labor Party (Mapai).

For both sides this is not simply a matter of political theory, to be shelved by them in their capacity as Zionists. As we said, state power is at stake. For the Americans, of course, it cannot directly be their state power, but it is state power in "their" Zion. Not less than their non-Jewish class-counterparts in this country, they are morbidly antagonistic to socialism, which they see in Mapai's controlled economy, labor base and program. For them the Israeli General Zionists' program (unreconstructed capital-ism) is not only the American Way but also ordained. They cannot take lightly the fact that the state which they fathered and financed and which is the incarnation of their dream is in the hands of men who stand for anti-capitalism.

The ZOA, for the first time in its history, at its convention earlier this year, voted overwhelmingly to identify itself formally with the Israeli General-Zionist party. It meant throwing down a gage. At the ZOA convention, as well as in Jerusalem, Silver went out of his way to take a crack at socialism. Part of the struggle at the world congress turned on "how much of a say in the development of Israel the Zionist movement outside the country should be entitled to in return for its economic aid," as the N.Y. Times reported (Aug. 26), and by "the Zionist movement" it is the American bourgeois Zionists who are meant in the first place.

"Translated into practical terms," continues the dispatch, "this, of course, means a measure of authority over immigration, the rate and sources of economic development, and inevitably Ben-Gurion's people believe this would have a political effect as well."

Naturally! And when the Israeli General-Zionists' allies from America yell that they want more determining power in fields which vitally affect Israeli economic policy, they can hardly be considered to be entirely naive. "The underlying issue ... is whether the world Zionist movement shall influence life in Israel or whether it should be a welfare organization," explained the Jerusalem Post (Aug. 14)—and what happens when the would-be influencers of life in Israel are enemies of the governing party?

The bitterest words in connection with the otherwise carefully restrained world congress flowed from this antagonism. Rabbi Silver started the very day before the congress opened with an open accusation at a press conference that the Israeli government had undermined American Jewry because it wanted non-interference from U.S. Zionists in political matters and "nothing pleased Washington more"—hence the drift of State Department policy away from Israel. He did not make explicit the inference that Ben-Gurion should tolerate interference from his American Zionist antagonists in the country's political affairs, or else.

On the other hand, Ben-Gurion's denunciation of the ZOA leaders had been even more slashing. At the congress Browdy had to stand up to rebut the former's statement labeling the ZOA "enemies of labor" and an outfit of labor-baiters. (He might have been more convincing if it had not been true, for one thing, that at the ZOA convention one of the chief speakers had waxed enthusiastic in praising the Israeli General-Zionists for supporting the right not to join a trade union.)

In a speech prior to the world congress on August 8, Ben-Gurion had cuttingly denounced the ZOA by name: "The leaders of this movement live in deceit... The nation must know that the Zionist Organization of America has ceased to be a Zionist organization": and pretty clearly referred to them scornfully as a bunch of "merchants, lawyers, and rabbis."

Perhaps the most heated moment on the open floor of the congress came when, after Rabbi Silver had been given time to speak his piece, Mrs. Golda Meyerson rose to answer him for Ben-Gurion, before a hall packed to see the sparks fly. Among other things she "demanded to know what Zionist leaders in America had done to refute the libels that the Israeli government was preventing private capital and foreign investors from participating in Israel's upbuilding. She asked whether some of these same leaders had not helped fan 'the fires of allegation.'"(Jewish Telegraphic Agency, Aug. 20.) The political struggle within Israel itself was being echoed.

It is, of course, not necessary to charge the gentlemen from the ZOA with the deliberate intent to substitute their own influence as foreign Zionists for the failure of the Israeli General-Zionists to do better in the last elections. The capacity of men to believe "sincerely" that they are acting not as "partisans" but only in the best interests of humanity is virtually infinite. But it is this which gave part of its heat to the congress issue of "special status" for the Zionist movement.

The Americans came to Jerusalem with the No. 1 demand that the world Zionist organization, rather than the Israeli government and its agencies, be given a monopoly on the activities of Jewry all over the world on behalf of Israel. As Silver said, demanding a "charter" for the Zionist organizations:

"What we mean by 'charter' is not just affording the [Zionist] Jewish Agency diplomatic status in Tel Aviv. ... We want the Zionist movement to be recognized as the channel for all important activities of Jews on behalf of the state of Israel."

They talked in terms of a "semi-governmental" status for the Zionist executive. The Israelis had more than good ground to suspect that what the Americans were demanding would mean in practice their assumption of a good measure of control and influence in Israel's foreign economic activities and consequently a long finger in all of Israel's affairs.

Under the circumstances this was more than a modest demand. Ben-Gurion rejected it, counterposing (perhaps only tactically) the demand that the Americans first recognize their obligation to aid Israel unconditionally regardless of their hostility to the political composition of its government.

Silver especially was quite clear on what he was demanding: "We do want, however, a say on how the money [raised for Israel] is spent. No taxation without representation, we say." There were the Americans, with the slogan of 1775 demagogically on their lips, demanding control over a vital part of another country's internal policies. The Israelis replied in effect that if Rabbi Silver wanted a voice in Israel's affairs, he would have to settle down as an Israeli citizen.

Browdy, at the congress, resorted to more weasely formulas: "We have no desire to interfere in the internal affairs of Israel," he said piously, "but we have every desire to make sure its foundations are firm and will resist the ravages of time." And later: "We are prepared to work unconditionally, but not at the expense of our self-respect."

The Americans had two weapons with which to enforce their demand against the position of the Israelis: their influence in the world Zionist organization—and the almighty dollar. And it can be argued that these two are one. Everyone knew, as the report to the congress later stated, that American Jews had given 75 per cent of all moneys received by Keren Hayesod, the Development Fund, in the last 5 years.

The Americans were not too bashful about waving the dollar in a threatening pose. Silver hinted broadly: "Jews are not automats which release coins upon the pressing of a button ..." And in his speech to the congress he "warned, however, that should Jews overseas begin to feel that Israel flouts them completely, 'they might cease to help you and there will be nothing you can do about it.'"(JTA, Aug. 20.)

At the World General Zionist caucus in Jerusalem just before the congress, the Americans threatened to make sure that the Jews would not act as "automats":

"The greatest impression was made by the speech of the chairman of the ZOA Executive Committee, Mortimer May, who said that the time had come to explain to American Jewry the internal problems of Israel. 'For a long time', said Mr. May, 'I was of the opinion that not everything about Israel should be told in the U.S., since I felt that it might harm the Zionist movement. But we must now change our way of thinking." (ZINS, the ZOA news service.)

Naturally, extreme threats by both sides must be taken with a grain of salt, since the American Zionists need their relation with Israel (otherwise how exist as Zionists at all?) as much as the Israelis need the former's dollars. But the threats were there, including May's to bring the Israeli election campaign home to New York. Everyone knew a compromise would be reached, as it was; it was a question of who got how much, and how the vague terms of the compromise would work out in the period ahead.

But it is too easy to see the conflict at the Jerusalem congress in terms of this political antagonism alone or primarily. That would be quite inaccurate. This element of crisis is here to stay, but it is not accidental that we have largely had to speak (as the congress did) in terms of the "Americans" and the "Israelis."

2. The Nationalist Antagonism

The Zionist axis is no longer, and has not been for 30 years, Tel Aviv-Odessa, but Jerusalem-New York.—Jerusalem Post, Aug. 14.

The axis has developed antagonistic national poles.

For one thing, the American Zionist leaders came to Jerusalem with roughly the same spirit and with the same psychology as the American delegation at the San Francisco conference on the Japanese treaty: as the world's aristocrats, with wealth and power behind them, and little inclined to play second fiddle to the leaders of a piddling country. That little country is dear to them, of course, because it is Zion, but it is dear to them as their Zion, not as a sovereign state with leaders of its own.

On the other hand, the development of Israeli nationalism (as distinct from Jewish nationalism, remember) and its effect on the character of Zionism in Israel would deserve a special chapter in a book on contemporary Zionism. "It is from here [Israel] that the principles of Zionism shall go forth," proclaimed Ben-Gurion a week before the congress.

In discussing the "special status" issue in terms of the political antagonisms, we had to be one-sided temporarily. Actually, the national sovereignty of Israel is also involved, and while the Americans could think of this concept only hazily, it meant a great deal more to the Israelis, and not Ben-Gurion's Israelis alone.

It was not just a matter of the Americans' "special status" demand versus national sovereignty as an abstraction. It is not hard to feel the reaction of an Israeli to the rich foreign tycoons, too many of whom apparently made manifest their scorn for "our alleged contempt for what a few among our guests consider to be elementary comforts of civilized life (e.g., hotel rooms with private bath)," as a Jerusalem Post article delicately put it.

The same paper editorialized during the congress about such people who come not as pioneer emigrants but as "alien experts with their talents for hire" and it urged that their contribution "be on this country's hard terms, without setting up two standards, one for those coming from the free, another from the enslaved world. Let not those that come cling to the return ticket as to a lifeboat in a storm; and let them embrace our civilization without a mental reservation about the size of the British Commonwealth of Nations or the United States of America."

As for the other delegations, it is likewise not hard to feel their reaction before the dollar-power of the Americans and the governmental power of the Israelis. Prior to the Congress, the London Zionist Review had editorialized:

"It is necessary for them [the British delegates] to oppose the idea that the two important centers of world Jewry are America and Israel." And the president of the British Zionist Federation, speaking at the congress, "expressed fears that Zionists in Europe would be caught in a struggle between the 'power blocs' of Israeli and U.S. Zionism."(JTA, August 17.)

Before the dollar-waving of the Americans, the Israelis reacted not as Zionists but in the first place as Israelis. We are not criticizing them for this. On the contrary, it would have taken miserable men—not men who felt they were building a country—to listen without bitterness to one of the American Zionist leaders who actually got up and said:

> You don't know America. It is too big for you to understand. You have fantastic ideas about the United States. ... We demand respect from the Zionist movement. Without the Zionist Organization of America, Israel will suffer." (Joseph Tenenbaum.)

The interests of Israel as a nation versus the interests of the Zionist movement could not have been more clearly counterposed than in the spectacle during Ben-Gurion's tour of this country earlier this year. The head of the Zionist state, the symbol of Zionism's great "victory," was here—and no reference to Zionism ever passed his lips at any of his meetings. More than that: he cut the whole American Zionist movement dead-cold.

He spoke at numerous meetings, but even the ZOA failed to secure his presence at their big "Salute to Israel" rally, where more than 19,000 waited for him. The president of the ZOA was not among the notables invited to sit on the platform during Ben-Gurion's Madison Square Garden bond rally. Zionism was never even mentioned in all the speeches and tableaus about the struggle for Israel's statehood. (He addressed not a single Zionist group until just before catching the boat—and then it was a semi-private meeting which we will discuss under Section 3.)

This is not to be explained by the political antagonism with the pro-General-Zionists of the ZOA; it is too extreme. Besides, he paid no more attention to his own Labor Zionists. And there is another very clear explanation for it, which the American Zionists understand only too well.

It is clear that Ben-Gurion looks on the Zionist movement as an obstacle to mobilizing the fullest aid to Israel from abroad, more than as an aid.

For now virtually the whole Jewish community, non-Zionists and anti-Zionists as well as traditional Zionists, are for aid to Israel. While Zionism was a dream, only the Zionists could be depended on. Now it is a state, a reality, and the old lines do not demarcate out the "friends of Israel."

The old Zionist movement is the old skin which has to be cast off in the moulting. As a state, Israel looks to and appeals to the Jewish community as such, and its appeal can only suffer if it gets involved with the traditional antagonisms between Zionists and anti-Zionists within the Jewish community. The Zionists, the Israelis feel, cannot hold back from giving. It is the others who are not to be offended, who are to be wooed. (Hence the Zionists' party hollow threats, in reaction, to hold back the dollars.)

A "prominent Israeli official" is quoted by the Times correspondent in Jerusalem"

> Zionism has had a long and useful life and should now be given a decent burial,"he said recently. "We Israelis, who pay taxes, maintain an army, fertilize the desert and bring in hundreds of thousands of new immigrants, cannot be expected to brook interference from Diaspora [non-Israeli] Jews.

At the Jerusalem congress, Nahum Goldmann, president of the congress, countered the demand for "special status" with the argument, among other things, that to give special status to the Zionists "would antagonize the good friends of Israel who are non-Zionists."

There is no doubt that the "special status" demand was opposed not only (though most sharply) by the Mapai Israelis for the reasons already explained, but by far wider Israeli circles whose motivations were not political-partisan but nationalist. Why should aid to Israel (as far as the Israelis are concerned) be forcibly channelized through a privileged section of the Jewish community—just because of this section's past services? Let it be given a decent burial, with a cheer.

But the Zionist leaders do not plan to be buried because their existence is inconvenient to the Israelis. Unfortunately for them, however, as we shall see, their chief gravedigger is not Israeli nationalism but their own ideological bankruptcy.

There is another and quite different aspect of the national question in Zionism which bedevils the diaspora Zionists, especially the Americans, as a result of the existence of the Jewish state.

It is the delicate question of "double loyalty." In words it can be and has been resolved easily enough: We are American Jews loyal to our own country but loving Israel; we are like good Irish-American citizens who love the old sod too; a man can have many loyalties, to family, party, religious group, country, etc. and they are not contradictory ... and so on. This is a perfectly consistent attitude for a non-Zionist "friend of Israel." Within the framework of the full, undiluted Zionist ideology (which we shall see even more clearly in Section 3) it is not so easy. It may be hard for American Zionists to understand this since the undiluted article is pretty rare in these States.

It was easier for the European Zionist (Labor-Zionist) leader, Jacob Yefroikin, editor of the Paris Kiyum. In the article which we shall quote he is talking what undoubtedly seems another language to most American Zionists. But thinking on the same basis, even though the question of double loyalty is the last question they would dream of bringing up. If Yefroikin is extreme, it is because he is following the heart of Zionism to its logical ends.

> President Truman at the beginning of 1948, in his message to the convention of the American Council for Judaism, said: 'Jews must in their own interests and as loyal citizens, think and act exclusively as Americans.' And if this hint was not sufficiently obvious, it found a clearer definition in a speech at the same gathering by Carol Binder: 'If,'he said, 'the struggle for a Jewish state ... would eventually have to cost the democratic countries the oil of the Middle East, the Jews of the United States would have to pay dearly for it' ... These words, veiled in Truman's and open in Binder's speeches, expressed not a passing mood; they are valid even now and their echo will be heard far and loud.

"Even now in peacetime, before the storm has broken out, there are Jews, even so-called Zionists, who have the sorry courage to justify morally the preference of American patriotism above the Jewish if there should ever come to a clash between the two." States the editor of the Reconstructionist in an open letter to Lessing Rosenwald that, in a not-improbable case, if the state of Israel should be involved in a war with the United States, American Jews will act exactly in the same manner as if another country were at war with America and in accordance with their 'exclusive loyalty' would fight Israel as Jews of one country always fought Jews of another country, just as American Catholics would fight any Catholic country. (Reconstructionist, March 5.)

There is a theory concocted by some Zionists, including Chaim Greenberg [American Labor Zionist theoretician], which says that we Jews are no exception to the general rule. Non-Jews too have many loyalties and this does not prevent them from being loyal citizens of their countries.

This is true. ... To each social cell man gives only a part of his loyalty. Only a totalitarian state demands the entire individual for itself. States which recognize a certain degree of individual freedom see nothing wrong in the pluralistic loyalties of its citizens.

All this is true, but our specific Jewish [that is, Zionist—H.D.] problem is not exhausted nor answered by this. For it is one thing to have many loyalties to different objects, and something else to have one's own loyalty divided and split between two objects of the same category. A man can be true to his father and mother, to his class and state at the same time. But a person cannot have two fathers and two mothers and remain equally loyal to both of them, just as a man cannot belong to two nations at the same time and have two fatherlands. [Italics in original. Quoted from the Jewish Newsletter, July 23.]

This question of "double loyalty" arises for the consistent Zionist (if there are any such left in the United States), and not for the Jew, not because the former "loves Israel" with the sentimental or philanthropic attachment of an Irishman for old Erin but because of the consistent ideology of Zionism on the "Jewish nation." This gets us to Section 3.

But before any American Zionist (as they virtually all do) rejects Yefroikin's views with sincere astonishment and an unwillingness even to consider such "absurdities" seriously, it would be well to look at Ben-Gurion's definition of Israel as a state. As a statesman, Ben-Gurion recognizes foreign Zionists' loyalty to their own country, but that is as a statesman.

> The state of Israel differs from all other states in that it is not only the state of its own citizens alone, but of the entire Jewish people, of every Jew wherever he lives." (Ben-Gurion at the Jerusalem congress.)
>
> The state is part of the nation [he is referring to the entire 'Jewish nation' in the world—H.D.] The state does not yet constitute the fulfillment of Zionism but it is the main and fundamental means for the Ingathering of the Exiles, and this is the content of Zionism ... Israel is a state not only in respect to its residents—it is a state for the Jewish nation. The constitution of the state of Israel is one small law—the 'Law of the Return.' That is the special historic quality designating the raison d'etre of the state of Israel. (Ben-Gurion in speech, Aug. 8.)

To be sure, Ben-Gurion does not want any "double loyalty" either. As we shall see, his demand is that every Zionist become an Israeli. But the American Zionists do not want to go to Israel; they want to remain Zionists in the diaspora even while "their own" state exists in the world. But their dilemma in this respect is only a part of their larger dilemma which is the content of the ideological crisis of Zionism, which underlies and embraces all that we have already discussed.

3. The Ideological Crisis

Like the political-partisan antagonism, and the nationalist antagonism in the Zionist movement, the present ideological crisis also arose automatically with the fact of the existence of Israel. As we have explained, what is involved is the very reason for existence of the Zionist movement, as a distinct movement, in the diaspora.

Before Israel came into being, the mission of the Zionist movement was clear: to work for the creation of the Jewish state. The non-Zionists did not support this aim, would not do so, and certainly would not contribute money to do so. But now, with Israel in existence as the Jewish state, virtually all in the Jewish community (not to speak of many non-Jews) are for aid to Israel, aid to its development, and interested in how the U.S. government treats it.

Of course, the Zionists can claim, probably with justice, that they are the best and most singleminded supporters of Israel, but this is hardly reason enough for the Zionist movement to continue in its present forms. Why not dissolve, for example, to give way to a broader "ginger group" of both Zionists and non-Zionists—that is, actually, a group not based on the Zionist ideology, in which the former Zionists can still be the spark plugs—if it is the broadest aid to Israel that is the object? This is what the soul-searching is about.

It is very clear that a large section of the Zionist movement has in fact decided that there is nothing for it but dissolution. This section is not heard from in the discussions that have raged because it consists of those who have already voted with their feet; for example, the more than 80,000 who quit the Zionist Organization of America in the last year or two.

In an important programmatic article in which ZOA leader Emanuel Neumann went through the problems before the World Zionist Congress at Jerusalem, to-be-or-not-to-be is the first question he raises (Zionist Quarterly, Summer issue). "We may now proceed on the assumption that the question has been answered in the affirmative," he says reassuringly, while indicating that "doubts were entertained by some leading personalities in Israel—men who only yesterday had held positions of highest responsibility in the movement."

It is easy to answer in the affirmative but to find a reason for existence is harder. He presents two: (1) "a strong Zionist movement in the diaspora, with high morale, is indispensable to the state of Israel, for an indeterminate period," because of the state's precarious position. But as pointed out, a broader "Society of Friends of Israel" could be even more effective by dissociating aid to Israel from Zionism as a special movement, to which much of the Jewish community is antagonistic. And (2) "a vigorous Zionist movement is equally essential from the point of view of Jewish life in the diaspora, its health and vitality, its spiritual bond with Israel and the bracing sense of world-wide Jewish unity." Here again there is nothing distinctively Zionist.

The same is true with all other proposals heard for what Zionism can do today: community work, cultural work, etc. They are simply irrelevant to the basic problem. An organization like the ZOA might continue to exist in some such way for some length of time but not meaningfully as a Zionist organization.

"The time has come," writes Neumann, "for the World Jewish Congress to be merged with the Zionist movement, which can take over

151

its functions as an important branch of its activity." It would seem to be more logical the other way around, to dissolve the Zionist movement into the broader organization, on the basis of Neumann's perspective!

But Neumann is aware there is another answer, which was indeed the answer which was shoved before the noses of the American Zionist delegation at the Jerusalem congress. That is: that the Zionist movement today can only be a movement, primarily and overwhelmingly, to bring all the Jewish people back to Zion, which is now incarnated in Israel—a halutz (pioneering emigration) movement.

This, of course, has always been viewed as one task of the Zionist movement, but only as one task, and especially in the U.S., a minor one. American Zionism has been primarily "philanthropic Zionism." Its day is over; such philanthropy could be distinctively Zionist yesterday; today it is not.

During the congress sessions, the Jerusalem Post took a bitter jibe at this type by quoting the definition of a "Zionist" as "a rich Jew who gives money to another Jew to help a poorer one go to Palestine." Reflecting the Israeli point of view, it is quoted bitterly and contemptuously. Now the Americans are wondering whether they can even be philanthropic-Zionists.

This soul-searching has been going on since 1948 but it was raised to new intensity and sharpness by Ben-Gurion's visit to these shores—on that occasion (at long last before catching the boat) when he finally appeared before a gathering of Zionists. He laid the meaning of Zionism before them, punctuated with table-banging. A Zionist, he told them, is a Jew who identifies himself fully with Israel by giving up all his allegiance and loyalties to the country of his birth or domicile and settles in Israel with his wife and children; no one can describe himself as a Zionist so long as he and his family remain living outside Israel!

If the American Zionists thought that this was a personal crotchet of his, they found at Jerusalem that the overwhelming majority of the congress agreed with Ben-Gurion, across all party lines. For convenience we shall refer to the "Israeli" point of view versus that of the Americans, but it was not limited to the Israelis. It was the Americans who were out of step and virtually isolated there on this question.

It has not been sensibly answered by the American Zionists, unless feeble squirming can be called an answer. They know they want to be Zionists and they just know that emigration to Israel is unthinkable for them—that's for the poor Jew who needs a refuge—and they find it hard to adjust themselves to the notion that there is a contradiction. But on the other hand, they also can see that their own view is no longer the basis for a movement.

In a very interesting article in the Student Zionist for February, the president of the student Zionist organization explains how this group groped its way through the question, spurred to quicker decision by the fact that, on the campus above all, lack of a clear viewpoint meant immediate disintegration. The viewpoint they came out with was that the organization could continue to exist only if its reason for being was to orient youth toward emigration.

While this is a basis for a movement, he rightly explains, it means a much smaller movement than before. But it is something.

But this decision cannot simply be made merely for lack of any alternative reason for existence. The whole situation brings the Zionist up before the question: Has this in fact, whether we recognized it or not, been the real meaning of Zionism all along, the rest being auxiliary or peripheral? If this is what is left of the Zionist ideology, what was that ideology?

What is left of the Zionist ideology is indeed its heart and soul. What stares the American Zionist in the face, clearly for the first time, is indeed that which has always been the essential basis of the Zionist ideology, now no longer overlaid by rationalizations. From the Marxist viewpoint, it is no new discovery. For many Zionists, it is. It took the creation of the state itself to confront them with it. Their crisis consists only in the fact that they refuse to look it in the eye.

Ben-Gurion is reported to have said in New York: "I deny that there is a crisis in Zionism. There is a crisis—in some Zionists." In a sense, he was right.

That which is left of the Zionist ideology, and which has always been its essence, is summed up in the Zionist slogan "The Ingathering of the Exiles." The Americans heard this phrase more often in two weeks in Jerusalem than they had in the U.S. in years.

Earlier this year an American Zionist commission headed by Israel Goldstein got up a new draft "Jerusalem Program." Its formulation of the task of Zionism was "to further the speedy ingathering into the state of Israel of all Jews who wish to go and live there ..."(Congress Weekly, May 28.) But they did not even try hard to get away with this sidestepping formula at the world congress. The slogan of the Ingathering of the Exiles rent the air at Jerusalem.

What "exiles"? Who are the exiles? World Jewry—the "Jewish nation." The tribes (Zionist term) were dispersed but are now to be rescued from the diaspora. The tribes have been in Galuth and are now to be brought "home" from their exile. This is the mission, the law, the constitution, the reason for existence for Israel, as Ben-Gurion said. Without this, Israel has no Zionist meaning.

Does that mean we all have to go to Israel if we are to be good Zionists? The American delegates were given a minimum program on this. Not that they were totally absolved from personal "self-fulfillment." Golda Myerson, in her rebuttal to Rabbi Silver, declared that "if American Zionist leaders had come to Israel and settled there after the state was established, it would have been an 'inspiring example' of immigration for American Jewish youth." (JTA, Aug. 20.)

At a press conference before the congress opened, Silver was asked whether he planned to settle in Israel; he countered with "Do you need another rabbi?" The smart retort was fittingly answered at the congress by an Israeli General-Zionist leader (anti-religious) who suggested to him that he come and establish a reform-synagogue movement in the country.

But the Israelis did not insist on the condition of personal "fulfillment." Their minimum demands were: (1) Send your children; (2) make emigration the main task of your organization; (3) compulsory Hebrew education in the Zionist movement.

On the last, Ben-Gurion had declared: "No one can be a Zionist who does not feel the duty of educating his children in the Hebrew language... Otherwise, neither they nor their children have any connection with the Jewish nation. A Zionist can either live in the state of Israel or he must at least live in that spiritual state of the Jewish nation which is the Hebrew language." Another Mapai leader urged the Zionist leaders overseas to Hebraize their names.

The Americans protested in effect: But these demands are impossible, absurd, unreasonable. You obviously don't know us Americans. Our American Zionists don't want to go to Israel. There's no use you or us agitating them. They just won't.

—Your job is to change that, to "Zionize" them, they were told.

The Americans protested but all they had to say, stripped of bluster, was: The Americans won't go because they're comfortable, secure and better off where they are ... which is perfectly good reason, for a non-Zionist.

It is difficult to say which side was and is more outraged by the other's viewpoint. But it is not difficult to say which has a right to be outraged from the Zionist viewpoint. The Americans were saying in effect: Zionism is all right in theory—for some poor Jews in other places—but not when it's a matter of exchanging the fleshpots of America for the hard realities of Israel. Their first and last argument remained something like the Talmudic one which Neumann had quoted in his pre-congress article, from Mordecai Kaplan:

> Nothing can be more fantastic than to assume that a considerable proportion of American Jews can be persuaded to migrate to Israel. The Talmud enunciates the principle that an ordinance by which the majority cannot possibly abide should never be issued. Such an ordinance creates an unnecessary sense of guilt. It is destructive of peace of mind and soul. To find fault with Jews who are satisfied to make their permanent home outside Israel is to violate that sound Talmudic principle.

It would seem from the reports that among the American delegates only the president of Hadassah had the guts to blurt out in so many words what they believed: "We cannot accept the concept that we are in exile." But the Americans accepted the "exile" concept for the others! "Exile" apparently is only where they won't let you live.

Most of the Americans were discreet enough not to be as plainspoken. They gave and give lip service to halutziuth and aliyah (emigration to Israel) but, resting on "realistic" grounds, mostly claimed to be helpless before the reluctance of their ranks. It was only thin concealment for the fact that they agreed with the ranks.

The Israelis blasted away. Dobkin of the Jewish Agency pointed out that the neglect of the halutz movement in the U.S. was illustrated by the fact that a single youth center in Brooklyn had a larger budget than the entire halutz movement in the country. It was reported that only 7,000 immigrants had come from the U.S., Britain, South Africa, and Australia since the creation of the state (and we do not know whether this figure includes those who later left).

"Zionist parents [in America] tremble at the thought that their children might become infected with the idea of emigration to Israel," charged Dobkin.

The Americans were informed, by Nahum Goldmann, that the Zionist Ingathering of the Exiles also applies to Jews in "free countries where they are not forced to depart for a safer area. ... So long as a majority of the Jewish people remains outside Israel, Zionism's aims have not been attained. ... The function of Zionism ... is to 'Zionize' both the Jews in Israel and those outside the Jewish state."

155

We have to quote further from Goldmann, perhaps the outstanding non-Israeli in the world movement and furthermore considered a "moderate," for both of which reasons he was elected president at the congress. In the polemic against the Americans, the overwhelming majority at the congress made the meaning of Zionism crystal-clear.

"Take away the Galuth," cried Goldmann, "and you take away Zionism." He is referring to the concept that Jewry as a "nation" is in exile.

This was re-emphasized and hammered home in more than one speech. Goldmann again: "Galuth does not cease being Galuth because Jews are happy and well-treated there. Galuth is not measured by good or bad treatment."

And he added: "Galuth is a mystical concept. If you deny that America is Galuth, you might as well deny the need for Israel." (My emphasis.)

Of course, this is the concept which is also behind Ben-Gurion's definitions of Israel as a state founded on the "Law of the Return." In his August 8 speech he had said: "a Zionist must himself come to Israel as an immigrant," as he had said in New York. And he made clear that this was no new interpretation: "From the beginning Zionism meant for us only halutzic Zionism"—that is, Zionism as a movement to return the Jewish "nation" to Palestine.

The concept is as "mystical" for the majority as for Goldmann. Goldmann's use of that word was not an aberration. Even Neumann—even Neumann, spokesman for the anti-Galuth Americans—had to put it that way (in the article above-quoted) in explaining why the philanthropic-Zionist Americans choose to direct their philanthropy toward Zionism:

> They [in America] were in dispersion but had little sense of exile. ... They wish to further the cause not only as a duty toward Jews less fortunately placed, but out of a deep, if mystic, sense of obligation toward the Jewish past, of identity with Jewish destiny and the vision of a nobler future.

The view that the Jews of the world, and not merely the Jewish yishuv in Palestine, constitute a nation in the Zionist usage is a view which can only have a mystical basis.

What in non-mystical terms is the "Jewishness" which they have in common and which is discussed at such great length? Religion? Not for the non-religious, secular Zionists, though we shall see what is happening on this. Common persecution? Yes; but if this is to be the basis for the concept of nationhood, it is an inverted acceptance of the anti-Semitic view of the Jewish people as a "peculiar people" with whom the non-Jew cannot live. The fact is that the Jews in their dispersion, have become even more varied than most imagine.

This is rather spectacularly illustrated by a passage in Ben-Gurion's August 8 speech, thrown in apparently not so much for its relevance in the context but because even he had just been "shocked":

> I was shocked to the core by the seriousness of the problems connected with the absorption and fusion of the Dispersions, when I saw the abyss lying between two types of Iraqi Jews that cannot live together, the townsmen and the hillsmen. Now we have brought them together at Halsa and at Bet Lydd and they cannot live together even though they speak one language and come from one country.
>
> I met a Yemenite, a Tunisian and a Moroccan. They demanded that separate synagogues be built for them. I learnt that where a Moroccan prays, a Tunisian will not perform his prayers, even though both pray according to Sephardic rites,although their cantillation differs. The Yemenite told me that Yemenites need two types of synagogues, one for the natives of San'a and another for those originating outside San'a.

It is rather extreme, but still these are Jews who speak the same language, come from the same country, and practice the same Sephardic rites. Then there are the others ...

Persecution, distress and need are driving the many and disparate Jews of the Dispersions to Israel, and the Israeli leaders have cause to be appalled at the task of welding them into one nation; this was a task also for the United States with respect to the many-nationed immigrants who were driven to its shores by persecution, distress and need, in spite of the fact that the pre-history of the United States (in its colonial development) had already provided a base. But if it is a difficult task, it is because it is not a "one-nation entity" (Ben-Gurion's term) which is "returning home." The great majority are fleeing their homes.

The "mystical" concept which is at the heart and soul of Zionism (in spite of the American Zionists' disclaimer) is that of tribal blood-solidarity. For the Zionist (in greater or lesser measure depending on the degree to which the individual's Zionist ideology is diluted by concessions to other ideologies), it is inevitable that this mystic sense of tribal blood-solidarity should be their overriding motivation.

To be sure, it collides with class solidarity, both for the bourgeoisie and the working class; and for the latter, both in Israel and in the diaspora Zionist movement, it is an alien and corruptive element in any attempt to build a consistent, genuine socialist movement. It collides with the solidarity of internationalism; and most specifically, it collides with the need for a policy of equality, toleration and peace with the Arab peoples. Scientifically, ideologically, philosophically if you wish, it does not have much to recommend it above the "Aryan" theories of the Nazi theoreticians.

The Zionists set as one of their tasks to "achieve the unity of the Jewish people." Aside from anti-Semitism, which is doing this job more effectively than they, the outstanding common element of the various Dispersions is religion. Religious Zionism has always been one kind of Zionism among many, but as Zionist ideology boils down more and more clearly to its mystic tribal core, it is the religionists who feel their ideological strength.

More boldly than ever could the Religious Zionist (Mizrachi) caucus at the Jerusalem congress adopt its manifesto, calling for greater efforts to preserve religious values and traditions "which have always been and must continue to be in the future the main guarantee for the unity of the Jewish people throughout the world."

But that's the Mizrachi, who have always said so. it is interesting to read the following from a leading theoretician of the traditionally secular American Labor Zionist movement, in a pre-congress article entitled "Notes for a Labor Zionist Program":

> A religious designation to denote the totality of Jewish life in this country imposes the duty upon the Jewish community to adhere to certain mores and observe certain rituals which have their origin in the Jewish religion.

It is, of course, not the "religious designation" which "imposes" this duty. It is the Zionist's search for the elements of nationhood. He continues:

> The same duty should devolve upon the individual Jew. The voluntary acceptance of a minimum of observances must be his spiritual membership dues to the Jewish community, even as his

158

participation in its budgetary requirements must be his financial dues. This is necessary both to preserve Jewish identity in this country and to integrate the American Jewish community into the unity of Jewish peoplehood. We are approaching a time when the Jews of the world will no longer have a common living language. The cultural barriers between the Jews of one land and those of another are getting higher every day. In proportion as a Jewish community becomes integrated into the affairs of its native land and shares with the rest of the population fundamental values which do not belong to the Jewish legacy, the factors contributing to the fragmentation of the Jewish people will be strengthened. Only the preservation of meaningful Jewish traditions, the observance of Jewish holidays and folkways, and the fostering of modern Jewish culture and education, centered about and supplementing the creative efforts of Israel, will prevent Jewish disintegration. (C. Bezalel Sherman, Jewish Frontier, June.)

By "disintegration" he means assimilation.

Sherman, no doubt, wishes the "observances" without the theism, making of them not a ritual for the unseen God but a ritual for the hard-to-see nationhood. But in dealing with masses, as the Israeli leaders have to do, it is easier to eliminate the subtle distinctions. In Israel itself religion and religious observances play the role of a national cement. We have no doubt that Ben-Gurion and the secular Israelis have little personal sympathy for many of the excesses that characterize Israeli society in foisting religious practices upon all the people; but if there is less separation between church and state in Israel than almost anywhere else in the modern world, that scandalous fact is not solely due to the pressure or influence of the Mizrachi or the rabbis. It performs a nationalist function.

At the Jerusalem congress, there was an attempt (most particularly, apparently, by the Mapam delegates) to put the Ingathering of the Exiles on another and seemingly less mystical basis. Mapam delegates repeatedly, while supporting the majority thesis in favor of the liquidation of the diaspora into Israel as the goal, direly "warned U.S. Jews that they might meet the fate of some European Jewish communities, which ignored the call to Zion and perished." The state of mind of the American Jews was compared with that of the German Jews before the rise of Hitler. Come to Israel, they argued in effect, because anti-Semitism will get you in the long run anyway.

Only a Lessing Rosenwald or his co-thinkers might deny the gross reality of this danger; it is surely true that anti-Semitism in the West may yet rise to the heights of Hitlerism. But this horrible prospect is only a part of another, with which it goes hand in hand: the deterioration, totalitarianization and brutalization of capitalist society in decay on the one hand and of Stalinism on the other. But the Mapam delegates were not making their point in order to urge a fight against anti-Semitism; their argument was: Flee from anti-Semitism, flee now before it is too late!

It is the theory of the inevitability of anti-Semitism. This theory can have only one of two bases: (1) The working-class, socialist and democratic forces in the world are inevitably doomed to defeat; or (2) anti-Semitism is inevitable as long as Jews live with non-Jews, for reasons which cannot be less mystical and "tribal" than those we have already discussed. And as far as Mapam is concerned—it considers itself to be "left socialist" (actually Stalinoid)—it hardly subscribes to the first thesis. If any do, one may ask how much of a haven can be provided in such a world by Israel, which is surrounded by hostility even today.

Actually, the motivation of this argument is, again, an inversion of anti-Semitism itself: there is "something about the Jews" as such which makes persecution inevitable..

At the Jerusalem congress, on this question of the Ingathering and emigration to Israel, a compromise had to be reached, as everyone knew in advance. Ideologically, it was a rotten compromise, as it had to be. The Americans accepted the formula "Ingathering of the Exiles" as the task of Zionism—with their own rationalizations in mind. But the draft formulation had read: "the redemption of the Jewish people through the Ingathering of the Exiles." They boggled at tying up the Ingathering with redemption, and the latter was struck out, in order to achieve a unanimous vote (the chauvinist Herut delegates abstaining). Furthermore, the document was represented as the "tasks" of Zionism, not the "aims" of Zionism, the latter being held over for the future.

We must mention, in addition, another aspect of the declaration adopted which did not figure in the debates (as far as the reports have shown, pending the verbatim minutes). But it appears in the text. Set as the task of Zionism is "the Ingathering of the Exiles in Eretz Israel."

"Eretz Israel" is not the state of Israel. It is the whole of Palestine, that is, all of the land which the Zionists from the very beginning set as their homeland goal. It can be achieved only by expansion beyond the borders of the present state in conflict with the Arab Near East.

The use of this term in the document is not simply a nostalgic nod in the direction of a sentimental aspiration. discussion of the use of this term as against simply Israel may or may not have taken place at the congress (though it certainly did in the commission which drafted the declaration). The difference is highlighted by what happened with the draft for a new program which was prepared earlier this year by an American commission and which we have already mentioned. This draft read "ingathering into the state of Israel." Writing in the Congress Weekly for May 28, Joseph Schechtman, a leader of the Revisionists who participated in the commission's deliberations, reports that he proposed to amend it to read "land of Israel" or Eretz Israel. He leaves no possibility for misunderstanding:

> The alert reader will easily discern the fine point of difference of emphasis in the term 'State of Israel'—a recently established, internationally recognized sovereign territorial entity—and 'Land of Israel'—the everlasting patrimony of the Jewish people, the unique object of Zionism ... A 'Jerusalem Program' cannot disregard the wider concept of 'Eretz Israel' in its Zionist program. In this respect, 'Eretz Israel' is different from the State, which is bound to be the bearer of the legalistic, static interpretations of the term 'Land of Israel.' The Zionist movement can and must remain the bearer of the dynamic interpretation.

It was "Eretz Israel" that appeared in the congress document. It was the Revisionists and their allies who particularly insisted on it. Quite possibly, the other might have preferred not to make explicit the expansionist aims which cannot be divorced from the Zionist ideology; if its inclusion was a concession to the Revisionists or under their pressure, as may possibly though not certainly be true, that was not because of any opposition to the concept. The mystic tribalism of Zionism cannot help being implicitly expansionist.

Labor Action, September 17, 1951

Chapter X
"THOU SHALT NOT CRITICIZE ISRAEL"

Two recent episodes have underlined some truths about the dilemmas involved in the relationship between American Jews and the state of Israel—American Jews in particular though to a very large extent the same applies to all other Jewish communities outside of Israel.

The first was the statement made at the World Jewish Congress in Geneva by Dr. Nahum Goldmann, the leading figure in the world Zionist movement (if we except Israeli premier David Ben-Gurion himself).

Goldmann said: "Israel is unique among nations. There is no other state where 90 per cent of its people live outside it."

The Zionist ideology is epitomized in this capsule statement, particularly the Zionist view of what Israel is: the homeland not of its own inhabitants Jewish and Arab, and not even the homeland of its own Jewish inhabitants alone, but of all Jews everywhere in the world, regardless of the latter's own views on the matter.

This view of the state of Israel is the official ideology not only of Zionism but, unfortunately, of the Israeli government itself and of its leading parties and spokesmen. It is the ideology of the "Ingathering of the Exiles" which Ben-Gurion and others have so often enunciated.

It is a view which (1) implicitly makes all non-Jews, especially the Arab Israelis, aliens and interlopers in the land, the short- or long-term objective being to drive them out; (2) makes the perspective of Israel expansionist, no matter what diplomatic declarations on that score are put out for occasional world consumption by its leaders; and (3) poses the question of dual national allegiance for all Jews in the world as the Israelis see them, regardless of the fact that only a very small minority of Jews are made happy thereby.

Nahum Goldmann's statement of the theory of citizenship-by-ancestral-"blood" is itself not unique, though the Israeli state is unique today as the one presently existing prominent government which holds and acts on such a theory. it has been seen before in the world, though the most recent historical instance cannot be mentioned without making Zionists froth with anger. His statement of it in such forthright fashion was enough to awake a storm of protest in Jewish circles, even though he was merely reiterating what the Israeli Zionists and other Zionists have said many times before in unmistakable language.

Now one must be clear, we think, on the main reason behind the indignation that Goldmann's statement evoked among most American Jewish organizations. This reason is primarily point No. 3 in the above-listed implications of the Zionist theory of Israel:it comes into conflict with their "Americanism," in some cases with their "American" chauvinism and bourgeois patriotism.Many of these elements have been able to swallow in silence, though perhaps not with equanimity of conscience, the Israeli anti-Arab policies; but when the same ideology which leads to Israeli discrimination against the Arab people in the land also points to a conclusion touching on their own patriotic allegiance, they rise up in horror.

But this only explains why this particular statement of Goldmann's led to such an outcry, as if he had been saying something new or unheard-of, when actually he was merely repeating the heart of the Zionist creed.

For example, the same thought which led to the "scandal" over Goldmann's speech can be found officially embodied in the last Israeli Government Yearbook, in the introduction by Ben-Gurion.Here, the premier and Zionist leader wrote (we quote from Zion, the monthly published by the World Zionist Organization in Jerusalem, November 1952):

> The establishment of the [Israeli] State did not mean the vision fulfilled.For by far the greater part of the Jewish people is still divided among the nations, and so the State is not yet the consummation of redemption, but only its instrument and principal means.

Twice Ben-Gurion sets down a curious formulation in writing: "The greatest victory won by the Zionist idea over the Jewish people was the establishment of the State ..." And again, a few pages later, "I cannot too often declare that the State is the greatest conquest of the idea of Zionism over the Jewish people." He is referring to the fact that before the establishment of the state of Israel, the majority of the Jews of the world were opposed to the Zionist idea.

Has this changed?Indisputably, the overwhelming bulk of Jews are enthusiastic supporters of Israel's health development and self-preservation and development as a state; nor are well-wishes for Israel confined, or to be confined, to Jews.But the same question persists, though changed in form.

It is not:For Israel or Against Israel—this is only the way the Zionists inside and outside Israel see it.It is:For or against the Zionist program and ideology for Israel.

And this is a program and an ideology which is harmful and even suicidal for the Israeli people, in the opinion of many, including ourselves as Independent Socialists.At any rate this is how the real question is to be put.

For the Zionists this is not in question.Ben-Gurion writes in the above-mentioned introduction to the Government Yearbook: "The Jewish people is not an abstract notion, or just a collective name for myriads of isolated and scattered individuals in various countries.It is a conglomerate whose actuality, will and common destiny are not open to question." This common destiny, etc., which is not open to question is the expansionist Zionist view of the manifest destiny of Jewry to be ingathered from their "exile." Therefore he writes also: "It is essential for the Zionist movement to ... comprehend that it, the Jewish people and the State now form together a close-knit and indivisible unity."

The Zionists have been amazingly successful in their obscurantist effort to identify the two problems:(1) For or against Israel, and (2) For or against the Zionist program and ideology for Israel.That is, pursuing Ben-Gurion's thought that the establishment of the state is "the greatest victory won by the Zionist idea over the Jewish people." They have sought another "victory over the Jewish people," and this would be a victory indeed:to identify the cause of Israel with the cause of the Zionist ideology, if not the Zionist movement.

How much they have succeeded is indicated by the degree to which they have convinced non-Zionist Jews that all criticism of Israel is "disloyal" to the Jewish people and Israel.In this connection, a document of the greatest interest must be cited.

The interest which attached it to proceeds from the fact that in no other place we know of is the conception written down with such frankness that Israel must be considered immune from criticism by Jews because it is "ours." It is a letter sent by the general secretary of the Workman's Circle, Nahum Chanin, to the periodical Jewish Newsletter edited by William Zukerman (August 17 issue).Here Chanin puts into words what few others would be willing to say openly though it is common indeed.

"I want to write to you about a painful subject which agitates Jewish life at present," begins Chanin.He introduces his remarks by explaining that he is "a friend" of the Jewish Newsletter, which is an outstanding liberal foe of Zionism among Jewish periodicals.He explains further, by way of preface:

I am not a Zionist.I have been a Bundist (a Jewish socialist) all my life.I cannot accept the Zionist philosophy of life particularly in its application to Jewish culture and Jewish life in the Diaspora ... Zionism, which preaches the liquidation of Jewish life everywhere outside of Israel, will never strike a responding chord in my heart ... Thus my entire approach to Jewish life is in contradiction to that of Zionism and I cannot be considered a Zionist.

And indeed the rest of this revealing letter has its point just because of this avowal of (at least) non-Zionism.(We note in passing Chanin's reluctance to call himself an anti-Zionist, even though his statement of views add up to this:this is an example of a small-scale "victory won by the Zionist idea over the Jewish people.")

"But, at the same time," Chanin's letter says as it comes to the point,

I believe that Israel will soon become an important factor in Jewish life and we have to help with everything in our power to put it on its feet.Your publication [the Jewish Newsletter] takes an opposite view.For instance, you frequently take the part of the wronged Arabs.I admit that great injustices have been committed against the Arabs.But to re-admit the Arabs to Israel now would mean a tragedy for the Jewish state.At the present moment, I dare to say that every Arab admitted to Israel would be a member of the Fifth Column for the state.Those Arabs who are in the country should, of course, remain.But to admit those who escaped would be a very grave mistake.I believe that the Arabs should receive compensation and reparation in money, but they should not be admitted to the country.

There are black spots on the sky of Israel, but they are natural in a country which has just begun to reconstruct itself.And where reconstruction is going on under conditions worse than that of any other new state.It would be a terrible catastrophe for the Jewish people if the state of Israel were to disappear.The difference between my position and yours is that I say without hesitation that we must do everything possible to avert such a catastrophe and to help and strengthen Israel, while you say:We are for the state of Israel; we wish her success, but you proceed to find fault with it.

There it is in all its naivete, set down no doubt with "painful" frankness by a prominent figure in non-Zionist Jewish circles.The key, of course, is the last sentence: "The difference between my position and yours" is that you criticize the policies and acts of the Israeli leaders.

That is what speaks eloquently about this non-Zionist frame of mind, though we have quoted the whole of the passage for its interest as a specimen in political psychology.Its lack of logic and internal contradiction only manifest the split-thinking which has gone into it.Chanin, for example, starts off by saying "Your publication takes an opposite view" when he seems to be talking about the desire "to help Israel with everything in our power to put it on its feet." He does not mean, of course, that the publication is opposed to helping Israel; on the contrary, he says in the next paragraph that it too agrees "We are for the state of Israel; we wish her success"—only ... only it still insists on "finding fault," criticizing.

His discussion of the Arab question in Israel is purely evasive, at the best.The biggest problem is the policy of the Israeli government toward the Arabs now within its borders; but while the government has lately struck new blows at these its own Arab citizens, Chanin talks as if the only problem for a non-Zionist well-wisher of Israel is the readmission of those Arabs who fled.But it would be a digression, however tempting, to discuss these remarks on the Arabs.Chanin's intention is not to whitewash the Israeli Arab policy.He is saying:If we publicly "find fault" with what they are doing, this will weaken Israel.

To socialists the pattern is a familiar one.It is the pattern of the best-intentioned apologists for Stalinism, more familiar some time ago than today, it is true, but familiar nonetheless.Chanin's letter is written in the same accents, with the same confused groping, the same combination of heart-burning and reservations, as characterized so many people who so long continued to denounce all criticism of Russia as "anti-Soviet" and "reactionary" at the same time that they muttered and protested and criticized privately or secretly.What we have here is an analogue of the frame of mind of certain American liberals who, although never Stalinists, long persisted in avoiding any criticism of Russia for fear of harming a noble experiment—and to some extent still so persist.

Chanin cannot understand that liberal Jewish leaders like himself (he calls himself a "socialist" but we can ignore this little concession to nostalgia) can best serve the interests of the Israeli people by refusing to whitewash the deeds and policies which put the Jewish people in jeopardy in their little island-state in the midst of an Arab world.He cannot understand that loyal criticism is often necessary to loyal support.

But there is very little to be said about this that has not long been said about the similar state of mind of non-Stalinist apologists for Stalinist Russia, and the rest of the argument will be well known to our readers.For a long time during the period of degeneration of revolutionary Russia under the aegis of Stalinism, this same type of liberal used to call the press of our own movement "anti-Soviet" because it devoted its columns to signalizing the crimes of the Stalinist leadership, instead of joining in the paeans of praise to the "great accomplishments" of the Kremlin.

Indeed, the Chanin-type is a victim of the Zionist euphoria which the establishment of the state of Israel caused.It is not unknown even among socialists, and our own criticisms of Israeli policies have met with reactions which stemmed from the same roots.

Such "friends of Israel" are no friends of Israel, we know from long similar experience with "friends of the Soviet Union," despite their excellent intentions. And the truth has to be said.Chanin has perhaps unwittingly done a valuable service in putting the question so clearly.

Labor Action September 14, 1953

Chapter XI
GERMAN REPARATIONS
AND 'BLOOD-RESPONSIBILITY'

The current uproar in Jewish circles here and in Israel over the question of German reparations to Jews offers a disturbing picture. It should at least be disturbing not only to socialists but also to genuine liberals, Jewish liberals first of all. To get perfectly clear about it, a general comment on approach has to be made first.

The excesses and mistakes of the victims of an outrage are by no means to be equated, or even discussed on the same level, with the barbarity of the perpetrators of the outrage themselves. We have at times had to make that point in a different but somewhat similar connection: the reaction of some among the Negro people to Jim Crow brutality.

There is the white chauvinism of the white-supremacy hoodlums and racists; and there is the "black chauvinism" of some misguided (and fortunately very few) Negro elements who react by becoming anti-white, instead of looking for allies among the white enemies of Jim Crow. This is no major problem for the Negro fight today, we are glad to say, and we recall it only for the lesson it teaches.

Such "black chauvinism" has been combated energetically by the best fighters for the Negro people, and it has to be, but this fight is on an entirely different plane from the fight against Jim Crow itself. The latter is the fight against the enemy camp; the former is a struggle against mistakes in that fight by people who ought to be in our camp. But unless those mistakes are set right, the enemy will not be beaten, but will be built up to greater strength.

Just as the "black chauvinist" reaction is understandable, in view of the horrible wrongs inflicted upon the Negro people by dominant elements of the white race, so also do we understand the emotional drives behind the attitudes being expressed in Jewish circles about German reparations. But these attitudes are wrong, self-defeating, and harmful to the Jewish people, and so it is not enough merely to sympathize with their motivation.

The question arose when the West German government, assuming responsibility for repairing the crimes against the Jewish people committed by the Nazi German regime, offered to pay reparations in order to help the surviving victims. A good part of such reparations would go to Israel.

The proposal has been greeted in the most prominent Jewish circles with an outburst of anti-German hatred. No, not anti-Nazi hatred—anti-German hatred.

The article by a Jewish liberal journalist which we reprint on this page describes the anti-German tempest in the American Jewish press. Along the same lines, on January 8 the N.Y. Herald Tribune reported a speech by the vice-president of the Zionist Organization of America, Jacques Torczyner, who denounced any acceptance of such payment as on a par with taking blood-money. "We shouldn't even sit down at the same table with murderers of 6 million Jews," he said.

The Israeli government is for accepting the reparations, because the money will help solve Israel's financial problems, but its leaders and spokesmen are making doubly sure that their vituperations against the German people as a whole are somewhere near as violent as those of the Israeli fascist and semi-fascist chauvinists, whose hysteria is being whipped up by Menachem Begin of the Herut party. Prime Minister Ben-Gurion argued that reparations should be taken because "the murderer shall not keep his loot."

On both of these sides the first principle is that the German people as such, and their leaders as such, are to be considered as murderers, Nazi exterminationists and on a par with the Hitlerites. They accept Hitler's theory of racial guilt and national guilt. They merely turn it inside-out, just as the "black chauvinists" turn inside-out the racism of their oppressors. And they apply their racist theory to those who were the first victims of the Nazi criminals—the masses of the German people who fought and were conquered by Hitler, whose best elements suffered in Hitler's concentration camps and whose survivors are not being recompensed.

Such a theory is a "natural," for the Revisionists like Begin. It is, as we said, only too "understandable" on the part of others. What is disturbing is that so many Jewish liberals and socialists, who ought to know better, do not raise their voice or, what is worse, go along with the anti-German hysteria.

How deep this hysteria is may be seen in the following contrast:

Last year, when the socialist parties of various countries came together in Frankfurt, Germany, to re-create the Socialist International, the socialist Jewish Bund entered a protest—against the fact that the conference was being held on German soil! Behind this protest was the same kind of thinking that has burst out so virulently now.

Contrast this with even the notorious issue published by the editors of Collier's magazine on how Russia was defeated in an atomic war. We deliberately refer to this horrific production because (as we sought to show in our article on it) there have been few more blatant examples of

American chauvinism. Yet, even in this product of chauvinistic thinking, we find, as the editors of the magazine envisaged it, that following Stalin's defeat and overthrow the world Olympic games are held in Moscow—as a demonstration of goodwill to the Russian people!

But is the German nation a nation of murderers, and the Russian nation is not? Were Hitler's crimes (including the numbers murdered) greater than are Stalin's? Did Hitler have that much more mass support or toleration or passive acceptance than Stalin? Or will Russia too become a nation of murderers if his mass holocausts extend to the Jews specifically as fully as they have blanketed the Russians—not to speak of the non-Russian subject nations within his empire?

It is to be hoped that this chauvinist poison will pass—not "forgiveness" for the crimes against the Jews, not forgetfulness of the ordeal of a people, but this chauvinist poison. Let the anger and hatred of the Jewish people, and for that matter of anyone who (say) has read The Wall—turn not against the German people in an inverted racist frenzy, but against the friends and heirs of Hitlerism still at large. Let them give support and encouragement to the most intransigent enemies of Hitlerism in Germany, the Social-Democratic Party, and remain less silent about the rehabilitation of former Nazi activists by the Adenauers with the toleration and even encouragement of U.S. officials! (That is, less silent about American responsibility for this development!)

There are still fascist elements in Germany, who are worming their way back; there are such in France and other Western countries, who have not yet built their gas chambers; anti-Semitism is blooming even more strongly in the Stalinist totalitarian world. It is not a question of races or nations, but of the totalitarian forces spawned by a decaying capitalist and Stalinist world. Not forgiveness and not racism—but a socialist fight against reaction is the answer.

Labor Action January 21, 1952

171

Chapter XII
ZIONISM vs. THE JEWS:
ISRAEL'S NATIONALITY ACT

The Nationality Act adopted by the Israel parliament on March 25, and which became law on April 1, once more illustrates the difference between two sentiments which are too often confused: on the one hand, Israeli nationalism, and on the other, Zionist Jewish chauvinism.

It is the Zionist Jewish chauvinism which has put its stamp upon the new law.

And in doing so it gives aid and comfort to anti-Semitism, it jeopardizes the future of Israel as a nation, it inflames precisely the reactionary forms of Arab nationalism in the Middle East, and it serves to encumber the road to a solution of Israel's pressing economic crisis.

The new Nationality Act does this in two related ways.

(1) It discriminates against non-Jews (mainly Israeli Arabs, of course) by depriving them of citizenship unless they were citizens of Palestine before the establishment of the new state and can prove continuous residence in territory now held by Israel and unless they were included in the official register before January 1, 1952.

(2) It extends the right of immediate citizenship to all Jews of any nationality, permitting them to hold double nationality—in the country from which they have emigrated and in Israel.

This makes sense only from the point of view of the Zionist ideology, and not from the viewpoint of building a united nation or of easing the situation of Israel as an island-ghetto in an Arab world or of making peace with the Arab world.

The grant of double citizenship and special privilege to Jews of all countries is, of course, not at all required by the desire to make Israel a haven for Jews oppressed in other lands, who could have no difficulty in becoming Israeli citizens without these special provisions. What it means is that the peculiarly Zionist aim of the "Ingathering of the Exiles" has been written into the basic law of the state. Its sponsors openly stated during the debate in the Knesset that it was designed especially to encourage the immigration of Jews from the United States without "burning their bridges behind them" as far as citizenship is concerned. (Though as a matter of fact U.S. law forbids double citizenship.)

In writing the "Ingathering of the Exiles" into state law, the Knesset made official the Zionist theory that Jews are "exiles" in an alien land wherever they live, outside of Israel, regardless of their traditions, culture, roots and conditions, and that it is the duty of the "Jewish tribes" everywhere to leave their "exile" and "return." (It was the Israeli Zionists at the last world Zionist congress who spoke in these terms of the Jewish "tribes.")

As William Zukerman, editor of the liberal Jewish Newsletter, points out,

> it revives a dangerous racist theory that smacks of the slogan of a previous generation, "A German is a German wherever he is.'

And further:

> this law, passed by a state which calls itself the 'Jewish State,'may be interpreted by some future anti-Semitic government as an invitation to deport its Jews to Israel.
>
> In any event, such a law strengthens the moral position of the anti-Semites in all countries by confirming their claim that Jews are aliens everywhere, that they cannot become a real part of any country or civilization, except in Israel. Such a law, abysmally false as its theory is, may in an age of propaganda cause irreparable harm to millions of innocent Jews in this and in other countries, who have nothing to do with nationalism in any form and do not even know of the existence of its fantastic claims, and yet may be made to pay the penalty of nationalistic excesses.

Before coming back to this point, we must also make clear what will be the effect of the provisions regarding non-Jews. Like the notorious "grandfather" clauses of Jim Crow laws in the American Southern States, the exact nature of the conditions set for citizenship by Israeli Arabs is not the main point; the point is that, quite beyond a doubt, the conditions have been devised for no other purpose than to exclude the vast majority of Israeli Arabs from nationality in the state. To become citizens, they must be naturalized, even though they and their ancestors have lived in the land longer than its present governors.

The difference between the Israeli Nationality Act and the aforementioned "grandfather clauses" does not reflect credit on the Israelis. The "grandfather clauses" and their successors today make no official distinction between Negroes and whites. This is hypocrisy, of course, but, as Samuel Butler said of hypocrisy, it is the homage which vice pays to virtue. The Israeli law pays no homage at all to any democratic concept of citizenship; it is unabashedly chauvinist.

174

Not only in Israel but also in Zionist circles in this country, opposition to the chauvinist content of Zionism is often assimilated to "anti-Semitism," with approximately the same type of methodology as when anti-Nazism in Hitler Germany was denounced by the regime as "anti-Germanism" or anti-Stalinism is denounced by the Kremlin as treason to the fatherland. Among the victims of this kind of smear campaign have been liberal Jews.

The fact is, however, that the consistent Zionist ideology is bisymmetric to anti-Semitism, and fosters it. Both take as their starting point the view that the Jews are a "peculiar people" who cannot live in harmony with other peoples, that they are an incurably alien element. The alienness of the Jews is given documentary and legal reinforcement by the extension of automatic double citizenship.

The proper commentary upon this with relation to the Israeli Nationality Act has already been made by prominent Jewish anti-Zionist spokesmen. Writing in the New York Forward of April 26, Dr. B. Hoffman-Zivion says, beginning with some gentle irony directed against the Zionist habit of excommunicating opponents from the Jewish community:

> If it is the sacred duty of a Jew to say that everything the state of Israel says or does is wise and good, then I will have to say that the Citizenship Law (recently) passed by the state is also wise and good; but if I am permitted to exercise my democratic rights to freedom of opinion, I will surely say that the law passes is very unwise and very unfair. I was even going to say that it is a very unjust law, but was restrained by the fear of being charged with taking sides with the Arabs, which, in this day of raging nationalism, is the greatest of crimes ...
>
> As I have said at the outset, I will not raise the question of justice in connection with this discrimination. I know that the morality of nationalism is generally of the Hottentot kind, holding that 'if I take your wife away from you, it is good; but if you take my wife away from me, then it is bad.' We holler murder when someone discriminates against us, but we think it perfectly in order for us to discriminate against others. But should we not take into consideration that only a small portion of the Jewish people lives in the Jewish land, while the bulk of Jews live among other peoples? ...
>
> Our perennial cry against the 'Goyim' has been that they discriminate against Jews, and we have always felt that it was a just

cry. Can we feel about it the same way now? Could they not come back at us and say: 'And are you Jews better people? Are you not, in fact, discriminating against the non-Jews who live in your land?'

A similar point is made by the assistant professor of sociology at New York University, Dr. Israel Knox, writing in the Jewish Socialist Vecker (May 1):

> Israeli's new citizenship law which has now been accepted by the Knesset is undemocratic and non-Jewish because it is a denial of the sacred rights of [morality]. The worst of the law is the part which deals with approximately 170,000 Arabs in Israel. Logically, these Arabs whose fathers and forefathers lived in Palestine for hundreds of years should be considered equal with Jews in the privilege of immediate citizenship. But reason is one thing and nationalistic fanaticism is something else ...
>
> Behind that law burns the fire of nationalistic chauvinism, and who will gain by this law? It will certainly play into the hands of the Communists. It will place mountains of obstacles on the road to peace with the Arab states without which Israel is sentenced to a tragically uncertain existence. The law must and will inflame the hatred in the Middle East and will destroy the loyalty of the more moderate Arabs in Israel. Certainly, it will not add to the health of the Jewish communities outside of Israel, especially in the United States, which must fight for liberal immigration laws. Why should Senator McCarran be better than Ben-Gurion? Why should Lehman, young Roosevelt and Celler get from the American Congress what Israel does not do in its own country?

But the most serious long-term disability of the new law is the one stressed by Dr. Knox—that it intensifies the Arab-Jewish cold war in the Middle East precisely at a time when even the reactionary Arab leaders have been reduced to pressing one main demand, the question of the Arab refugees. It is a slap in the face for all the Arab people and can only serve to push them closer to the rulers with whom they are saddled. At the same time that the hope of Arab-Jewish peace, which is essential to the economic well-being of the state of Israel, is pushed further away, Israel has to devote more and more of its inadequate resources to the crushing burden of armaments, which oppress the Israeli Jews also and make their lot bitter.

Labor Action, June 2, 1952

Chapter XIII
ANTI-SEMITISM AND ARAB PROPAGANDA

A new book published by the Anti-Defamation League of B'nai B'rith—Cross Currents, by Forster and Epstein—has created a bit of a stir as an expose of anti-Semitic propaganda in the United States, especially as connected with international "plots." A press conference to launch it rated prominent write-ups in most of the New York papers and a black front-page scream-head in the Scripps-Howard outlet New York World-Telegram.

I am concerned here with the last third of the book, entitled "Cross-Currents in the Middle East," which deals with Arab pro-paganda activities in this country and their connections with native anti-Semitic agitation. This part of the ADL book is an excellent example of a disturbing trend, with reference to the fight against anti-Semitism, about which some honest words need to be said but rarely are.

*

The background fact, of course, is the war of propaganda in this country to line up the government and public opinion on one side or the other of the Israel-Arab conflict in the Middle East. Given U.S. power in the world, the stakes are considerable for the rivals.

In this propaganda war, it is also not surprising that the Arabs are hopelessly outclassed, outpointed, outthought and out-argued.

Sympathy for Israel is far from limited to the Jewish population. Leaving aside here the rights and wrongs of the Palestinian disputes: it is a fact that there is, or at any rate has been, a vast fund of sympathy for Israel which stems from vivid knowledge of the horrors and atrocities committed against the Jews by the Nazi regime's exterminationism, and a view of Israel as simply the place where the pitiful remnant of European Jewry found refuge.

There is also more than an element of a guilty conscience involved: if hundreds of thousands of Jewish DPs had to go to Israel, it was (among other reasons) because the gates of the United States and other virtuous democratic countries were closed against them. Outside of socialists like ourselves, there were few who shouted very loudly against this "democratic" compounding of the atrocities against the Jews. A few liberals took it to heart; there was not even a respectable-sized campaign to demand that the doors be opened.

There are other strands in the pattern of pro-Israel sentiment in this country, and there is a well-organized movement, with massive institutions of its own, to develop this sentiment to the full. This is the Zionist movement, plus its "non-Zionist" allies like the American Jewish Committee and the B'nai B'rith, who are ready to go down the line in defense of Israel's interests in spite of their ideological and in part muted disagreements with the Zionists' theories of Jewish nationalism.

The above description attempts to skirt the question of the comparative justice or injustice of Israel's case at various times in the last few years and its relative appeal, in order to put the spotlight on the constant factors behind the judgments of public opinion on an episode like the Kibya massacre (which had an anti-Israel effect) or like the Egyptian arms deal (which had an opposite effect).

For the apparatuses which are drawn up in such a propaganda war are not built by justice or injustice though their effectiveness is conditioned by it. Certainly that is true in this case.

For comparison, think (say) of the wide American sympathy for the Irish struggle against Britain in the years especially before the First World War—a sympathy that lost nothing because of the large numbers of Irish in this country, and which was enhanced by combination with historical factors like traditional anti-Britishism here.

If anything, the advantages possessed by pro-Israel sentiment are even greater. Certainly, there are few impulsions to sympathy with the case of the Arabs, about whom Americans in general know little and who have only a small number of their people among our population. Most Americans have never seen an Arab except in movies about the French Foreign Legion.

So in a propaganda war in the U.S., under the best of circumstances for them the Arab states have two strikes against them in every respect, not excluding the financial one.

In addition, they suffer from a self-created handicap: their propagandists are stupid, incompetent, understand little about this country, and would never be effective even if a couple of millions were put behind them (though, of course, with a bankroll that size, more knowledgeable agents could be purchased).

This is said on the basis of personal acquaintance with Arab propaganda material here, which I happen to be looking into particularly in connection with the question of Israel's Arab minority. Take the matter of falsification of facts, for example: this can be done by propagandists in either a professional or an amateurish way.

178

The Israel Government office in New York, for instance, puts out a pamphlet on "The Arabs in Israel" which is a slick, persuasive job, guaranteed to convince anyone who knows nothing at all on the subject that the Arab minority in Israel is a pampered group with completely equal rights and opportunities. It is a polished and professional job of combining half-truths with falsification.

Its opposite number is a pamphlet on the same subject distributed by the Arab Information Office in New York (run by the Arab League). It was not smart of the authors of this pamphlet to prove Zionist crimes by (say) quoting "the Zionist paper Kol Ha'am," as if they were citing an indictment out of the mouths of the Zionists themselves. Anyone who tries to use this ammunition would find out quickly enough that Kol Ha'am is the organ of the Israel Communist Party, not a "Zionist paper," and the real bullets in his ammunition would explode along with this dud.

Or take another bombshell put out in the war of propaganda which is our subject: a pamphlet published last year for English-language consumption by the Syrian government and distributed through the Syrian offices in this country. It is entitled Tension, Terror, and Blood in the Holy Land, published in Damascus, prepared by one Musa Khuri of the Syrian University, under the imprimatur of the "Palestine Arab Refugees Institution."

From the purely technical point of view, this 253-page booklet is terribly written, terribly organized, wandering, a mass or mess of documentation, comment, quotations, side excursions, etc. But we were speaking not simply of garden-variety incompetence but of stupid-type falsification.

One of the sections of this compendium purports to be excerpts from the excellent article by Dr. Don Peretz on "The Arab Minority in Israel" in the Middle East Journal for Spring 1954. Naturally this article appeals to the Arabs because it tells a good part of the truth about the mistreatment of this minority. The writer, Peretz, is a sincere follower of the ideas of the Israeli Ichud and believes in Jewish-Arab cooperation; therefore, simply by telling the truth and not by polemic, he indicts the government policy. It is natural that Arab propaganda likes to quote denunciations of authoritarianism in the Arab states. All this is fair game for the machines.

But the Damascus authors were not content simply to print it. Incredible as it may seem, they rewrote sentence after sentence in the quoted paragraphs to make it say not what Peretz wrote but what their own propaganda line demands.

Now this is the sort of crude falsification which shows lack of sophistication, unnecessary heavy-handedness. It has the gaucherie of the feudal reactionary who has never had to take account of how modern minds work, and therefore how to deceive them.

It is also typical of Arab propaganda. The stupidity to which we have referred is not individual but social. It reminds one of the fantastic degree of incompetence in modern methods of procedure which the Arab armies displayed in the Palestine war of 1948, and why the Israelis were able to plaster them in spite of numerical and material inferiority. It is the stupidity of a dinosaurian social organism that is socially obsolete.

Nothing could be more ridiculous than to paint these people as Middle Eastern Fu Manchus subtly weaving their oriental webs of intrigue and deceit around us poor unsuspecting fresh-faced upstanding Americans. The truth is exactly the opposite. When it comes to propaganda, these Arab propagandists are babes in our woods—and this is part of the reason they play with some of the animals in our woods rather than with the humans.

But we are not through with this Damascus pamphlet which is being circulated here, since our subject is anti-Semitic propaganda, and not simply the troubles of Arabs in a modern civilization.

The booklet opens with a disclaimer of anti-Semitism and recurs to this disclaimer in many ways; but this does not prevent it from falling into anti-Semitic ruts. It purports to be denouncing only Zionism, which it often and clearly differentiates from the Jews as a whole; but this does not prevent it in other sections from slipping into blatant anti-Jewish expressions.

On page 20, for example, there is a passage which may or may not be quoted from another book called This Sword for Allah, by one Lawrence Griswold, though the passage lacks quote marks. In any case, the following occurs:

> ... Men who come [to Israel] from the United States with firm pro-Zionist convictions returned a few months later with bitter hatred toward all Jews, excepting perhaps, those whom they personally knew to be fair. One American Jew, a prominent man in his city, told me with a groan, after his visit to Israel: 'Why, those kikes aren't even human!'

On page 4, the booklet refers to Protestant clergymen who are sympathetic to Zionism and, in a slip, calls them "Protestant

Judaizers"—hardly making sense for people who claim to distinguish so insistently between Zionism and Judaism.

But the longest such passage occurs on pages 62–3, in a section entitled "Zionist Organization in the United States," which has nothing on the subject of Zionist organization in the U.S. (a vulnerable subject even for Arab propagandists), but rather devotes itself exclusively to a certain obscure article in the Brooklyn Jewish Examiner which dealt with Jewish life in a typical American small town—Lorain, Ohio. The article, apparently, was (for its source) a more or less typical account in glowing terms of a strongly maintained Jewish community life.

The Syrian booklet peppers it with its interpretations:

...A remarkable example of the cohesiveness which has typified the Jew, not only in the U.S. but in every other country where he has settled ... . the Jews of Lorain, Ohio have set themselves apart from the American community in which they live... They stress Jewish culture [stated as an accusation]... . In all this the Jews of Lorain, Ohio follow an age-old tradition. If you go to Cairo, or London, or Buenos Aires, or Casablanca you will find the Jews there practicing the same mode of racial exclusiveness as they do in Lorain. And if you check closely you will observe that the Jew of Cairo, no less than his brethren in London, regards himself as a Jew first and as an English or Egyptian citizen secondly. By the same token American Jews give a necessary allegiance to the U.S. while reserving their first loyalty for 'Israel.' That is the pattern which has been followed for centuries; it is the pattern they follow today.

Whatever else may be said about this tirade, it is certainly clear at least that it is a harangue against Jews as such, all Jews, the Jewish people as a whole, and not against "Zionists" alone; and that the stereotypes implied or insinuated are derived from well-known anti-Semitic routines.

Since the Forster-Epstein book Cross-Currents devotes its last part precisely to trying to prove an anti-Semitic strain in Arab propaganda here, as we shall see, it is hard to see how they have overlooked this booklet, since nothing so far published by official Arab authorities in this field equals it in the brashness of its anti-Semitic thrusts. Certainly there is nothing in the ADL book which approaches it as public and documented evidence for the thesis. If the small army of espionage agents and undercover operators, not to speak of agent-provocateurs, employed by the Anti-Defamation League have not been able to turn it up for the reading of Messrs. Forster and Epstein, then I gladly contribute this bit of information: You can get a copy of the incriminating evidence by making a phone call to the Syrian Consulate in Manhattan.

But before we turn our attention to what is in the ADL book, let us now raise the question: what is this Arab "anti-Semitism"? Is it simply Machiavellian guile that the Syrian authors repudiate anti-Semitism on one page—on many pages—and practice it on others?

A favorite Arab gambit, of course, is the well worn bit about how Arabs cannot be anti-Semitic because they are Semites themselves. This remark is not completely pointless, to be sure, because it does illustrate the terminological inexactitude of the term Semitic has any more scientific meaning than the term Aryan. But this is only a bit of curiosa.

What is really involved, as the Arab authors know quite well when need be, is the difference between anti-Jewish and anti-Zionist, for one thing. When we cite derogatory stereotypes against the Jews as a whole, the Jews as such, then whether we call it anti-Semitism or no, it is the same thing, isn't it?

...Well, is it? There is a question that pops up once we start calling it anti-Jewishness, rather than the more trickily connotative term anti-Semitism.

Take, for example, the sentiment of anti-Britishism, or anti-foreignism in general, in the Middle East, especially backward portions of it. Legitimate nationalist feelings and aspirations have often, of course, taken the British imperialists as their butt, since the crimes of this imperialism are most immediate and best known there. A politically better educated populace, or section of the population, may be able to distinguish sharply between being anti-British-imperialism and being anti-British—between attacking a British imperialist cop, and denouncing British culture—between taking action against an occupation army, and xenophobia. The more advanced a nationalist movement the more likely such distinctions will be made; the more backward the social base of a nationalist movement, the more likely is the element of xenophobia.

But however regrettable it may be, however much one may condemn it, is it "racism," in the sense connoted by anti-Semitism, when nationalist sentiment spills over to a virulent anti-Britishism, or a bitter anti-Americanism in the course of a struggle against these states?

And is the Arabs' "anti-Jewishism" of the racist type or of the nationalist type—given the fact that it is the state of Israel itself, and the whole world Zionist movement, that insists heatedly and inflexibly that "the Jews" not only of Israel itself (the immediate enemy seen by the Arabs) but of the whole world are a single nation indivisible?

There is reason to inquire whether or not the charge of anti-Semitism, as applied to the Arabs, is itself an unthinking stereotype, especially when we find that the charge is made in a fashion which has all the attributes of a smear. This is not an easy question, especially since one type can shade into or evoke the other.

Let us approach the ADL book with this question, and go from there to some other cases where the anti-Semitic label has been thrown about for purposes which can only harm the interests of the Jewish people and of the fight against anti-Semitism.

The actual butt of this book is far from just being allegedly anti-Semitic Arabs. One of its main victims is the organization known as the American Friends of the Middle East. At various points, stabs are made in the direction of any anti-Zionism. Under the head of what purports to be merely an expose of anti-Semites, there is adroitly woven in a thorough whitewash of Israeli policy on the Arab refugees and other matters; such a whitewash is the authors' democratic right, of course, but we are speaking of the way it is done; by smearing together, as if inextricably linked, criticisms of Israel policy with anti-Semitic rubbish.

The book, in other words, is a noteworthy example of a tendency on the part of Zionist circles, and their friends, to use and abuse the cry of anti-Semitism as a means of intimidating or discrediting any critics of Zionist or Israeli policy. This is what the present article is concerned with.

But first on the Arab angle:

The Forster-Epstein book presents a certain amount of evidence purporting to link up Arab officials here with notorious American anti-Semites like Gerald L.K. Smith, James Madole, Allen Zoll, Merwin K. Hart, Robert Williams, etc. The latter's names pepper the whole section.

Briefly, the evidence adduced in the book, stripped down to its essential content, would indicate that: these American anti-Semites use Arab charges against Israel as part of their anti-Semitic propaganda; they have pressed Arab officials to accept their help in "fighting Zionism"; Arab officials have had lunch with them and discussed with them what they can do; some of them have toured the Arab countries and have been received in friendly style; certain Arab officials have given them money for publishing articles supporting Arab charges; Arab officials have helped circulate pamphlets on the same subject published by such anti-Semites.

In most cases of a serious charge, the proof rests on the assertion that so-and-so did or said such-and-such in private conversations or at meetings such as could be reported only by undercover agents. The weight of most of the evidence would depend on one's evaluation of the reliability and nature of the ADL's undercover agents and sources.

There are almost no distinctions made among Arabs: an Arab is an Arab. An Arab may be quoted without necessarily bothering to mention whether he has any connection with the Arab Information Center here or not; whether he has any connection with others cited; whether he has any connection with any Arab government. Each is quoted as if he were an official representative of the Arab world. At any rate, this is the effect achieved by the method of presentation used in the book, which consists of inter-bureau "memos" of ADL offices, juxtaposed one after the other, with no necessary relationship or explanation.

Anti-Jewish or even pro-Nazi tirades from Arab newspapers in various countries are quoted with no indication whether these quoted newspapers are responsible spokesmen for any significant Arab viewpoint, or which viewpoint, or what they are. This looks like the other side of the coin of the Arab office's habit of quoting Israeli papers as if they were all identical, even when one of them is Kol Ha'am, the Israeli Communist Party organ.

This will have to do for the "Arab" part of this book's target; for we repeat it is not this aspect that we are most interested in at this point.

Students in the art of propaganda-slanting would do well to study the methods of Forster and Epstein.

The main method is to interweave, juxtapose, and sandwich-together the activities and ideas of known anti-Semites with all other activities and ideas which the authors are interested in discrediting. We have already mentioned that the literary method—a series of compiled office "memos"—allows for complete free-wheeling in the interweaving process; there is no necessary continuity between successive memos, and often there isn't any relation.

Thus, at one moment the reader will be reading some hair-raising statement quoted from (say) Allan Zoll in vilification of Jews; in the next paragraph he will be reminded of the Arab demand that Israel take back refugees; somewhere along, there will be thrown in some link between anti-Semite and the Arabs—say, a note that so-and-so came to lunch. If we look at the "filling" of the "sandwiching" process, it turns out in many cases to be a number of criticisms of Israeli policy which are common among all kinds of critics of Israel, including Jewish critics, and which have nothing whatsoever to do with anti-Semitism.

184

This, as a matter of fact, is systematically done in the introduction to the whole section. This introduction is not put together in the form of "memos." It is written out as a setting of the stage for the "memos."

Here, in brief, as their introduction to a study of anti-Semitism, Forster-Epstein go through Arab charges against Israel. Then the connection is made: "Whatever the themes of Arab propaganda may be, one of its goals in this country is precisely similar to that of every dyed-in-the-wool American anti-Semite... This calculation [by the Arabs] determines the goal of their propaganda here, and that goal is also the over-all aim of the professional American anti-Semite, whatever his motivations: it is the utter destruction of Jewish prestige in America."

This—and it is the heart of the book's discussion—seems quite similar to the well-known Stalinist proof that Trotskyists are fascists: for do they not share the fascist's goal of discrediting the Socialist Fatherland?

Here is another important Forster-Epstein connection: "When Arab sources inspire a propaganda argument in their continuing anti-Jewish campaign, its theme immediately becomes a regular part of our native bigots' stock in trade."

Now Forster-Epstein are not here referring to themes like the "Elders of Zion" fable. Not at all. They immediately list two. Both are charges not against "the Jews" but against (a) Israel, and (b) Zionists. Both are criticisms that have been made plentifully by responsible, liberal, Jewish and pro-Jewish critics of Israel and Zionism. Much can be said about them. But this book is interested only in weaving them in as Arab and anti-Semitic "lies."

This procedure is the typical sort of thing about which we are concerned. It colors the character of the whole book.

In a subsequent disclaimer of this very method, the authors protest that it would be "inaccurate to equate Arab representatives with native hate-mongers." This sounds very fair. They are not interested in "equating." They are intent upon the effective "amalgam," the tie-in, in a context where charges against Zionist and Israeli policy are indignantly mentioned and indignantly rejected as tainted with the anti-Semitic amalgam.

In this context the authors permit themselves to write that those Palestinian Arabs who did not flee during the war "have retained their property" and "enjoy equal rights" with no qualifications. This assertion has little resemblance to the far more complicated and much less pleasant truth.

With regard to the method of equating anti-Semitism with anti-Zionism, there is an especially simple example on page 361; a memo ("Middle Eastern Correspondent to Research") quotes the Cairo radio—"verbatim," it emphasizes, so as to imply that here is something damning. The entire quote is as follows:

> The information office which was opened several days ago by the Arab countries in New York is the first step. ...There is no doubt that Zionist propaganda and influence in the United States is strong. The new Arab bureau in New York should expose all Zionist plots and propaganda to the American people. We must not squander any more time in agreeing on a policy for that bureau.

That's absolutely all. No comment, as often. Presumably some revelation has been communicated. It is the memo before and after which have something to do with anti-Semitism. There is no connection at all among them, except that they are printed one after the other. And the only reason we chose this particular example to quote is that it is short.

As a mirror-image of the method used by the anti-Semites themselves, the authors play fast and loose with the equation: Zionists = Jews. Compare the following two passes, for example.

On page 328, a "memo" says Rahim of the Arab office has told friends that "Most Americans do not distinguish between Zionists and Jews,"and this fact has to be carefully exploited. On page 369 a "memo" quotes from a "directive" to students put out by the Arab office itself. It is a remarkable memo. There was obviously absolutely nothing in this "directive" that has the remotest appearance of anti-Semitism. Yet a page and a half is spent on it. Among other things, the following sinister note is found:

> This little gem of propaganda by omission [says the memo, apparently cognizant of the fact that there is nothing really quotable] is all the more significant in that the students are also directed: "... the most important point is to stress the difference between Jews and Zionists."

That's all on this!

The "memo" was an undercover report on what Rahim was supposed to have told friends. It is, if anything, refuted by the "directive" which the same Rahim's office puts out semi-publicly. Both are equally evidence of some sinister intention.

Now, of course, as everyone knows, it is a basic tenet of Zionist education and ideology precisely to identify Zionism and Jewry. Zionists always speak in the name of "the Jews." If anti-Semites, for their own purposes, systematically refuse to distinguish between Zionists and Jews, it is equally true that Zionists, for quite contrary purposes, systematically do likewise. There is scarcely a paper or publication in the land which does not headline actions by the government of Israel as having been taken by the "Jews."

In fact, the only people who systematically insist on distinguishing between Zionists and "The Jews" are anti-Zionists.

Yet, in a system of doublethink which has few parallels outside the Stalinist world, Zionists frequently denounce criticisms of Zionist as being "anti-Semitic" as such.

Take, for another example, the smear campaign against the organization called American Friends of the Middle East, headed by Dorothy Thompson, Garland Evans Hopkins, and including many outstanding and prominent American figures. References to and attacks on it and on Hopkins take up pages and pages in Cross-Currents. There is not the slightest evidence of anti-Semitism on the part of this organization that is adduced in the book, even by undercover "memos." Yet, I am willing to bet a week's salary that many a reader of the book will come away with the conviction that the AFME has been implicated in anti-Semitism. "Implicated" is indeed the world: it has been done solely by the Forster-Epstein interweaving method of innuendo.

The case of the AFME is typical of a broader field.

As this writer interprets the politics of the AFME people, they represent that school of thought in American policy-thinking which believes that U.S. imperialist interests lie in cultivating the goodwill of the Arab states rather than Israel. This view represents the opposite of the often-heard Zionist and pro-Israel argument that American imperialist interests lie in an alliance with the "democratic bastion in the Middle East," Israel.

In this sense the AFME and its similars are "pro-Arab," i.e., within the framework of American imperialism.

The Zionists and their spokesmen are reluctant to make this type of analysis. The very last thing they want to say about this school of American "patriotic" thought is that is motivated by such considerations. They often like to claim a monopoly on "respectable" motives for themselves.

Hence the constant, unremitting campaign of these propagandists to paint their opponents as tainted, not simply with an objectionable view of American imperialism's best interests, but with something dirty and discreditable: anti-Semitism.

This is what is behind the large role played by the AFME in the pages of Cross-Currents.

Only a few weeks ago, in the pages of the N. Y. Post, the long-time-Zionist Max Lerner published one of the most disreputable smears printed anywhere about Garland Hopkins and anti-Semitism. When Hopkins made a defensive reply, Lerner came back with a rejoinder which in virtually so many words argued flatly that anyone who criticizes Zionism is going in for anti-Semitism, for don't we know that anti-Semites slyly use "Zionism" as a cover-word for the Jews ...?

It is usually done more subtly than in Lerner's disgraceful way.

It is under this head also that one must understand the wide-spread insinuations and charges that old reactionary, ex-Secretary James Forrestal, was an anti-Semite, as "revealed" in his published Diaries. Forrestal was "merely" a prime example of a thorough American imperialist hard-headedly trying to choose allies for the "American Century."

The same thing goes for the late Foreign Secretary Ernest Bevin under the last British Labor government, and his "reputation" for anti-Semitism. Bevin's policy in the twilight of the Palestine Mandate was (again, in this writer's opinion) one of the most vicious and malevolent in the evil history of British colonialism, but there is not a shred of evidence that it had anything to do with anti-Semitism, whereas it clearly flowed from the line taken by British imperialism in the period.

One of the most prominent contemporary victims of the anti-Semitic smear has been Professor Arnold Toynbee, since the appearance of the eighth volume of his Study of History. Toynbee very forcibly takes the side of Arab rights as against Zionism. It is perhaps needless to say that I do not agree with much that he writes on this subject or on anything else; but that has nothing to do with the loud charges of anti-Semitism that have been made against him for his stand.

The anti-Semitic smear has been increasingly used by pro-Zionist propagandists and apologists as a substitute for political argumentation and as a means of evading an accounting of their own positions.

Cross-Currents does this, on a booksize scale now.

It works. It intimidates, it discredits. It takes a fair amount of courage even to stick your neck out in front of the charge, which you know will not be slow in coming, with powerful amplification behind it. The subject is a tender one. The field is sensitive. Why bother?

However, it not only "works," but is being overworked. It is bound sooner or later to discredit itself, but this means also discrediting the cry of anti-Semitism. Even while it "works," it does not help the cause of a real fight against anti-Semitism.

It is not the interests of the Jews as a group that are promoted by this Zionist method. It is time that more democratic voices were raised to warn against it.

Labor Action, April 9 & 16, 1956

Chapter XIV
SACRILEGE & ANATHEMA:
Notes on
CHRISTIANITY & JUDAISM TODAY

A while back, we expressed the idea that some good real Christians (by which we merely mean people who actually believe what Christianity preaches) would be of some help on the scene in this country today; and we'd like to make the point again, provided readers understand that we make the point objectively from a strictly non-theistic angle.

If there were any real Christians around, for example, there would unfailingly have been a flood of letters to the N.Y. Times on that Easter morning when the paper came out, fresh and crisp, with a photograph on its front page depicting a cross in the sky—a cross formed by army bombers.

If we were Christian, we'd have considered this sacrilege, but there did not seem to be any believers around.

And if there are any considerable number of Christians left in this country, we cannot understand how Hollywood can get away with the sacrilege which regularly appears on its screen, especially in historical films dealing with the development of Christianity.

Rarely, for instance, have we seen pictures which were as contemptuous of the ideals for which early Christianity stood as that CinemaScope pair consisting of "The Robe" and "Demetrius and the Gladiators." We admit that the sacrilegious propaganda which imbues them is very subtle, since probably not even the makers of these wretched films were consciously aware of it. But sacrilege it is.

Consider: A big point is made in both pictures about the principled pacifism (insistence on non-violence) of the early Christians. The filmmakers could have chosen to ignore this ancient peccadillo; but no, they insist on flaunting it before the audience. And in each case, this principled pacifism is systematically shown to be absurd, futile, self-defeating. In fact, in each case the deus ex Hollywood, who saves everybody at the end, is not the man whom Christians like to call the Prince of Peace on holiday occasions, but is rather the man of violence who brings the plot to a triumphant conclusion with an act of violence.

In the case of "The Robe," the Christian protagonists are saved as the armed (pro-Christian) legions pour into the arena, glittering with shields and javelins. The case of "Demetrius and the Gladiators" is even worse.

In the latter film the climax hinges around the renewed pacifist convictions of Demetrius, who has been forced into the gladiators' arena and told to defend himself. Dramatically in the face of certain death, he faces the emperor and flings down the sword symbolically. A symbol? It turns out to be a signal for rebellious guardsmen to shoot an arrow into the breast of the bad emperor Caligula, revolt, and crown the good emperor Claudius. The Christians have been saved—by stark violence and murder—in a film which revolves around the theme of Christian ideals and non-violence.

We are "complaining" of all this as unbelievers in either theism or pacifism, ourselves.

We are merely interested in pointing out how the American bourgeoisie and its dream merchants and entertainment-propagandists spit upon and revile the ideals to which they give lip-service, the religious homilies without which no speech by Eisenhower is complete.

No one is in any doubt about why they do this—it is in the interest of the militarized capitalism which goes along with militarized institutional-Christianity. And with the exception of a small band of Christian pacifists, whom of course we know, the ideals of the dominant religion in this country are a thing to be mocked at, not lived. It is a paradox, but not hard to understand, that it should be revolutionary socialists writing this in some regret, not the spokesmen of the church.

While on the subject of the sociology of institutionalized religion in the United States today (to give our comment an academic air), a recent event turns attention to the Jewish synagogues, and raises an interesting problem.

First of all, here is the news as summarized in the Jewish Newsletter, published by the liberal William Zukerman:

A reform of Orthodox Jewish marriage laws which have not been changed for 1000 years has been introduced last week by a group representing Conservative Judaism, which occupied a middle-of-the-road position between traditional Orthodoxy and Reform Judaism. The Conservative group, which claims to represent 40 per cent of all religious Jews in this country, announced a revision of the old Jewish marriage contract known as Ketubah which imposes many hardships, indignities and discrimination on Jewish women. The Ketubah goes back to the time when women were considered and treated as chattel slaves and when wives were sold and bought as property of man. It is not a marriage agreement freely entered by a man and a woman on the basis of equality as a marriage contract is in all civilized Western countries. It is a one-sided contract according to which the man 'acquires' a wife, and has all the rights and privileges of the property owner, while she has none. A man may divorce his wife at will for any reason or for no reason at all, without her consent, while she cannot do the same. Under this contract, a Jewish widow is not allowed to marry unless actual evidence of the husband's death is furnished, nor can a childless widow remarry without obtaining a property release from her late husband's brother. These and similar inequities prevent thousands of Jewish women from remarrying and result in untold suffering for thousands of others.

The new marriage contract of the Conservative Jews provides for the establishment of a special Religious Court (Bet Din), which is to be empowered to consider all complaints arising from the backwardness of the Orthodox marriage laws and to try to settle family claims in the light of modern conditions. The announcement of the Conservatives has met, however, with the instant fanatical opposition by the Union of Orthodox Rabbis of America who issued a declaration that the Torah laws given by Moses cannot be changed under any circumstances, no matter what human misery they cause. The rabbis threatened with dire consequences, including excommunication, if the Conservative Religious Court is established.

We can add to this account that (as reported by the Orthodox New York Day & Morning Journal), the prohibition pronounced by the Orthodox Rabbis included the following threats:

The Bet Din and the reformed Ketubah will lead to forbidden cohabitation and to bastardy, leading to a split in the Jewish people and to a breach in Jewish family life...

We declare that the false reforms of the Conservative Rabbis undermine the foundations of the Jewish religion, and they will lead to a situation in which we shall feel ourselves compelled to prohibit marriage unions with families who married under such reforms; and it will be necessary to keep a roster of families married under such reforms in every city.

All this has the smell of authentic medievalism. What is paradoxical about it is that we are not dealing here with a backward people. On the contrary, in all other respects, it is perhaps no exaggeration to say that the body of Jews, even those who follow the Orthodox rabbis, are probably more "enlightened,"not less, than the average in the United States.

Yet, a not inconsiderable section of the American Jews, those for whom the Union of Orthodox Rabbis speak, permit themselves to be bound by certain social customs (at least in form) which have few if any peers in backwardness in the modern and civilized world.

The mystery may seem to be deepened—or, from another point of view, an answer may be indicated—when we see that in the state of Israel the medieval customs of Orthodox Judaism (for example, the marriage laws) are not only insistently imposed on the population by the rabbinate but even reinforced by the state. And here we are dealing with a state whose leadership claims to be modern, indeed "socialistic" (God save us), and beacon lights of progress in the world.

Yet in this otherwise modern state, today mobs of zealots can conduct a campaign of terror on the streets of Old Jerusalem in order to force strict Orthodox practices on the Jewish population: stoning passing vehicles, beating up people caught smoking on the Sabbath, attacking mixed gatherings of men and women (forbidden by the Torah), etc.

Are we not dealing here with a pattern of desperate attempts to preserve intact a crumbling whole, lest any change whatsoever cause the whole structure to fall apart?

The student of sociology can scarcely fail to conclude, from the statement of the Orthodox rabbis, that they consciously fear that any change whatsoever in the laws of Judaism will open up some rift which will inevitably widen, that therefore the whole edifice must be defended with the cry of No Change.

But this is typically a phenomenon which accompanies a social structure which is already dead, though not yet buried. Only such need be defended by such methods.

What is it that is dead—not, we stress, necessarily in our opinion, but in the eyes of the desperate Orthodox who hurl such anathemas at Change? What is it that they fear so much?

Their own answer—varying in form for the Orthodox or for the Israeli Zionist—is (1) Jewishness, in answer to the first question, and (2) assimilation, in answer to the second.

Consider, for example, the following statement by David Ben-Gurion, former Israeli premier, as he hammers away in the Jewish press:

The Jewish people in the Diaspora [dispersion] ... is now faced with a question of uncommon urgency and importance. It is this: Will it be able to survive for a long time, and if so, what kind of Jewishness will sustain it? A Zionist movement that does not endeavor to give a positive answer to this question, thereby denies its own purpose and the reason for its existence...

It is true that we do not have an official Jewish assimilationist party in America. On the contrary, there are very few Jews who are ashamed of their Jewishness and hide it... Yet there can be no doubt that practical Jewish assimilation is proceeding apace, as the old obstacles to Jewish integration in other cultures are being swept away. It is an undeniable fact that the old religious traditions and observances have lost much of their power over the masses. The same is true of the language of the Jewish masses. There is hardly a barrier left to hold back the onrush of Jewish assimilation in the free lands of the world.

It is ironic that in this process of assimilation and integration into a non-Jewish culture there is hardly any difference between Zionists and non-Zionists ..."(Day-Morning Journal, March 7.)

Here Ben-Gurion ties together the joint fears of the Orthodox and the consistent Zionists (note his reference to religion), and indicates how the same phenomena can appear in both circles. In both cases the religious forms, no matter how reactionary, are important to preserve as guardians against the devil of "assimilation," the "danger" of which Ben-Gurion perhaps exaggerates.

Now Independent Socialists do not believe, on principle, in having a "party line" for or against assimilation (as we have stated in our resolutions), for we consider that this is a matter to be freely chosen by the Jewish masses themselves in the course of their free development. What we do insist on, as socialists, however, is creating and maintaining the preconditions of free choice.

What is socially and politically reactionary about the Orthodox anathemas and the practices of the Zionist state and zealots in Israel is that they are directed toward destroying freedom of choice for the Jews with respect to assimilation and other courses. They insist on forcing all Jews, by political or spiritual terror, into a predetermined separateness which their ideology insists on.

Such a course can have only reactionary social consequences, as we have been seeing. Nor can it help any genuine religious feeling, for those to whom this is important.

Labor Action, December 20, 1954

Chapter XV
TO BREAK THE VICIOUS SPIRAL

In discussing the crisis in the Middle East, we are dealing with one of the most difficult problems in a torn world. There are no very easy or ready-made solutions. As someone has said, it is "a conflict of rights"—it is not a simple matter of right on one side and wrong on the other. By the same token, it is a conflict of wrongs too.

Although this article will try to present a very concrete and immediate program—one which is even brashly numbered from 1 to 12—I want to emphasize right at the start that this will be done mainly in order to illustrate the type of approach which is pointed to. The intent is to suggestive, certainly not "definitive," and not to cover all aspects of the dispute.

The question is how to break out of a vicious circle.

One of the poles of the situation is the threat by the surrounding governments to wipe out Israel as a state. As I tried to stress at a recent symposium on the subject, on which this article is based, this discussion is within the framework of the question of how to defend Israel—against this threat.

"How to Defend Israel" in this sense is also the question we addressed ourselves to in the Palestine war of 1948. At that time we supported Israel in the war against the invasion of the Arab states; but we predicted that if the war were carried through as a war against the Arab people, rather than as a revolutionary war of defense appealing to the Arab people against their own rulers, only grief would come of it. And we were indubitably right, as events have shown.

It was also from this point of view that a year and a half ago we engaged in a polemic against the anti-Israel position of Arab socialists on this question, as represented by Clovis Maksoud.

But we have always stressed that we expect more from the Israeli working-class movement, precisely because of its relatively more advanced social and political character. This is why we have addressed ourselves in the first place to a program for Israel— how to break out of the vicious circle.

What is at stake is the survival of Israeli Jewry, and also all of its considerable accomplishments in many fields, all of the many sacrifices that were made by or exacted from so large a part of its population since the exodus from Nazism.

We fear that what is happening may be a new act in the tragedy of the Jewish people. Yesterday it was played out in Europe; now it has been shifted to the Palestine arena, which according to the Zionist ideology was supposed to be the scene of the final solution of the Jewish question.

Last November, Israel army head Yaakov Dori, at a rally in Haifa, said: "If war breaks out here our enemies will be fighting to kill every Jew, and for us it will mean a fight against extermination ..."

Yesterday Jews were faced with Hitlerite exterminationism. Now, today—again—there is talk of extermination. This is an appalling fact. It cannot be explained away by a devil theory, not even by a theory about Arab devils.

In 1953 when Foreign Minister Sharett reported to his Knesset on world reaction against the Kibya massacre, he said: "It is ... false to assume that Israel cannot survive without peace. We exist and can continue to exist indefinitely without it."

Exist? Perhaps. But how?

As a state ghetto in the Middle East?

As a fear-palled fortress?

As a militarized garrison?

As a satellite of Washington?

Even before this present alarm of war, two years ago, two leaders of the Ichud of Israel regretfully put a spotlight on the following fact, which speaks volumes: "The State of Israel ... is today almost the only country in the world where the life of Jews is in danger—now, and even more so in the future."

Think of it!

If the outcome of the "Zionist fulfillment" is not to be simply another act of Jewish tragedy, then some way of breaking out of the vicious circle must be found.

In fact, it is not a vicious circle but a vicious spiral, a spiral down. The present situation is not some entirely unforeseen result of unpredictable factors. From the beginning of Zionism, the opponents of Jewish chauvinism insistently pointed to the fatal results that would flow from trying to displace a people from their land by colonization under the aegis of an imperialist power. The Zionists always underestimated the "Arab question," though usually giving it lip service. Reactionary Arab leaders utilized the justified resentment of their people, against the interlopers who came under the protection of the imperialist's flag, and turned it into fuel for their own dynastic and feudal power-politics. So reaction on both sides has jacked up mutual antagonism first on one side and then on the other.

This jacking-up process has been especially virulent in the last few years. It has even been systematized with the adoption by the Israeli authorities, under Ben-Gurion's inspiration, of the policy of "massive retaliation" (as against Kibya, Gaza, and Syria) in response to Arab attacks; which in turn were exacerbated by Israeli injustices to its refugees; which in turn took place on the background of the Arab states' aggressive assault on the sovereignty of the new State of Israel in 1948; which in turn of Zionist transgressions in the Jewish-Arab relations in this land which they were infiltrating with the hope of taking it away from its inhabitants ...

This vicious spiral is still moving down. The program proposed below aims to break it from the Israeli side.

There are four guiding principles on which any such program has to be based, in our opinion. These are four things to realize about the position of Israel. Or four ways of looking at it.

(1) First and foremost, Israel must be looked on as a Middle East state.

Not as the "fulfillment" of the Bible or Theodor Herzl. Not as a ghetto (a very large ghetto with national boundaries) in the midst of an Arab world. Not as a regional beachhead for NATO or American imperialism.

Israel will either accept its being as a Middle East state, as against any of the other concepts, or it will remain an alien splinter-state festering in the body of this region where three continents meet.

(2) Israel must be a state of two peoples, Jews and Arabs—a bi-national state in this sense, even though the Jewish majority will inevitably be the dominant element.

The policy and orientation signified by the Zionist concept of "Jewish State" is a danger to the Jews and a provocation to the Arabs at home and around it.

In this country the question of Israel's relation to its own Arab population is not separate and apart from its relation to the Arab people outside. The close tie makes it one question, not two. Its situation is not like that of the U.S. where people can better afford the error of thinking of domestic and foreign policy as being in two compartments. Here internal Arab policy and external Arab policy are intertwined like the fingers of two hands—hence the one question of survival.

(3) The problem of breaking out of the vicious spiral is not how to appease the Arab rulers, not how to tickle them under the chin with concessions.

Even when and where the Israeli leaders have thought to make concessions, it has been with this false perspective.

The aim is how to appeal to the mass of Arab people against these rulers, how to mobilize them against their own government cliques.

In this sense, it is a revolutionary approach, and the very opposite of appeasement.

The question of concessions to the Arab population, or a new approach in Arab-Jewish relations, takes on an entirely different coloration from the standpoint of this objective.

In contrast, Israeli policy has lurched between appeasement on the one hand and provocation on the other, always with the eye fixed on the Arab tops. The way out of the vicious spiral is: from below.

(4) The Arab countries, it must be recognized, are not simply backward and zombie-like societies, with passive but bloodthirsty Arab hordes firmly in the grip of feudal devils. This is a chauvinist caricature.

The Arab countries today are rent through and through with revolutionary ferment. They are filled with anti-government and anti-status-quo dissent—more so than Israel. Their masses are stirring.

There is no paradox in the following statement: The same hatred of the Arab regimes by its people which today even takes the form of anti-Israel extremism could, given a revolutionized Israeli policy, be channelized in a progressive direction—to blow up from within the dictators and feudal powers who are today the joint enemies of both their own people and the Israeli Jews.

There's the direction to look! Certainly not to the Big Brothers in the imperialist camps; not to cynical manipulators like Dulles and his colleagues in Washington, who are ready to sell out the so-called "bastion of democracy" at the drop of an oil barrel. Not to the totalitarians in Moscow.

A "security pact" with the U.S., which the Israelis and Zionists are demanding, would afford Israel no security in making this little country the local branch office of the Atlantic Pact in a hostile environment.

An Israel which is "guaranteed" by U.S. armed "police action," as is demanded, is more likely to make Israel a Korea than to integrate it into the Middle East where it exists.

When the Israeli regime faces in this direction, it is of course in response to immediate dangers from its threatening neighbors; but to face this way is to ensure disaster. There is no safety in becoming the satellite, satrapy or stooge of the imperialists.

So Israel must about-face. It has to go in the other direction, to integrate with the peoples of the Middle East as a force for political freedom in friendship and peace.

What these "four principles" add up to, we admit, is a revolutionary transformation in the Zionist policy-basis of the state—no slight change.

200

The question is whether the realities of life in the Middle East will batter this into the Zionist-stuffed heads of the political people of the country before the last act of tragedy is played out.

But in any case it is a change in direction that is vital, not an overnight transmogrification. The direction would have to be toward winning the support and friendship of the Arab masses, away from and against the reactionary rulers of the Arab states—instead of the present policy which pushes them together.

This program begins at home for Israel.

In Israel the Arab question is first of all internal, not external.

Israel can show the world how to make peace with the Arab people without waiting on the power-politics or whims of neighboring kings or colonels.

Israel will never achieve real peace with the surrounding Arab world, even after a settlement with the Nassers, as long as it is at war with its own Arab minority.

This is the first place to start, to reach the Arab people.

This is precisely the opposite of the prevailing Israeli line—prevailing since 1949 at least. It early became the government practice and the Zionist norm to treat all Israeli Arabs as if they were enemies as long as the neighboring states breathed war clouds.

Spoliation of Israeli Arabs has been excused on the ground that they are fifth-columnists, potential or otherwise. Discrimination against Arabs at home has been condoned and officially fostered in vital economic fields—even Arabs who were never hostile to the state; even Arabs who fought with the Israeli Jews against the Arab armies.

For seven years, with zigs and zags, Israeli policy has pushed itself into the pattern of making bitter enemies out of even friendly Arabs, in spite of sectors (like health and education) where real benefits were bestowed.

Arabs were juridically turned into second-class citizens by a Law of Nationality which discriminated racially and put obstacles to citizenship in the path of Arab families whose ancestors had lived in the land for a thousand years.

It was this Law of Nationality which caused Norman Thomas to write that "An Arab, without too much exaggeration, could complain that the Jews were practicing Hitlerism in reverse ..." If the comparison seems shockingly extreme, it is an index to Thomas's sense of shock.

The overwhelming majority of Israel's Arabs are confined to areas under military rule as if they were a conquered people under occupation by an enemy. To all intents and purposes the military commanders over them are dictators with wide powers over their lives. They cannot even travel out of their areas without military permits, whether to look for a job or to sell their produce on the market or to visit a doctor outside.

The barbarous system of collective punishments (of a village, for example, for an individual's offense) stems from the colonialist code of the British, but has become an anti-Arab weapon of the Israeli government. It has been applied even to a village that fought on the side of the Jews in 1948.

The system is justified as a security measure. Is it wise security which seeks to turn every Arab into an enemy even if he was not an enemy to begin with?

Is it a security measure that Arabs from the border zones are not allowed to move away from the border, so that presumably their ethnic sympathies will not be so dangerous?

Is it entirely for security reasons that Jewish citizens (by state definition, "racially" loyal) are not allowed into Arab zones?

Is it entirely for security reasons that an Arab cannot leave one of these military areas and come to Tel-Aviv without a military permit?

Nor is it in the interests of security that the Arab population (including some who never moved from their villages during the war) have been systematically robbed of land, by a series of laws.

The large majority of the Arabs who remained in Israel territory during the war were peasants—people who, uprooted from their land, were uprooted in life.

From 1948 to a culmination in 1953 a systematic land-grab went on—"legally." By an Absentee Properties Law of 1950, Arabs who fled from their village to a neighboring village, to get out of the way of the bullets, or some even because they were ousted by Israeli troops, were declared technical"absentees" even though they were in the country, not to speak of those who were caught on the other side of borders as refugees. The government took away their land.

By another set of laws, the government stripped Arabs of land by declaring an area a "security zone," then making it Araberrein, ousting all Arabs, taking over the land and handling it over to Jewish settlement.

By the Land Acquisition Law of 1953, even land-grabs that had been perfectly illegal up to then were sanctioned ex-post-facto, and Israeli Arabs were despoil of land which was added to Jewish settlements.

Aside from the inadequacy and trickiness of the government's compensation provisions, no money compensation could keep these Arabs' lives together.

It is little justification for these gross acts when pro-Zionist apologists, in extenuation, point to the U.S. crime against Japanese-Americans who were stripped of their property and herded behind barbed wire for the duration of the war.

These are the two main grievances which work to turn Israel's Arabs into "security risks" against their own will: military rule and the land-grab.

To this, add the problem of the Arab refugees from Palestine who were caught on the other side of the truce lines at the end of the war, after a mass flight from the war-torn land which was caused by three pressure working in close harmony: the threats of the Arab military forces; fear of the Israeli forces especially after the atrocious Deir Yassin massacre, and ejection from villages even by the regular Israeli troops; and evacuation by the British forces when they left Palestine.

The refugees too have been turned, unnecessarily, into a festering pool of hatred and hostility—incidentally, not only against the Israelis but also against the Arab leaders, and almost anyone else.

Insistently, the Israeli government and Zionist parties have taken the position that they can do nothing to change the lot of these Arab masses until the Arab war lords become willing to make a peace settlement.

They keep their eyes fixed on the tops.

They were willing to think in terms of a deal with Abdullah of Jordan, till he was assassinated. They are willing to think in terms of a peace deal with Nasser, if he will change his tune.

But they have shown no capacity to think in terms of a "deal" with the discontented masses, that is, of a revolutionary approach to them—from below.

They too look on the Arab people as pawns of their leaders, doomed to be somebody's victims—victims of oppression by an Israeli overlord or an Arab overlord.

If this is true, then Israel is probably doomed as a free and independent state and a decent home for its people.

The conditions that have been sketched point to another way. This road leads from unity with the Arab population at home to the implementation of a bi-national approach to drive a class wedge inside the encircling Arab states.

It is a road that can turn the socialist and democratic currents of Arab life from enemies of Israel's existence to friends of a revolutionary Israel which fights for two peoples.

It is a program which starts with proposals that are demanded by elementary feelings of justice, to remedy political sins which today lie heavy on the conscience of every decent man in Israel.

(1) An end to the land-grab from the Arabs of Israel. Repeal of the discriminatory laws. Rent from occupied land and possessions to go to the Arab owners immediately. Return of a maximum of such land and real property to Arab owners. Compensation at full current value in all other cases.

(2) Full and equal citizenship rights for Arabs.

(3) Abolition of the segregation system, restrictions, permits, etc., in Arab zones, and turning over of a maximum of functions to civilian self-government.

(4) Abolition of military rule over Arab areas.

(5) Extension of the right to all members of an Arab family to rejoin parents in Israel.

(6) Encouragement—not just toleration, but encouragement—to Arabs to enter into every field of life and work on a plane of complete equality. Extension to Arab workers of the right to vote in the Histadrut elections.

The above six proposals give examples of the type of change that involve the present Arab minority in the country.

(7) The Israel government should return to the proposal it made once before, albeit grudgingly under U.S. pressure: admission of 100,000 of the refugees.

(8) Acceptance of the principle of repatriation or compensation for other legitimate refugees—not conditioned on a prior peace agreement with the kings and colonels but as part of an Israeli political offensive. Few observers expect an overwhelming number to insist on repatriation.

(9) The Jewish fund-raising network in the United States and elsewhere has raised millions of dollars a year for Israel. Let the American Jewish fund-raisers announce a campaign to raise such millions to resettle the Arab refugees, and the whole world would be electrified!

(10) The abandonment of the theory and practice of Israel as a "Jewish State," as explained above.

(11) Border changes to straighten out the frontier so as to reunite Arab villages with their own land where the truce lines ran through them: one of the biggest single contributions possible to stopping "infiltration" and border incidents.

(12) And lastly, on the basis of such a deep revolutionary transformation of Israeli policy, which ranges the Jewish people of Israel with the Arab people: launching of a massive initiative and political

offensive inside the whole Arab world to rally support for the new Israel and against any and all of the provocateurs and fanatics and dynasts who want war.

It is in such a context that an enormous initiative could be taken to do, within such a transformed framework, what Nahum Goldmann of the Jewish Agency proposed the other week: a program of Israeli-Jewish economic development and investment for the whole Middle East.

This idea, with all of its huge potential, was suggested in a speech by Goldmann, who was speaking as a top leader in the World Zionist movement, but he did it in the traditional Zionist way: as a dangled piece of bait to reward some "good" Arab leader who would accede to Israel's demands.

But the idea itself, in the framework of our own program, is dynamite. Not as a reward for capitulation, but as the spearhead of a political offensive. Propose it now. Of course, the Arab states are busy pretending that Israel does not even exist, or at least refusing to recognize its existence—except to implement their economic boycott against this non-existent state. Let them reject such an economic offensive, on the basis of a transformed Israel policy ...

Instead of hedging in Arab students at Hebrew University with restrictions and red tape and suspicion, let Israel make efforts to bring Arab students there, and press for cultural exchanges of all sorts.

Above all, and this applies to the program as a whole, it is meaningless to act along these lines in a half-hearted fashion; or (as the Israeli government has typically done) suggest that one is willing to make a couple of concessions along these lines only provided the other side (meaning the kings and colonels and feudals) reciprocate.

The whole point of such a program is its sweep. A policy of half-hearted appeasement, alternating with sporadic retaliation and provocation, is a combination of sure poisons, bringing together everything that is self-defeating.

What unites and inspire such a revolutionary program is its aim: the eventual integration of Israel into a Federation of the Middle East to unite the region for development and independence from outside pressures and imperialism. This may be a more or less distant aim: that is not the point. Every step in the direction of Arab-Jewish unity is a step in its direction.

This is not only the road of survival for Israel's Jewry; it is more. It means the end of the state's ghetto existence. It means the liberation of its none-too-plentiful resources from the crushing burden of armaments. It means the normalization of its economy, which can make sense not by indefinite dependence on international charity but by correlation with the complementary economies of its Arab neighbors. It means the end of its process of satellization by the American dollar—both the dollar of charity and the dollar of imperialism.

And still more: it means that for the first time, Israel can really play the role it deserves where the superior cultural and technical resources of much of its population can legitimately give it the position of a beneficent leader and guide in Middle Eastern development, as a part of a whole.

Today its boast of being the "bastion of democracy" and progress in its part of the world is only a boast. Tomorrow it could really play that role—not over the Arab peoples but as a partner with them, as one Middle Eastern people among others.

Labor Action, March 5, 1956

Reference Notes

1.Chaim Weizmann, *Trial and Error*; see especially pp. 149, 170, 177–9, 182, 191–3, 205, 223, 324, 366, 393, 396, 435.

2. *The Arabs in Israel*, Israel Office of Information, NY 1955, p. 9.

3. Ibid., p. 11.

4. Don Peretz: *Israel and the Arab Refugees*, vol. II, pp. 232–3, 237. This is an unpublished Ph.D. thesis (Columbia), 1954, available in mimeographed form; it is the most authoritative work on the subject in English. Peretz writes from the Ichud viewpoint.

5. Ibid., vol. II, p. 240, 270.

6. Ibid., vol. I, p. 9.

7. Raphael Patai: *Israel Between East and West*, Jewish Pub. Soc., Philadelphia, 1953, pp. 242–3.

8. *Arabs in Israel* (n.2), p. 7. For this version, see also Joseph B. Schechtman, *The Arab Refugee Problem*, Philosophical Library, N.Y., 1952, p. 1–2. (Schechtman is the present leader of the world Revisionist group and his book is a straight Zionist party-line argument.)

9. Arthur Koestler: *Promise and Fulfillment*, Macmillan, N.Y., 1949, p. 155. In the pages following, Koestler details activities of the foreign irregulars without in any way indicating Palestinian cooperation.

10. Patai (*Israel Between East and West*), p. 256.

11. David Ben-Gurion, "The Fight for Freedom," *Palestine and Middle East* (Tel-Aviv), Jan.–Feb., 1948.

12. Y. Shimoni, "Inside the Arab Camp—Arab Masses Unwilling to Fight Jews," ibid.

13. Harry Sacher: *Israel, the Establishment of a State*, British Book Centre, N.Y., 1952, p. 149. Rufus Learsi: *Fulfillment, the Epic Story of Zionism*, World Pub. Co., N.Y., p. 371. Misha Louvish, "Arab Minority in Israel," *Zionist Newsletter* (Jerusalem), Apr. 7, 1952. Special Correspondent, "What Is Happening in the Arab Camp?" *Zionist Review* (London), March 19, 1948.

14. For quotes purporting to show this, see the Israel government pamphlet *The Arabs in Israel* (ref. n. 2), pp. 9–10. None of the quotes is from the AHE or its leaders. Another question not satisfactorily handled is why, from their own standpoint, the Arab leaders should have issued such a general sweeping call. A quite different explanation for the flight is given in the book by McDonald, first U.S. ambassador to Israel (ref. n. 27) who was and is more pro-Zionist than the Zionists, and who is undoubtedly merely retailing what he was told in Tel-Aviv in

1948 (p. 175). See also the different explanation in the propaganda book by the Revisionist Schechtman (ref. n. 8), Sayegh (official of the Arab Information Center in New York), *The Palestine Refugees*, Amara Press (Wash., D.C.), 1952. A pro-British historian recommends that the Zionist story about the AHE call for a mass exodus at this time "should be treated with reserve in the absence of positive evidence to corroborate it. . . ." (George Kirk, Royal Institute of International Affairs, anti-Zionist from British imperial angle, *The Middle East 1945–1950*, p. 263).

15. *Arabs in Israel* (ref. n. 2), p. 9. Likewise in Schechtman (refr. n. 8), pp. 3–4.

16. "Facts and Figures on Israel's Arab Citizens," *Israel Digest* (Los Angeles, Isr. Off. of Info.), Apr. 5, 1949.

17. Michael Arnon, "Arabs in Israel," *Israel and Middle East* (Tel-Aviv), Jan. 1949.

18. Y. Shimoni, "The Palestine Arabs—The Breakdown of a Community," *Zionist Newsletter* (Jerusalem) Aug. 9, 1949.

19. J. C. Hurewitz: *The Struggle for Palestine*, Norton, N.Y., 1950,
p. 313–4. See also the similar observation by the American Mid-East scholar C.B. Richardson of Columbia, in his paper "The Refugee Problem," *Proceedings of the Academy of Political Science*, Jan. 1952 (standpoint not known to me; tone academic).

20. Dvorah Metlinsky, "New Deal for the Arab", *Jewish Standard* (Montreal), June 1951.

21. Hal Lehrman, "The Arabs of Israel,"*Commentary*, Dec. 1949.

22. *Arabs in Israel* (ref. n. 2), p. 10.

23. Schechtman (ref. n. 8), p. 6.

24. Pierre van paassen: *Jerusalem Calling!* (Dial Press, N.Y., 1950,
p. 177—8.

25. Sacher (n. 13), p. 149. See also Patai, (ref. n. 7), p. 256–7.

26. Gideon Weigert, "The Arabs of Western Galilee," *Youth Horizon* (Jerusalem), Oct.–Nov. 1949.

27. James G. McDonald: *My Mission in Israel, 1948–1951*, Simon & Schuster, N.Y., 1951, p. 29.

28. Dr. W. von Weisl, "Hard Facts About Israel's Arabs," *Jewish Herald* (Johannesburg), Feb. 17, 1950.

29. M. Bligh-Grotto & E. Koigen, "These Arabs Came Back," *American Zionist* (N.Y.), Nov. 1955. Their story was also summarized in the *N.Y. Times*, Feb. 12, 1953. with some varying

details, at time of resettlement.

30. Although Koussa is Arab (Christian, not Moslem), it is within my ground rules to cite him here because, on this matter, he is also cited as an approved authority by the Revisionist propagandist J.B. Schechtman (ref. n. 8), pp. 12–13, and by Barou (see ref. n. 32). The same applies to Msgr. Hakim. I may add also that Koussa, who is perhaps the leading Israeli Arab defending his people's rights within the state as a loyal citizen, is a collaborator with the Ichud and its organ *Ner*.

31. *N.Y. Herald Tribune*, June 30, 1949, cited in Schechtman (ref. n. 8), p. 13.

32. *Congress Weekly* (N.Y.), Apr. 4, 1949.

33. For example, see Hal Lehrman (n. 21).

34. According to the *Bulletin of the Council on Jewish-Arab Cooperation* (a then-existing U.S. group based on Ichud's type of Zionist ideology), as quoted in *Labor Action*, Aug. 23, 1948, the terrorists worked up to it during the preceding days: "On April 4 Irgun Zvei Leumi stole 1,000 head of cattle from Arab villages in the coastal plain; Haganah pursued them and succeeded in returning part of the loot to the Arabs. On April 5 terrorists hijacked an Arab truck laden with citrus fruit. On April 6 the Stern group blew up the deserted Arab village of Bir Adas, when the Arabs began to return by day to work in their fields."

35. Jon Kimche: *Seven Fallen Pillars—The Middle East 1945–1952,* Praeger, N.Y., 1953, p. 227..

36. *Labor Action*, Dec. 27, 1948.

37. Kimche (ref. n. 35), p. 227.

38. *Labor Action*, Apr. 19, 1948.

39. Text of letter given in Menachem Begin, *The Revolt, Story of the Irgun,* Schuman, N.Y., 1951, p. 163.

40. For example, at the time the *Palestine Post* (Apr. 12, 1948) editorialized that "No good reason can be given even for the action as a military operation"—i.e., even aside from the massacre aspect. It went on to say that the Irgun "scored a cheap victory, 'capturing' a village which was peaceable and constituted no menace, even if some few Iraqis or other armed Arabs were in it against the wishes of its inhabitants."

41. Sacher (ref. n. 13), p. 192.

42. Ibid., pp. 193–4.

43. For example, see: Koestler (ref. n. 9), p. 160; Hurewitz (ref. n. 19), p. 214; M. Begin (ref. n. 39), pp. 164–5; Richardson (ref. n. 18); McDonald (ref. n. 27), p. 175.

44. Kimche (n. 35), p. 233.

45. Begin (ref. n. 36) p. 165.

46. Zionist sources like to quote the British police reports on Haifa: "Every effort is being made by the Jews to persuade the Arab populace to stay. . . ." See Schechtman (ref. n. 8), pp. 7–9. In M. Pearlman's *The Army of Israel,* these British reports are reproduced in facsimile. The effort is to make it appear as if this applied to the Arab flight in general.

47. *Labor Action,* Jan. 12, 1948.

48. Ben-Gurion (ref. n. 11); Shimoni (ref. n. 12); a longer account of their efforts will be found in Kimche (ref. n. 35).

49. For the British role, see ref. n. 31 and ref. n. 33.

50. Koestler (ref. n. 9), p. 207.

51. Kimche (ref. n. 35), p. 229.

52. Ibid., p. 230.

53. Arnon (ref. n. 17).

54. McDonald (ref. n. 26), p. 176.

55. Kenneth W. Bilby: *New Star in the Near East,* Doubleday, N.Y., 1950, p. 31. (Bilby was the N.Y. *Herald Tribune* reporter in the war; his book freely criticizes both sides; no evident bias either way.)

56. Jon Kimche, "The Arabs in Israel," *Jewish Observer & Middle East Review* (London), Feb. 15, 1952.

57. Kimche (ref. n. 35), p. 265.

58. Kirk (ref. n. 14) adds that expulsions also took place of the Arab population of Acre, Beersheba and Western Galilee (p. 264). The UN Mediator, Count Bernadotte, in July 1948 reported to the Security Council on Israel's expulsion of 8,000 Arab inhabitants of three villages south of Haifa and the destruction of their homes.

59. Bilby (ref. n. 55), p. 43.

60. Arab sources charge other massacres (by Haganah), though none as bad as Deir Yassin: e.g., at Nasr-el-Din. Regarding this village, see *Palestine Post,* Apr. 13, 1948, for the official Zionist report, which says that "Before the Haganah counterattacked, the women, children, and older inhabitants were warned to leave the place." It does not go on to say what happened to them. The next day the same paper reported, without comment, the charge by

the British colonel in the area (Tiberias) that "twenty Arabs, including women and children, were killed and the houses set on fire." The Ichud's organ *Ner* has stated that one cause of the Arab flight was "the Jewish leaders, who took advantage of Dir Yassin and similar deeds, *not all perpetrated by 'dissident' (Jewish) forces,* to spread terror among the Arab masses and to drive them away." (May 1954, as published in *Freeland,* May–July 1954. Emphasis added.)

61. Kimche (ref. n. 35), p. 265.

62. Koestler (ref. n. 9), p. 199.

63. Bilby (ref. n. 55), p. 3.

64. Sacher (ref. n. 13), p. 149.

65. Norman Bentwich: *Israel,* Benn, London, 1952, p. 158.

66. Hal Lehrman: *Israel, The Beginning and Tomorrow,* Sloan, N.Y., 1951, p. 66.

67. Peretz (ref. n. 4), vol. II, p. 242.

68. Yaakov Aviel, "The Arabs Among Us," Article III, *Haaretz* (Tel Aviv), Jan. 7, 1955.

69. Peretz (ref. n. 4), vol. II, pp. 257–8.

70. Ibid., vol. II, p. 256.

71. Quoted in Peretz, vol. II, p. 242.

72. In *Haaretz* (Tel-Aviv), July 26, 1949; quoted in Peretz, vol. II, p. 254.

73. Don Peretz: Israel and the Arab Refugees, v. II, p. 233.

74. Ibid., p. 230.

75. Ibid., p. 231–2.

76. Ibid., p. 237.

77. Ibid., p. 240.

78. Ibid., p. 236, 238.

79. Yaakov Aviel, "The Arabs Among Us," Article III, *Haaretz* (Tel-Aviv), Jan. 7, 1955.

80. Peretz (ref. n. 4), v. II, p. 229.

81. Ibid., p. 228, 244.

82. *Laws of the State of Israel, Authorized Translation* ... Vol. I. Government Printer, Jerus: Abandoned Areas Ordinance, No. 12 of 5708-1948.

83. Peretz (ref. n. 4), v. II, p. 244.

84. Ibid., p. 258-9.

85. Yaakov Aviel (ref. n. 68).

86. Peretz (ref. n. 4), v. II, p. 248. Also Joseph B. Schechtman: *The Arab Refugee Problem,* Philosophical Library, N.Y., 1952, p. 96.

87. Peretz (ref. n. 4), v. II, p. 250-1.

88. Ibid., p. 248.

89. Ibid., p. 248-9.

90. Ibid., p. 248.

91. Ibid., p. 249.

92. Schechtman (ref. n. 8), p. 97.

93. Peretz (ref. n. 4), v. II, p. 251-2.

94. Ibid., p. 260.

95. Yaakov Aviel (ref. n. 68).

96. M. Stein, "The Arab Minority in Israel," *Lebensfragen* (Tel-Aviv), organ of the Jewish Labor Bund in Israel (socialist anti-Zionist), Jan. 1956.

97. For the legal reference, see Peretz (ref. n. 4), v. I, p. 204.

98. Peretz (ref. n. 4), v. II, p. 229.

99. Ibid., p. 277.

100. Ibid., p. 278.

101. Schechtman (ref. n. 8), p. 102.

102. Peretz (ref. n. 4), v. II, p. 279.

103. Don Peretz, "The Arab Minority of Israel," *Middle East Journal* (Wash., D.C.), Spring 1954.

104. Hal Lehrman: *Israel, the Beginning and Tomorrow*, Sloane, N.Y., 1951, p. 260. See also Norman Bentwich: *Israel*, Benn, London, 1952, p. 157–8.

105. Peretz (ref. n. 1), v. II, p. 281–4.

106. Ibid., p. 288.

107. Ibid., p. 285.

108. Ibid., p. 297.

109. Ibid., p. 299.

110. Judd L. Teller, "Israel Faces Its Arab Minority Problem," *Commentary*, Dec. 1951.

111. Lehrman (ref. n. 21), p. 260.

112. Peretz (ref. n. 4), v. II, p. 279.

113. Ibid., p. 279.

114. Bentwich (ref. n. 21), p. 78–79.

115. Peretz (ref. n. 4), v. II, p. 294.

116. Text of law in *Middle East Journal* (Wash., D.C.), Summer 1953.

117. Maier Asher, "The Arab Minority in Israel," *Jewish Chronicle* (London), Dec. 18, 1953. (Datelined Haifa.)

118. Yaakov Aviel (ref. n. 68).

119. *Jewish Newsletter* (New York), May 25, 1953. (Liberal anti-Zionist.)

120. Peretz (ref. n. 4), v. II, p. 308.

121. *Ner* (Jerusalem), Apr. 1953.

122. Moshe Keren, "The Arabs Among Us," Article V, *Haaretz* (Tel-Aviv), Jan. 14, 1955.

123. Peretz (ref. n. 4), v. II, p. 306.

124. Peretz (ref. n. 4), v. II, p. 306.

125. Peretz (ref. n. 4), v. II, p. 307. See also text of law as quoted in my article.

126. Peretz (ref. n. 4), v. II, p. 310.

127. Ibid., p. 310.

128. Ibid., p. 308.

129. Yaakov Aviel (ref. n. 68).

130. Peretz (ref. n. 4), v. I, p. 168.

131. Peretz in *Middle East Journal* (ref. n. 103).

132. Moshe Keren (ref. n. 122).

133. Stein (ref. n. 96).

134. Lehrman (ref. n. 21), p. 260.

135. Peretz (ref. n. 4), v. II, p. 255.

136. Ibid., p. 305.

137. Ibid., p. 305.

138. "Arabs in Israel," *Business Digest* (Haifa), July 23, 1952.

139. Peretz in *Middle East Journal* (ref. n. 103).

140. Peretz (ref. n. 4), v. I, p. 213.

141. Ibid., v. II, p. 308—9.

142. Ibid., v. II, p. 309.

143. "The Position of the Arabs in the State of Israel," *Ner* (Jerusalem), Feb. 1953 (English section).

144. Schechtman (ref. n. 8), p. 98–9.

145. Ibid., p. 111–2.

146. For a more general discussion of what has been happening to the Israeli kibbutz, see the interesting comments by Stanley Diamond in the current *Dissent*.

147. This border happens to be the only one in the history of the world which has been under constant military observation for a number of years by an impartial, international organization of supervisors—the UN truce commissions. Their reports have never gotten any currency in the U.S. press. A recent book by one of the UN observers, Commander E.H. Hutchison, "Violent Truce" (Devin-Adair, N.Y.) reflects the findings of the UN agencies on the spot. It has succeeded in getting reviewed practically nowhere, with one exception, but is "must" reading for anyone trying to get acquainted with all sides of this story. The exception is a bitterly hostile review by Hal Lehrman in *Commentary*, which proves (by what it does not say) that Lehrman can find nothing to refute in the general factual picture drawn by Hutchison.

148. The *J.A. Digest* article, says a note, "is based on an article by Shabetai Tevet in *Haaretz*,"which is the leading daily of Israel. The information in it is "based on official Egyptian documents" captured, and on testimony by captured fedayeen.

www.ingramcontent.com/pod-product-compliance
Lightning Source LLC
Chambersburg PA
CBHW072129270326
41931CB00010B/1708